MW01505451

Rockefeller In Retrospect:

The Governor's New York Legacy

Edited by
Gerald Benjamin
and
T. Norman Hurd

The
Nelson A.
Rockefeller
Institute
of
Government

Albany, New York

Acknowledgements

The Conference upon which this volume is based, and the book itself, would not have been possible without the support of Clifton R. Wharton, Jr., Chancellor of the State University of New York, and Warren Ilchman, Director of SUNY's Rockefeller Institute of Government. The Rockefeller Retrospective Advisory Committee, the members of which are cited in Chancellor Wharton's introductory remarks, provided invaluable help in defining the form and scope of the conference. Participants in the Retrospective, named in the Appendix, were most generous with their time: first as conference attendees and later in editing their remarks for publication. Finally, the support provided by the Rockefeller Institute staff, especially the editorial and organizational efforts of Roberta Bensky, was central to the successful completion of this project.

Our thanks to all who assisted us.

T. Norman Hurd   Albany, New York
Gerald Benjamin   New Paltz, New York

The
Nelson A.
Rockefeller
Institute
of
Government

State University
of New York

Clifton R. Wharton, Jr.
    Chair, Board of Overseers

Warren F. Ilchman
    Director

James K. Morrell
    Deputy Director

Alison M. Chandler
    Publications Associate

Barbara A. Plocharczyk
    Marketing Associate

William J. Moran, Cynthia Wilson
    Special Assistants

Design, Telecommunications/Composition: The Type & Design Center, Inc., Latham, NY

Printing: The Saratoga Printing Co., Inc., Saratoga Springs, NY

Direct inquiries to:
Publications Department
Rockefeller Institute of Government
411 State Street
Albany, New York 12203
(518) 473-5328

ISBN 0-914341-01-4

Table of Contents

Rockefeller In Retrospect: The Governor's New York Legacy

Edited by: T. Norman Hurd and Gerald Benjamin

Preface

Rockefeller in Retrospect

T. Norman Hurd

This volume explores the legacy of Nelson A. Rockefeller, the State's distinguished fiftieth governor, who served over a period of 15 years, from 1959 to 1973. About 100 people — many of them participants with the Governor in State Government during his tenure — gathered at the State University's Nelson A. Rockefeller Institute of Government in Albany's historic downtown district on December 10 and 11, 1982. It was their purpose to discuss, ten years later, the governor's long term impact upon politics, institutions, and policies in the Empire State. This volume is the record of that two day program.

The Rockefeller Institute was created by the Board of Trustees of the State University of New York in 1981. It is most fitting that the Institute, designed to focus the enormous resources of the University in support of the public policy needs of State Government, be formally launched with this program, a survey of its namesake's activist leadership; leadership that, indeed, created the University in its modern form.

This retrospective represented a unique and unprecedented effort by many of the Governor's closest colleagues and assistants to systematically review and appraise the efforts of one of New York's most famous, important, and controversial governors. Nelson Rockefeller's achievements were so significant and wide-ranging that it was difficult to decide upon a limited number of areas that might be addressed in a two-day meeting. Finally, eight of special importance were chosen. They included the Governor's methods as a manager; his financial innovations; his political leadership; his performance as a "master builder"; his efforts on behalf of workers in the State; and his initiatives in social, educational, and criminal justice policy-making.

Outstanding among Nelson A. Rockefeller's many achievements was his remarkable ability to identify public problems facing the people of the State, to develop feasible solutions, and to press for legislative and public approval to enact them. The consensus of those who took part in the retrospective was that these efforts made an indelible impression upon the government and people of the State.

The Nelson A. Rockefeller Institute is prepared to play a major continuing role in contributing to the on-going study of current and future public problems of responsive state government functioning in a democratic society. Its goal will be to seek sound solutions to these problems, in conformance with the Nelson A. Rockefeller approach, and thus improve the service offered by State Government to the people of New York.

Introduction

The Plan and Purpose of the Conference

Clifton R. Wharton, Jr.

It is for me a very singular pleasure to welcome you to the Nelson A. Rockefeller Institute and this conference, "Rockefeller in Retrospect: The Governor's Legacy." In doing so, I am reminded of the words of John Kennedy when he addressed America's Nobel laureates at a dinner at the White House. Kennedy quipped, and I quote, "Never has such genius been assembled at the White House at one time since Thomas Jefferson dined there alone." I am quite confident that a similar comment might be made for those who are assembled here today.

The subject of our conference is Governor Rockefeller's profound impact upon the policies, processes, and institutions of this State. It is an appropriate inaugural for this SUNY-wide Institute that bears his name. Surely, few people in the history of this State have had such a determinative influence on our lives as has Nelson A. Rockefeller. Throughout the State are the physical reminders of his vision. Our contemporary problems and opportunities very much bear the mark of that long distinguished and sometimes controversial governorship.

So important do my colleagues and I at the State University of New York feel this contribution of Nelson Rockefeller to be, that we felt analysts of State politics and future generations of New Yorkers alike needed to have a record, a transcript of the judgments of the chief participants and chief architects of that era. Those persons with active engagement with the Governor and the gift of hindsight can do what no historian or political scientist can do — to "tell it as it was" and evaluate how it has become. The people here assembled can produce an oral history that will be unique in the annals of state politics. This will be a legacy in itself for future governors to consider (perhaps even with a bit of anxiety as they realize that their colleagues, too, might be called upon to appraise their tenure at some future date at this very same Institute).

I would like to take a moment to identify one person who could not be here. It is, of course, Mayor Erastus Corning of Albany. He was a lifelong friend of the Governor, beginning with their boyhood summers together in Maine. Mayor Corning wrote to me recently from his hospital bed in Boston regretting his inability to be here and to chair a panel.

While the contributions of this conference, I believe, will be unique, it is also true that every subject of every panel deserves a conference of its own and at least a full-length book. That such rich experience as you have must be summarized and economized upon to the degree that it must, is unfortunate. Our solace is that the transcript and eventual volume of this conference will be seen as a source for further scholarship and, indeed, even a goad to you to put in writing your views of the Rockefeller era.

Whatever limitations the sheer importance of the subject places on the necessary brevity of the conference, the success of the conference, the success of the event, indeed, the virtual reason we have achieved this gathering, is the fruit of the Rockefeller Retrospective Advisory Committee, whose members include Governor Wilson, Bill Ronan, Stanley Steingut, Manly Fleischman, Donna Shalala, Bob MacCrate, Al Marshall, Bobby Douglass, Hugh Morrow, Joe Zimmerman, James Underwood and Gerald Benjamin. I would particularly like to thank and congratulate the acting director of the Institute, Warren Ilchman, whose tremendous energies have led to this outstanding congregation. In particular, an enormous debt is owed to the chair of the Advisory Committee, T. Norman Hurd. He devoted to this conference the same energies and dedication that I'm quite confident he devoted to the annual budgets of Governors Dewey and Rockefeller—and yes, to everything that he touched during his many years of service to New York State. We are all in his and their debt.

Finally, let me speak for a few minutes about the Rockefeller Institute. The Institute, along with the Rockefeller College of Public Affairs and Policy at the University Center at Albany, was created by the Trustees of the State University last year to mobilize the public affairs activities of the 64 SUNY campuses and to make them more accessible to those in Albany concerned with research and training with regard to State problems. The Institute has three programs at present. The first is a fellowship program that brings students, faculty and others to do research on subjects of pertinence to the State. There are, for instance, five junior and four senior fellows in residence this academic year. The second activity is a public affairs publications program which brings recently published articles and work-in-progress by SUNY faculty to the attention of New York policy makers. Third, the Institute will be the setting for seminars, workshops and conferences such as this one, the first. Finally, internships, consultantships, and contract research are expected to be a part of the Institute's work.

The goal of the Institute and this marvelous facility is to provide a site to provide a service to the State Government of New York whereby the scholarly resources of the State University and our sister independent institutions may be engaged with the ongoing, critical problems of the State.

The Institute is governed by a Board of Overseers with official, SUNY, and citizen members. Among its citizen overseers are three participants in this conference — Norm Hurd, Evelyn Cunningham and Bill Ronan. The finances for the Institute's program and for the restoration of this extraordinary building have come from the SUNY Research Foundation. Contrary to appearance, this is not an official grantee of the Rockefeller family or the estate of the late Governor.

I look forward to your panels today and tomorrow and extend to you once more our appreciation and gratitude for your coming and our anticipation of the tremendously valuable time you will spend here with us.

Chapter I

The Man and Public Servant

Malcolm Wilson

Norman, Chancellor Wharton and friends. I'm delighted to have had the opportunity to join with all of you for this two-day session. And I want to express my personal appreciation to Chancellor Wharton for the inspiration which led to the convening of it and to Dr. Thomas Norman Hurd and to the other members of the Advisory Committee.

I recognize, ladies and gentlemen, that I rise in the presence of men and women, most of whom were very much a part of the administration of our late friend, Governor Rockefeller. And hence, I feel very much like someone who would rise to give a travelogue with Lowell Thomas in the first row. To attempt to add at all to the sum total of your knowledge is a very formidable task. As a consequence, I feel that I should not plan to write the Lord's Prayer on the head of a pin by giving you a synthesis of the accomplishments of Nelson Rockefeller as I understood them over a period of 15 years. Rather, I thought that I might most usefully just speak of Rockefeller the man as I knew him, because the man and the qualities of the man were obviously very much a part of what he accomplished.

Christopher Wren, as we all know, was one of the great architects. He specialized in churches, and after he had built St. Paul's, Wren felt that it was his crowning achievement. When he died, Wren's son put a small plaque, lettered in Latin, in St. Paul's. That plaque reads: *Si monumentum requiris, circumspice,* which, in English means: "If you seek the creative product of the man, look about you." That certainly would have application to the things we'll be looking at today and tomorrow.

We meet under the auspices of the State University of New

York which, under the leadership of the Governor, became the largest public university in all the world. But its growth was not only quantitative, it was qualitative as well. And at the same time, virtually in the shadow of the Capitol, we have the College of Saint Rose — one unit of the State's far-flung private college system. The Governor also had concern that the young men and young women of our State should have complete freedom of choice in higher education between the private sector and public sector institutions. Therefore, he increased the number and value of Regents' Scholarships, provided financial grants called "Scholar Incentives" for students attending tuition-charging colleges and universities located in our State, increased the loans available through the Higher Education Assistance Corporation, and established a system of direct grants, called "Bundy Aid," on a per degree basis to independent colleges.

If we crane our necks a little, we can see what we started calling "The South Mall." It is the Nelson A. Rockefeller Empire State Plaza — the result of the innovation of Nelson Rockefeller and his determination that we would have here in Albany the most beautiful and most functional Capitol among all of the states in the nation. And it was not easy. But interestingly, "those who came to scoff remained to pray" — because among those who boast the loudest about it are many who were the most critical during the course of its planning and construction.

It is of such things that I thought I would speak to you, as I talk about Nelson Rockefeller the man, hoping that scholars with a desire to know more about him than they can find either from contemporary accounts of Nelson Rockefeller during his 15 years in the governorship, or even from the many books which have been written about him, will be advantaged by the recollections of so many of us here who worked closely with him on a day-to-day basis. I apologize to those who are intimately familiar with some of the things that I am going to say, but if even only one of you learns or hears something which he or she has not heard before, I will be pleased.

It was shortly after he was graduated from Dartmouth College that Nelson Rockefeller was approached by the then Chairman of the Westchester County Republican Committee, Mr. William Ward. He sent for him and told him that the Rockefellers had a commitment to Westchester County. They were enjoying the benefits of living there, as Mr. Ward reminded him, and Mr. Ward felt that they should do something in terms of serving in county government. He told Nelson Rockefeller that he would like to bring about Nelson's appointment as a member of the Public Health Board of Westchester County, and Nelson accepted. He was, I think, about twenty-five years old. The interesting thing is that he continued as a member of that Public Health Board until just before he took the oath of office as Governor of New York. I really think that of the various public services which he rendered, that was the one which he enjoyed the most. I mention this so that historians will remember that Nelson Rockefeller had an early commitment to the service of his fellow citizens through government.

It would be idle for me to recite in the presence of this company the very significant nationwide and worldwide services which Nelson provided while serving by appointment of a series of Presidents, beginning with the late President Franklin D. Roosevelt. Among the more significant of them were his work in Latin America and his leadership in the organization of the United Nations. It is easy for us to forget some of these things because we focus on what is recent and sometimes we forget those things which were — and still are — of great importance.

I come now to the public service he performed which really made him decide that he wanted to run for Governor of New York, namely his service as the Under Secretary of Health, Education and Welfare under Oveta Culp Hobby. Nelson threw himself with great vigor into that, as he always did in every undertaking. He had a well of energy which was the envy of everyone and which made those of us who were weaker, physically and emotionally, nervous wrecks. He proposed legislative approaches to the problems faced by that agency; he went to Capitol Hill and talked to congressmen and to chairmen of committees, and he testified before committees. He felt totally frustrated because, with few exceptions, his proposals met with something less than enthusiasm on Capitol Hill. And so he decided that the way to get things done was by the executive branch, and that's why he decided that he would seek the governorship of New York.

In 1956, Senator Walter Mahoney appointed Nelson as chairman of a committee which was to prepare recommendations for consideration at the next Constitutional Convention. It was then, I believe, that one of the participants here met Nelson Rockefeller for the first time. And that's Bill Ronan, who was the executive director of the commission. And a man who is not here, and I wish he were, is George Hinman of Binghamton, who was the counsel to that commission. Through that mechanism, Nelson had an opportunity, without indicating the use to which he planned to put the knowledge he gained, to get some rather detailed information about the government itself, about how state government functioned. Bear in mind that up to that time he had always been a national and international man, except for service on the County Board of Health in Westchester County. The Constitutional Convention was never held because the people voted down the proposition to convene one, but nonetheless, Nelson did serve as chairman of that preparatory commission.

I move you now to 1958. In 1958, the aspirants for the Republican nomination for Governor were Ozzie Heck of Schenectady, the long-time Speaker of the Assembly; Senator Walter Mahoney of Buffalo, the Majority Leader of the Senate; Leonard Hall of Nassau, who had served in the Assembly, in Congress, as Surrogate of Nassau County, and Chairman of the Republican National Committee; and Paul Williams, who was a former United States Attorney for the Southern District of New York.

These were the aspirants, and as late as April of 1958 our friends from the press were speculating as to which of these men would receive the Republican nomination and would be defeated by Averell Harriman in November.

In late January of 1958, on a Sunday night, Nelson Rockefeller and I met with the Republican Chairman of Westchester County, Herbert Gerlach. A little background might be helpful. The Westchester County Republican Committee pioneered fund-raising dinners, priced at $50 a plate in those happy, pre-inflation days. When Tom Dewey became Governor, he picked up the concept for the Republican State Committee. It was Westchester's custom to have a speaker from Washington and a speaker from the State at each of these dinners. In January of 1954, Nelson Rockefeller was the Washington spokesman and I was privileged to be the speaker from the State. And that happened again at the January 1958 dinner. Nelson Rockefeller, although not actually from Washington at that time, was billed as the speaker from Washington and I was the State speaker.

It was on the Sunday night following that January 1958 dinner that we met at Mr. Gerlach's law office in White Plains. I learned, when I got there, that Nelson Rockefeller had told County Chairman Herb Gerlach, at that dinner, that he would like to talk to him about the possibility of his seeking the Republican nomination for Governor. The Sunday night meeting was set up, I was asked to come over, and we talked about the matter. Nelson said that he would appreciate it, if he made the decision that he would seek the nomination, if he would have the support of his County Committee. Mr. Gerlach responded that if I aspired for the nomination, the Westchester County Committee would back me. I said that I had no such aspiration for 1958 and expressed the view that Nelson would be an excellent candidate, and one who could defeat Governor Harriman. I added that I knew what strategy could be best employed to win the Republican nomination for him.

One day in late April I received a telephone call at my law office in White Plains from Nelson Rockefeller, asking if he could come up and talk to me on his way home. He said he would be driving from New York to Pocantico and would like to have a visit about the subject which we had discussed at the end of January in Mr. Gerlach's office. I told him I would be glad to see him, and he said he would be at my office at 4:00 p.m., but he arrived at 5:15! Nelson said that he had decided to seek the nomination and wanted to see me because at that meeting in January I had mentioned that I knew the strategy to pursue the nomination successfully. I outlined what I had in mind, and he asked whether I would be willing to undertake it on his behalf.

Since I was perceived as being a conservative during my 20 years in the legislature, and Nelson Rockefeller was perceived as being of liberal bent, I said that I wanted to know more about him than I did before I would undertake to talk to my upstate friends. And as I talked to him over a two-hour period, it became very evident to me that, in fairness, Nelson Rockefeller should not properly be labeled a liberal.

We lived in a time then — and we live in a time now — when our friends of the Fourth Estate insist on applying labels to public figures. And the label which they had attached to Nelson Rockefeller was "liberal." To the contrary, it became evident to me during our talk that he was someone for whom there was no label. Our late friend Ken Keating had a somewhat similar problem and he said there was no label for what he really was, philosophically, unless one coined the word "conserveral." During our talk, I discerned that's what Nelson Rockefeller was. He was conservative in fiscal matters, but in terms of what you would call human rights, he was liberal. How frequently, how incessantly, ladies and gentlemen, did all of us hear him speak, in public and in private, of his deep commitment to spiritual values and the dignity of every human being!

I felt completely comfortable after that discussion, and I told him that I would undertake the responsibility of executing the plan I was certain would get him the nomination.

In those days, statewide candidates were chosen in a convention, with the delegates chosen by the county political organizations, referred to by the press as the "smoke-filled rooms." At the state level, the "smoke-filled room" has produced giants like Al Smith, Franklin D. Roosevelt, Herbert Lehman, Thomas E. Dewey, and Nelson Rockefeller. Now we have direct primaries for state-wide office. Look what they have produced! National conventions with "smoke-filled rooms" produced giants — winners and losers — men like Franklin D. Roosevelt, John W. Davis,

Wendell Willkie, Al Smith, Tom Dewey, and Adlai Stevenson. Now we have presidential primaries, and look what they have produced!

The custom before Nelson and I undertook our effort was that those who were aspirants sought to enlist the support of every county chairman to get his delegates to vote for that aspirant. That was the pattern which Ozzie Heck, Walter Mahoney, Paul Williams and Leonard Hall followed. However, what we did was to go underneath, to get to the men and women at lower levels of leadership within each county, as well as the county chairman and vice-chairman.

The pattern I employed was to call a county chairman — I knew each of them well — and asked him or her to arrange a dinner or a luncheon at my expense, and to invite county officials as well as city and town chairmen and vice-chairmen and any other prominent Republicans of his or her choice. I always requested that, if possible, the table be set up as a hollow square, to avoid head table "problems."

I emphasized the fact that this was to be done at my expense. I felt it essential that Nelson be presented as a man and not as a Rockefeller, lest it be felt that he was seeking to "buy" the nomination. I had made an arrangement with Herbert Gerlach, the Westchester County Republican Chairman, that I would pay out of my personal checking account the cost of all the dinners and luncheons that would be scheduled, and that after those expenses, so advanced by me, had reached a level of $5,000 or so, I would furnish the receipted bills to Mr. Gerlach who would see to it that the County Committee gave me a reimbursement check. Furthermore, although Nelson and other members of the Rockefeller family had been for 50 years the principal financial supporters of the Westchester County Republican Committee, I told Nelson to be sure that neither he nor any other member of the Rockefeller family made any contributions whatsoever to the Republican County Committee either during the pre-convention period or, if he was nominated for Governor, during the ensuing campaign. My reason for this instruction (which was scrupulously observed) was to avoid any charge that Rockefeller money was being used, even indirectly, to secure Nelson's nomination and election.

A further, and very important, extension of this same concept was my insistence that as we moved about the State, we would do so entirely without the "trappings" of wealth. We traveled mainly in my Buick, with me at the wheel, and the "traveling party" consisted of Nelson, his son Steven, and me, with Nelson's wife, Mary, accompanying us on some occasions. I have thought many times about the physical discomfort Nelson bore by this mode of travel. His preference had always been, and continued to be, travel by plane, with as little automobile travel as was necessary. He understood what I was trying to do, however, and never grumbled. As a matter of fact, a corollary advantage accrued to Nelson by this mode of travel, because he learned more about the geography of all parts of the State, traversing them by automobile, than he had ever known by flying around the State. Before we undertook our travels, he was familiar with the major population centers of upstate New York — Buffalo, Rochester, Syracuse, Utica, Binghamton, and Albany — all of which he had visited when he was serving as chairman of the commission planning for the Constitutional Convention which I had mentioned earlier. But during our automobile trips, his eyes were opened to the range and beauty of the wide areas of our State: the smaller cities, the towns and villages, the breathtaking beauty of the Finger Lakes area and many of our state parks, and the Southern Tier counties out to Westfield on Lake Erie at the extreme western edge of Chautauqua County. That experience was immensely helpful to him when he undertook his responsibilities as Governor.

There were some very amusing incidents which occurred as we utilized this mode of travel. For example, one of the luncheons which I had arranged through the County Chairman of Cortland County was scheduled for the American Legion Hall in the small city of Cortland. As we approached the building, I noted that there was a rather large crowd in front of the building and that there were barriers at the curb line making parking space available for the several automobiles which were obviously expected in the entourage. When only one vehicle — my Buick — arrived, and Nelson alighted with no — as I put it — "acolytes, synchophants or baggage handlers," the County Chairman who greeted us asked whether the other vehicles had lost their way. I must say that on that occasion, and on many similar occasions, it was clear to Nelson and to me that this low profile type of travel helped immeasurably in the successful effort to have Nelson received as a man rather than a Rockefeller.

The first such experience we had was on the evening of the day in June of 1958 when Nelson announced his candidacy for the Republican nomination at an afternoon press conference in his office on the fifty-sixth floor of 30 Rockefeller Plaza. After the announcement, he and I got into my Buick and drove to Kinderhook in Columbia County where a dinner had been scheduled, at my instance, by Myrtle Tinklepaugh, the County Chairman. About 50 men and women were in attendance, and at the end of the dinner all present, representing the full Republican leadership of Columbia County, including the five persons who were to be delegates to the convention, unanimously endorsed Nelson's candidacy. I was very anxious that this be done so that the same newspaper stories that carried the announcement of Nelson's candidacy on their front pages included mention of the fact that the first county which endorsed him was an upstate county — Columbia County — one of the most rural counties of the state.

It was at that dinner that I discovered the real secret of Nelson Rockefeller's appeal; namely, that he loved people as people. I saw demonstrated for the first time on that occasion what all of you who knew him no doubt noted; namely, that when Nelson was talking to any person, it was clear that for that particular period of time, whether it was ten seconds or one minute, the only two people in the world, insofar as Nelson was concerned, were Nelson and the person to whom he was speaking.

You and I have had the experience many times of observing people going through a receiving line. Almost invariably we note that the person at the head of the line is really not concentrating on the person whose hand is being shaken, but is rather looking over the shoulder of that person to try to figure out whether he or she knows the name of the next person in line. Nelson was a clear exception to that rule for the reason I have just indicated, and this was a major part of his appeal to people.

I think that the impact of this "love of people", which was Nelson's particular hallmark, was rarely more dramatically evident than when he attended county fairs, which is something we started to do in July 1958. The first of them was the Empire State Potato Festival, an annual event held in Savannah, in southern Wayne County. Within moments after our arrival, Nelson had taken off his coat and tie, rolled up his shirt sleeves and plunged into such activities as driving a tractor, engaging in a "tug-of-war," visiting the cattle barns and impressing the exhibitors with his knowledge of the fine points of their animals, walking down the midway with stops to purchase a hot dog or spun sugar candy on a stick — and devouring both with evident relish — and shaking hands with all the people he encountered. On that and subsequent similar occasions, as well as when we would get to some community and Nelson would immediately "take off" to walk up and down the main street, he reminded me of nothing but the Pied Piper of Hamelin, because people flocked to him and sort of formed an entourage accompanying and following him.

I am convinced that Nelson's love of people, as individual human beings, underlay most of his legislative innovations after he took office for — as all of you are aware — Nelson was nominated at the Republican Convention in Rochester in August and went on to defeat Averell Harriman quite handily in the November election, confounding all the political pundits of the Fourth Estate in the process.

I feel that I am taking much more of your time than I should, in view of our schedule for the day. By way of excuse, I can only observe that I admired Nelson so greatly and loved him so much that it is hard to stop talking about him. However, I will try to hurry to my conclusion by citing a few other specific traits of character I discerned in Nelson and, out of the vastness of his accomplishments in the interest of the people during his fifteen-year tenure as Governor, select a few examples to support my thesis.

Nelson was a man of courage.

Governor Rockefeller conferring with Lieutenant Governor Malcolm Wilson.

I will not mention his demonstration of courage in meeting crises in his personal life, such as the tragic loss of his son, Michael, in New Guinea, nor in his political life, such as his standing up to the hooting, jeering crowd of Goldwater supporters at the National Convention in San Francisco in 1964, insisting that he was going to complete his remarks rather than fold under mob pressure. Rather I will mention a couple of actions he took as Governor which demonstrated that courage. The first I will mention is his presentation to the Legislature in January 1959 of his first Annual Budget.

You will recall that this budget called for the imposition of additional taxes. Traditionally, governors simply sent to the Senate and Assembly, by messenger, their Budget Message and accompanying legislation. Not Nelson, however, in the case of his first Budget Message. Overruling the objections of all of his advisors, including me, Nelson insisted that he was going to present his Budget Message in person at a joint session of the Senate and Assembly — and he did so.

From his point of view, he felt it was necessary to proceed in this fashion because of the propensity of the Legislature, each year, to vote increasing appropriations for State aid for education —which was mother's milk to them — in a pattern which postponed much of the cost to the next ensuing State fiscal year. The increased State aid helped secure their re-election and the unpopular step of enacting new revenue measures to pay the bill was postponed to another day. The principal thrust of Nelson's Budget Message was that, while he fully shared the desire of the Legislature to ease the burden of local real estate taxpayers in meeting the cost of primary and secondary education, he was firmly committed to the proposition that the taxes to finance the cost of such increased State aid should be imposed simultaneously with its grant. He knew what he proposed to say would be far from popular with the legislators in that joint session, yet he felt he should tell them face-to-face rather than merely sending up his Budget Message by messenger. That was an act of courage.

As just one other example, I would mention his "taking on" the whole public school lobby — PTA's, the school boards, and the teachers' organizations — in insisting that the State, to the extent it constitutionally could, should help the parents who, while paying their taxes to support the public schools, chose to send their children to non-public schools — mainly operated under religious auspices. His first of many proposals in this area — the Textbook Bill which narrowly passed the Legislature — was signed into law by Nelson and was upheld as constitutional by the Court of Appeals.

Nelson was a balanced man.

From the very beginning of his first administration, Nelson made clear his recognition of the fact that, with the constantly increasing sophistication and technological innovation in industry, business and commerce, a high school diploma which sufficed for a job opportunity when I first entered the legislature in 1939 was grossly inadequate for young people of the 1960's and thereafter. He recognized, too, that the facilities of the State University were grossly inadequate in terms of providing educational opportunities for young men and women who, born during the "baby boom" which followed World War II, would be graduating from high school in the 1960's and 1970's. Therefore, he launched a huge, ambitious program for quantitative and qualitative growth of the State University, including community colleges and professional schools, which, within a remarkably short time, made ours the largest state university in the nation.

At the same time he wanted to make certain that the colleges and universities in the private sector of higher education would be financially able to survive and to meet their expansion needs, because — as he so often put it — he felt that every young person in the State who seeks and desires a college education should have complete freedom of choice as to whether he or she should seek it in the public or non-public sector. Consequently, he successfully proposed to the Legislature over a span of years a great variety of programs to assist the private sector colleges and universities: a huge increase in the number and value of Regents' Scholarships; expansion of Dormitory Authority's authority to finance class-rooms and residential facilities; the innovative "Scholar Incentive Program"; and Bundy Aid, providing direct payments of State funds to private sector, independent colleges and universities of New York on a "per degree" basis. Those were but some of his programs to help maintain the traditional partnership of public and private higher educational institutions in our State.

So, too, did he take a balanced approach in the field of public welfare, for while he saw to the appropriation of increased State funds to provide food, clothing and shelter for the economically deprived, he also established the Office of Welfare Inspector General to help weed out the welfare cheaters or — as he put it —"separate the greedy from the needy."

Nelson was a man of vision.

All of those who worked closely with him — a company which includes many of you here today — are aware of the fact that Nelson always acted on the premise that it was best to try to discern a problem as it was emerging over the horizon and undertake to transform it into an opportunity, rather than to let the problem grow and grow until it blew up to such proportions as to make it difficult, if not impossible, to effect a satisfactory solution. If anyone were to attempt to characterize in a few words the whole thrust of Nelson's major programs during his fifteen years as Governor, it would best be done, in my judgment, by the expression "transforming problems into opportunities."

An example which comes immediately to mind was the manner in which he dealt with the problem of inadequate higher education facilities for the children born during the post-war "baby boom" which I mentioned a few moments ago. That problem was just peeking over the horizon when he recognized it, dealt with it effectively, and transformed it into massive opportunities for hundreds of thousands of young people.

He discerned that all involved in all aspects of the visual and performing arts were finding it increasingly difficult to secure the financial resources required, not merely for the growth, but even for the survival of those activities. Therefore, he proposed the creation of the New York State Council of the Arts with an initial appropriation of $15 million — if my memory serves me correctly — to fund grants for the support of all aspects of the arts, including bringing into upstate areas symphony orchestras, ballet companies and other performing artists, where their talents could enrich the lives of vast numbers of people who would not otherwise have had the opportunity to have lives so enriched and ennobled. It was not easy — in face of all the other demands on the public purse — to persuade the Legislature to support his proposal. Nelson brought his fabled suasive efforts fully to bear and succeeded in having his proposal enacted into law. Thereafter, the Federal government and most of our sister states began to provide taxpayer support for the arts, and I venture the observation that but for Nelson's innovation, our nation would never have had the richness in performing and visual arts which it has today.

Nelson Rockefeller was a man of strong convictions, but he did not have false pride in the validity of his own views.

Throughout his whole administration, Nelson had staff meetings, at least weekly beginning in November, when the broad outline of the next budget began to be discussed in depth, and two or three times a week once the legislative session commenced. As each annual session of the Legislature neared its close, such sessions were held at least once daily. The nucleus at those sessions consisted of the Governor, the Lieutenant Governor, the Attorney General, the Secretary to the Governor, Counsel to the Governor, the Budget Director, the Press Secretary (later known as the Director of Communications), and the Governor's personal secretary (the last of whom was Ann Whitman). Depending upon the nature of the matters to be discussed, other members of the administration were invited to attend. It was in such meetings that the Governor, among other things, unveiled his proposals for new programs. Everyone present was expected to join in discussion and to offer his or her comments or criticisms. Although he was the Governor — and a Rockefeller — if Nelson discerned that criticism was valid, he modified his proposal to meet the objection or dropped it from consideration. He fought hard to defend his proposals against criticism but he acquiesced with grace when he could discern that the intellectual weight of the evidence was against him.

Nelson was an indefatigable worker.

In a long life, I think I have never encountered a person with more energy than Nelson Rockefeller. He seemed to have an inexhaustible supply.

As a legislative session enters its final weeks, there are tremendous pressures on those who are involved in the ultimate decision as to what bills, especially major program bills, should be passed by the Legislature and signed into law by the Governor, and what precise articulations should be used in each case. This process invariably involves intense negotiation between the legislative leaders and their professional staffs on the one hand, and the Governor and his top staff on the other, as efforts are made to reconcile differences and, on the Governor's part, to try to be sure that in the resolution of those differences the major features of his program bill survive. Insofar as the Executive Branch is concerned, the Governor is the "bottom line" and Nelson himself, especially during the final ten days of each session, would often devote sixteen or eighteen hours a day in meetings with his own key staff, with legislative leaders, with individual legislators, and with groups of legislators who shared, in common, some objection or another to a particular feature of a program bill. Very often these meetings would start with a breakfast conference at the Executive Mansion beginning at 7:30 in the morning and end late the same night — again at the Executive Mansion — sometimes following a dinner meeting.

Frankly, it always seemed to me that it was that aspect of his responsibility which Nelson enjoyed most, and in those settings his quick mind, his suasive talent, his charm, his determination, and his willingness to accommodate opposing views (provided that accommodation did not blunt the major thrust of his proposal) combined admirably to accomplish the result he desired in the public interest. He was as intellectually sharp and apparently physically unweary at the end of such a day as he was at its beginning, and leaped into the fray early the next morning with the same unbounded vigor. He had great "staying power," and, in instances too numerous to mention, the fact that he was able to outlast, in energy, those with whom he would be negotiating — many of them younger than he — led them to make the concessions Nelson wanted, just so that they could get back to their hotels and get to bed!

Except that he generally succeeded in spending a couple of weeks each August at his home in Seal Harbor, Maine, Nelson took very few vacations in the usual sense of the word. Whenever he took vacations, however, those of us who were close to him soon became aware of the fact that, away from day-to-day responsibility — his responsibility — his creative talent came to the fore. And, sure enough, it was a rare occasion when, upon his return from vacation, he did not unveil in a staff meeting the outlines of one or two new major programs.

Nelson was a loyal man.

I do not speak of his fierce loyalty to our country and our system of government, but rather of his loyalty to fellow man. Let me mention just two instances.

Judson Morhouse was the Chairman of the Republican State Committee in 1958 and was helpful, behind the scenes, in securing Nelson's nomination for Governor. Unfortunately, a few years later he became involved, along with Martin Epstein, Chairman of the State Liquor Authority, in an attempt to "shake down" the Playboy Club in connection with its application for a liquor license at one of its establishments. He was convicted and sentenced to jail. The appeal process was a long one, and during its course he was afflicted with a form of muscular dystrophy which became progressively worse. When all his appeals from his conviction were exhausted and he faced the prospect of incarceration, he applied for executive clemency in the form of a commutation of sentence. With few exceptions, all of those whom the Governor regarded as his close advisors warned him that his grant of the application could well cause an adverse political reaction and would surely precipitate editorial criticism. Nelson put those considerations aside and granted commutation out of his loyalty to a man who had been loyal to him.

When, after the resignation of President Nixon, Vice President Ford became President of the United States, Nelson, who during all of his political career from 1958 had steadfastly refused to be considered for the Vice-Presidential slot on the national ticket on the ground that he did not want to be "standby equipment", was anxious to be appointed Vice-President by President Ford. I would add, parenthetically, that at President Ford's request relayed to me through Nelson, I wrote a confidential letter to President Ford giving my assessment of Nelson, in the course of which I emphasized the fact that he was always a "team player" and an intensely loyal man. As you know, the President appointed Nelson as Vice-President in August 1974, but the Democrat-controlled United States Senate dragged out the confirmation process — including its requirement of detailed disclosure as to the nature and extent of Nelson's finances — through the balance of August, all of September, October, and early November in order to get the greatest political mileage they could.

President Ford's naming of Nelson as Vice-President met the disfavor of the conservative groups. The Republican Party's collective hearts clearly belonged to Ronald Reagan, their allegiance having shifted to him after their successful effort to nominate Barry Goldwater in 1964 resulted in the political disaster to the party nationwide which that nomination had produced. Bo Calloway (of South Carolina, I believe) was the one who had been charged by President Ford with the responsibility of securing support of delegates from the southern states for Gerald Ford's nomination for a full four-year term. He told Gerald Ford that the southern delegates would not support him, unless he gave assurance that Nelson Rockefeller would not be his candidate for Vice-President. The President reported this to Nelson, who had clearly wanted to run for Vice-President with Gerald Ford. Whereupon, Nelson wrote a letter to the President, and released it to the press, stating that he did not wish to be considered by the Republican Convention for nomination as President Ford's running mate. Basically, it was his loyalty to Gerald Ford that prompted him to take that action.

Ironically, Bo Calloway did not deliver a single delegate from the deep South in support of President Ford's nomination. They all went to the standard of Ronald Reagan. Equally ironic, Ronald Reagan would have been nominated instead of Gerald Ford at the 1976 National Convention, unless Nelson — despite many adherents of Ronald Reagan among the county chairmen in New York State — had delivered virtually the entire New York State delegation in support of President Ford. Despite the bitter disappointment, Nelson's sense of loyalty motivated his action in this regard, and no one campaigned more vigorously for Gerald Ford during the election period than did Nelson.

One final observation and I am done. One of the greatest disappointments which I have experienced in my life is the circumstance that Nelson was never able to secure the Republican nomination for President. Had he been nominated in 1960 he would have beaten Jack Kennedy — and in 1964, Lyndon Johnson. He would have won in 1968 far more easily than did Richard

Nixon. My assertion is based on the fact, demonstrated time and time again in his candidacy in heavily Democratic New York State, that Nelson had tremendous appeal in the polling booth not alone to Republicans but to massive numbers of Democrats and Independents. Had he been elected President, he would have gone down in history as one of the great ones.

Chapter II

Experimentation in Social Policy: Medicaid, Community Mental Health, Drug Abuse

ABE LAVINE: On July 7, 1947 I came to work for New York State as one of the first three public administration interns. Another of these three was our theme setter for today, Al Marshall. We were appointed by the Director of the Budget, John Burton, without much formality; fortunately, because neither of us was able to pass Civil Service tests!

One of Al's early projects was the reorganization of the Public Service Commission (PSC). After he did that study and rendered his report, Chairman Ben Feinberg agreed to accept it if Al would go to work for him in the PSC. That's what happened.

After a few years of stirring up things there, Norm Hurd brought him back to Budget as Deputy Director. From there, he became Executive Officer to the Governor and later Secretary to the Governor. There probably weren't too many policy decisions that were made without his involvement, as you know. And he had major impact not only in policy and politics of the time but also on a lot of careers in the State.

For example, I got a call one day from Al. Some of you may never have seen him in his office when he's dealing with a problem. He paces the floor, he runs his hands through his hair, he bites his fingernails, he flails his arms, and so forth. He may have dealt with 20 different things that particular day, but at that point in time the whole world rests or falls on the problem that he's dealing with at the moment. Well, in this particular case, he was having some labor pains with one strike by AFSCME (American Federation of State, County, and Muncipal Employees) recently settled, another by CSEA (Civil Service Employees Association) threatened, and all sorts of problems and issues ensuing from the passage of the Taylor Law. Al simply said to me, "I want you to take over all this." Being somewhat stunned, I said, "Al, you know, you and I have been friends for a long time. What are you trying to do to me?" He shrugged that off and said, "Never mind, we've got a problem here and you've got to do it." He didn't even smile. I said, "I don't know anything about labor negotiations." He said, "You'll catch on in a few days." Of course, the School of Industrial and Labor Relations would not appreciate that comment. In any event, that's how Al influenced a lot of careers.

He tried to leave the State several times, but, as Joe Persico has said in his book, Governor Rockefeller didn't like valued staff members going out on their own. Al finally did leave the State, but not the Rockefellers. He became President of Rockefeller Center — one of the top corporate presidents in the country. Now, most recently, Al has indeed gone out on his own as president of his own consulting firm, Alton G. Marshall Associates, where he continues his unique style of "shaking things up" that we who knew him in the State are so familiar with.

Two months ago, Al and I celebrated our thirty-sixth consecutive birthday party together. Not only did we come to work together on the same day but, we have the same birthdate and we haven't missed a year. So without further ado, it's my pleasure to introduce the man who I'm privileged to grow old with, your friend and my friend, Al Marshall.

AL MARSHALL: Thank you all. Abe gets concerned as he's grown old. But I stay the same, because I've had this white hair since I was 30.

I would like to emphasize some things in our area, Experimentation in Social Policy, that may sound to you as though I'm taking exception to what Malcolm had to say, but I'm not. There's no question but that this man's personality affected the administration of government more than any other governor whom I have witnessed or read about. We all know that we all felt this, so we don't have to dwell on it.

But in this particular area of social experimentation, I'd like to dwell on two things that Malcolm said. One was his drive to be an elected official so he could have the power, not to just recommend, but to decide. The Governor had a favorite Spanish saying to the effect that the power lies in the elected official. This was a hell of a drive, and I want to emphasize it.

The second was, Malcolm described him as "a doer." He wanted things done. On the basis of these two characteristics and others, I'd like to suggest to you that during the Rockefeller administration we had experimentation in social policy without having an experimenter as a head of our government. He was not, in my judgment, what normally is thought of as an experimenter. He did not care about discovery for the sake of discovery. The experimentation was not what motivated the variety of programs we put into effect. He never said to me, "I am motivated to find the fundamental basis of this particular problem." The comment always was, "Goddamnit, we want to recognize the problems in this particular area and we want to have some program that will meet them." I think this drive to find solutions to problems was as key a factor in that man's administration as any humanitarian or experimental motivation.

As a matter of fact, I would submit to you that in many cases the impact he had on me was not like that of a Schweitzer or a Helen Hull or a Claire Booth or Jane Addams or anyone like them. No, that never came through to me. What came through to me was this absolute drive for planning solutions to State problems. I never sat down with the Governor and developed new programs in deeply emotional sessions. This is not to say that he didn't care about people. I believe that he did. He had, however, as an official, disassociated himself from that emotion, to address in a rather objective way the whole matter of the solution to the problem.

And speaking of problems, we got confused sometimes. And you all were part of this. We got confused about whether we had a problem or whether we had an alleged problem or whether we were just searching for a better way to do things. This all goes back to that absolute drive for doing things. I am sure we tried to solve, or attack, problems that had not yet reached problem stage to permit a solution.

It may very well be considered by historians as one of the negatives of the Rockefeller administration, that because of his own personality, drive, and perception he sometimes did not permit the ripening of a problem. Sometimes we did not always recognize the necessity for governmental lag between what society's needs are and what the government's reaction to them can be. This man sold solutions to problems which may not have reached, in normal terms, historical terms at least, the state where they were to be addressed.

And when I tell you that I think that the "doer" characteristics of the man were more important than his humanitarianism or experimental trait, the other program result that arose was that he did not wallow in the one best way to solve a problem. He did not want to be that democratic, because in order to do that it would be months and years of wrangling, and he wanted to get something done. If he had to do several things at the same time, he

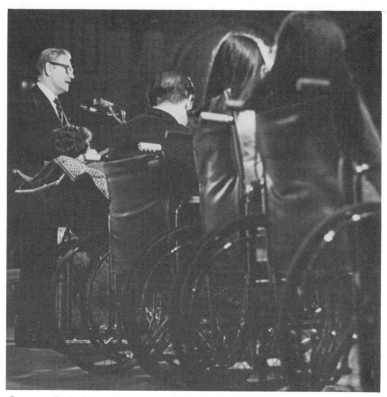

Governor Rockefeller addressing an "Employ the Handicapped" luncheon on May 27, 1970.

did several things at the same time. I'm not sure we didn't sometimes have programs that were antithetical because of this sense that we had to get on. Where I come from, they would call it "throwing more stuff at the barn, hoping some of it will stick." I think that is a real factor in my stand about his so-called "experimentation," which I do not characterize as experimentation, but as drive.

I think the other thing that I would like to bring to your attention for further shaking around is that Rockefeller had his own version of "states' rights." That version, again, grew out of this "doer drive," this executive power function. He insisted that we would address problems, sometimes without really giving a damn whether it was a local problem or a national problem. We were going to address it. The great State of New York could do something about it and address it irrespective of the root causes of that problem. I think that when we look back we will find this state's rights mixed with the doer and executive drive, and he operated one of the most expensive administrations that we ever had. And I think probably Malcolm was right in saying that I happened to be in the spot, along with others, where we made revenue sharing necessary.

The third point I want to make again ties in to these two characteristics. I think the structure of government, particularly at the top, had a great deal to do with the activities in the social areas. The very fact that we set up this system of program associates in the Governor's office caused, as Alan and Hollis know particularly, this constant drive by the associates for new programs in their particular social field. The concept was that established operating agencies were more apt to want to keep things status quo in government than to change them. Therefore, the program associates needed to reach in and excite that group to come up with some new ideas and also to encourage them to know that they had a friend in court for any new program they might wish. That very structure alone led to the goddamnedest number of programs!. Look at the annual messages of Rockefeller in the social area. Perhaps this was experimentation, but I never thought of it that way.

The other point I wanted to make, which again ties with the "doer" concept, was his concept of campaigning. I think Bill Ronan had the greatest hand in this, but we were all swept up in it. Rockefeller's concept of campaigning was to do a substantive campaign. Boy, we had to have an A.M. and a P.M. When we had to have something for the evening papers, we might come up with a rat control program. If it was some kind of strange mental aberration we had not addressed, Alan had to come up with one because we had to put something out for the morning papers.

We used to have a big book after the campaign: it was called "Campaign Promises." And I remember we had one person who kept track of it. It was a cardinal sin if we hadn't done something about what we had promised in the campaign. So we went ahead and we redesigned programs, because we had promised to do so in the campaign. I know, and my colleagues speak for themselves, that from the second floor the situation got to a point where we felt we were straining to get those programs, particularly when we had to put them in in the last year of a term, and we were getting ready to run the next campaign.

Specific examples of social program innovation will be spoken about by others, but the thought or direction that I'm trying to set for you can be examined in connection with Medicaid. Medicaid was a political decision. It was not some deep-rooted emotional humanitarian drive. I stood on the podium of the Speaker of the Assembly and negotiated the number that we were going to set in respect to the level for Medicaid eligibility.

You will recall, and others will speak about it in more detail, that since we had been very generous in the State of New York over time, as opposed to other states, we had an eligibility level of $4,800 for a family of four, or something like that. The Federal law on Medicaid was interpreted so that we had to improve on what we had in existence in order to be eligible for the Federal program. Bob Kennedy was insisting, through Travia, on a new level of $6,000. I started at $5,000. We ended up at $5,600. Rockefeller didn't know what that would cost, and I'm here to tell you that his own staff didn't know what it was to cost. It probably was the biggest financial boo-boo that we had in the history of the administration, except perhaps for the South Mall. That was a political decision.

I do not say that Rockefeller did not take comfort in the fact that other persons were going to be treated. But I don't want you to see this as experimentation, or the action of a governor who was a "bleeding heart." There have been plenty of bleeding hearts who have been elected who couldn't get a thing done. This was a man who was a doer and hence the most comprehensive Medicaid plan in the country was established.

Now consider "The War on Drugs" as we described it, as you probably remember, in the Annual Message. We all went down to see Wilbur Cohen who was then head of H.E.W. We were going to have a big drug program, and even then Rockefeller was in the stage of what we called a "criminal modality." We were going to set up great big, what we laughingly called "Happy Farms." We were going to have barbed wire around and practically put people into concentration camps.

I had already had the word from guys who were a lot smarter than I am, like Ed Van Ness, who said that the Federal government was committed to the "health modality." I told the Governor that the Feds would see this as a health ticket: "They're not going to watch you lock up everybody." Well, unfortunately, this was right. They insisted on a health modality. He came back. He was going to do something about that.

We threw more money at the drug problem than any other government had ever done — and I think has done since — and we did everything from A to Z. If playing a cello might help you, you did that. If yoga could help you, you did that. We built facilities, we found facilities, all in an effort with this crash program. He was constantly chewing me out because we weren't getting enough places.

Bob remembers the classic story of when I got a buzz one morning and Rockefeller said to me, "I want to buy the Queen Mary. We're going to put it in a slip and we're going to make it a drug rehabilitation center." And I said, "My God, I'm from Fenton, Michigan and the Queen Mary represents all the elegance in the whole world. You can't have junkies running around the Queen Mary." The Governor's response: "I want you to buy the Queen Mary." I called up O.G.S. and asked, "For God's sake, have we ever bought an international steamship before in the State of New York?" They said, "Call us back." Then they said "Oh, we can try the Admiral T. Panz, a shipper in London." I called Al Haight, then Deputy Controller. I said, "How the hell do you pay for a steamship in England?"

And after I had struggled with this prospect for what I had thought was a reasonably short time, the buzzer went off again. I failed to look at my *New York Times*, and right on the front page was a story that Lindsay had announced he was buying the Queen Mary, but he was going to make a high school out of it. In those days, remember, it was schools that were needed in New York City. McDonald had convinced him to do this. Rockefeller was in a rage, an absolute rage. I was insubordinate. I had not bought the Queen Mary because I did not want to buy the Queen Mary. What he was really mad about was that Lindsay had announced the idea publicly and it was for a better use. And we had about an hour of face-to-face shouting and screaming at one another. He questioned my loyalty and could not understand why in the hell we couldn't buy a steamship in a much shorter time.

I believe that Rockefeller was not the great social experimenter that his record might show, and that is a remarkable record. Rather, his drive as an executive, his use of his position as the elected executive, his urgent state's rights views (which cost us so much money and had us address problems without local help and in many cases without Federal help), his campaigning techniques, and his structure of government to take advantage of that executive power resulted in one of the greatest assaults on the greatest variety of diverse social programs that any state has undertaken.

There is no comparable experience in any state government. The two that I can think of that would even come close to matching the variety and scope of activities, of course, are national — Lyndon Johnson and his "Fair Deal" and Franklin D. Roosevelt in his early days in the 1930's when he had to address the Depression.

Perhaps, then, Nelson Rockefeller will not be seen as a social experimenter, but a social mechanic.

ABE LAVINE: O.K. We'll take our discussants now in the order in which they are shown on the program. And the first is our former Commissioner of Mental Hygiene from 1966 to 1974, Dr. Alan Miller.

ALAN MILLER: I don't want to debate Al and I'm not sure it's important about the meaning of the word "experiment" or "experimenter". I think, and I will illustrate that, at least in my experience, Governor Rockefeller may not have been the designer of experiments in the sense that an experimenter would be, but he was intrigued by experiments and was not afraid of them.

I could start with a brief reminiscence of my first official encounter, my first meeting with Nelson Rockefeller. Immediately after my appointment we were sitting in his office and he said, "There are two things I want to get straight right away. The first is, I want to make things all right between you and Senator Kennedy." Robert Kennedy had stormed through Willowbrook a little over four months before and had received a lot of publicity about the problems of the mentally retarded. (Incidentally, Nelson Rockefeller had done that about a year before Robert Kennedy had done it, without any fanfare to speak of.) But there were still afterwaves of the Kennedy visit and he said, "It's not fair for you to have to start as if coming from behind. I want to make things well between you and Senator Kennedy. Mental health, mental retardation, human service programs should not be partisan, should not be political."

That was very heavy stuff for me; the idea of sitting down with Robert Kennedy and Nelson Rockefeller and working this all out. But the fact is that when Kennedy was here, about ten days later, he called and said, "There's a meeting. Come on down." And we met. And, in fact, it worked that way for a long, long time.

The other thing the Governor said to me was, "I'm awfully sorry. We're now about a year and a half behind in our master plan of building thousand-bed hospitals." This had been started several years earlier and the notion of building thousand-bed hospitals in many parts of the State had been highly publicized. And I said, "Well, I think that's a good thing. Maybe it's good that we are a year and a half behind." He was surprised and said, "Why is that a good thing?" I said, "I'm not sure we know exactly what kind of hospitals we want to build, what their programs should be, or how they should be working with local programs."

Now this is a program that he had been identified with; there had been a lot of publicity about it. And here was an upstart, a new appointee who was saying, "I don't know if we should go ahead with this. Maybe there's some merit in our mistake in not having gone on ahead with this." He didn't say, "That's ridiculous. You go ahead and do this." He said, "Oh, I see." And he seemed to be intrigued.

About a week later, I was asked to prepare a briefing — a lengthy briefing in the new chart room — explaining what we had in mind. And so that was our first big chance to talk about some of the ideas, and a very attentive listener he was. And at the end of that time, he said, "O.K. You're right. I think we'll try it that way."

The thing that was really interesting to me at that time was that he was not asking us for certainty. He wanted something that seemed plausible. He was intrigued, it seemed to me, that we had suggested a way to proceed which had a certain flexibility from which we could learn as we went along, with a chance to correct our course when we made the inevitable errors. And that mode, of interacting with and developing programs, was one which characterized, as I view it in retrospect, my work with him.

Let me talk about community mental health a little more specifically. The first big initiative in community mental health actually had not been during Nelson Rockefeller's administration. In New York State, it was during the Dewey administration that the idea emerged that the local government should have some responsibility and develop a capacity for providing services for the mentally ill and the mentally retarded. At the time it was proposed — 1951, 1952 — it was an astonishing idea. Nowhere else in the country was it done, though it sounds so commonplace today. But, by 1958, '59, '60, it was established. I think virtually every state was doing it — had copied it. It needed a lot of strengthening, fixing up, tinkering with, enlarging, monitoring, and critical review, but the idea was set and it was no longer an innovation.

But the idea that grew out of some of the new ways of thinking about hospitals, and how local boards and the services that they provided could be integrated with long established State purposes, really was something which might be more interesting. At no time did he not support us in our efforts to try to do it. These local programs, up to that point, had been concerned primarily with a group of people who were younger, less disabled, tended to be more middle class, less unattractive, less dependent — people who had never been extruded from their communities. And the population the State hospitals had been involved in taking care of was an entirely different group. It was older, sadder, poorer, more disabled and more unsavory. The idea of trying to put these systems together may not have been an experiment which he designed, but it was an idea that interested him. It involved new forms of governments, new ways of looking at State government and local government which may have different capacities, different responsibilities, but not essentially different ranks nor unequal talents. So something which required new kinds of planning, new kinds of funding, new kinds of concepts, new habits, new kinds of accountability, was an idea that I think interested him more.

He also sensed that and assumed that some risk-taking was healthy for individuals as well as organizations. He didn't resist the notion, call it humanitarian if you like, of opening mental health systems, which was likely to lead to the relocation of people in institutions back into the neighborhoods. It was an idea which I think he sensed was moving in the direction of health. He wasn't a reckless innovator. He wanted us to anticipate, as carefully as we could, the consequences of our actions. And he liked the probabilities of benefit to be high. But this may be, in my opinion, one of the most important variables, and I think it is part of being an experimenter. He knew that no venture was free of miscalculation, untoward events, and unplanned events. And he knew that there was no growth in symmetry.

And since he knew that errors were inevitable, and I think he had a flair for errors, he knew that the only way in which we and he could learn from errors was not to conceal them from ourselves. The only errors that we could grow from were the ones that we knew about. He was not intimidated by the possible exposure of mistakes, but rather, he had the capacity of turning the mistakes into new growth.

In the attempts to balance the needs of the mentally ill, the mentally retarded people, the needs for autonomy and also structure, I think he knew as well as any of us that there was no perfect and permanent solution, and that the balance would need constant correction and adjustment. But that kind of adjustment could only happen if the mistakes were open, were exposed to view. And I think, in some ways, that may have been a moving force in the community mental health movement.

I am thinking of the idea of a new State hospital as part of a complex of services and responsibilities engaging the local government. This was something, again, which intrigued him. And that was one of the reasons why he was interested in unified services legislation. He was actively supportive of any of the efforts we might make to resettle some people in neighborhoods. I don't know to what extent he was prompted by the impulses of the healer, which is not to say that he was without sympathies and empathies. In fact, I think, in his relationships with people, there was almost a quality of passion. But I would agree with Al that the engine moving him was more the intrigue of seeing problems and trying to find solutions to them, not intimidated, but in fact growing from the fact that none of our ventures would be perfect throughout.

I learned very quickly that my small preoccupations were not necessarily central to him. But I also learned that even though we knew we weren't central, our ideas were of consequence. He took in ideas incredibly from all sources, and somehow the elements combined and emerged in some new, often unpredictable form. But even in that process, each one of us could trace the contribution of what we had thought, what we had done, and recognize it as a transformed idea. That made it possible for each one of us to feel as if he were somehow a part. The ideas we had took on a life all of their own when they became part of him. But we also, as it happened, felt included in the process.

ABE LAVINE: Our next speaker has the unique vantage point of having served not only in various posts in the Rockefeller administration but also in the subsequent administration. As Commissioner of Social Services, Barbara Blum has also taken an active part in national affairs, where she became the President of the National Council of State Welfare Administrators. Barbara.

BARBARA BLUM: Thank you. I think my remarks today should be prefaced by the fact that my observations come from different points in time and most of those observations will be from outside the Rockefeller administration. I was in the Lindsay administration at the Mental Health Agency in New York City and then at Human Resources during much of the period that was described by Dr. Miller. Subsequently, I had responsibilities for mental health, drug abuse, and Medicaid programs. Each, in one way or another, impinged on my professional life, so that I found preparation for this discussion particularly stimulating. I think, when we talk about the term "experimenter," that different people define experimentation differently. Dr. Miller points out that Governor Rockefeller was eager to try new things — that's part of experimentation. However, testing new approaches doesn't assess impact.

Measuring impact is necessary in order to identify errors so that we can correct mistakes — something particularly necessary in government. Bureaucracies can be so stultifying that we must have admiration for the changes that Governor Rockefeller brought to the State of New York. There are also a great many lessons that can be learned from these changes, and what interests me the most are some of the questions that arise in relation to the changes.

For instance, how can more extensive analysis be used when decisions are being made? That may be particularly difficult when a Governor is a "doer," as Al Marshall defined Rockefeller. The second question I would ask is, how can we use more rigorous evaluations to measure the impact of changes when massive shifts in policy are being implemented in the public sector? And finally, what is it that we might do to further an approach involving incremental changes so that corrective action can be taken periodically? This would permit implementation step by step as we are trying to shift many of our outdated policies.

With regard to Medicaid, it is interesting that the level of eligibility was seen as providing political advantage. Subsequently that became a great disadvantage, of course, to the State of New York. To have a high eligibility level and to have such an extensive array of services, caused New York to become the national target cited when the problems of Medicaid were discussed. All of us who've been in government know that once you have a very extensive, very full program, reduction becomes almost impossible. To take something away after it has been provided is politically very difficult. The Medicaid program was further complicated by the fact that there was a lack of careful analysis, and constant review, of demographic trends. Heavy investment in nursing homes and in certain kinds of institutions was stimulated and those costs became massive and have made even more difficult the change that is needed in the Medicaid program here in New York State. Medicaid is a generous program. There are many, many benefits, particularly for the older citizens and the disabled, and to a lesser extent for ADC (Aid to Dependent Children) clients.

With regard to drug abuse, I would agree entirely that we got these programs, as a state, at a point when the Feds should have been taking much more responsibility. Drug abuse is a national problem. We continue not to move vigorously on the sources of the problem to the extent that this nation should. In my opinion, it was necessary with the drug programs to try many approaches. We were deficient with the drug programs simply because we did not evaluate carefully the program results. There were many ways in which random assignment or comparison groups could have been used very effectively, to learn a great deal more about whether our resources were used appropriately for certain groups.

In the community mental health area, there is much to be said for the development of community based services. The shift to community was very important. My concern is that de-institutionalization was pressed with great momentum before the mental health services in the community were totally in place.

Since mentally ill people are so vulnerable, they do require extensive programs, not *only* mental health services but housing programs and networking. There was a serious timing problem with the thrust in mental health. Again, testing with certain groups in different models might have brought us further, had we had analysis and evaluation.

But Rockefeller was great because he wanted to solve problems in the human service area. Some of these problems are enormously complex. They need time in testing that our Governor Rockefeller did not have the patience for. In closing it would be marvelous to imagine how one could find, combined in a single person, the social mechanic effectiveness that Rockefeller had as well as social experimental interests. Rockefeller really was more than halfway home.

ABE LAVINE: Moving from mental health to mental retardation to health in general, our former Commissioner of the Health Department, Hollis Ingraham.

HOLLIS INGRAHAM: It was fascinating to hear Al Marshall getting excited over the programs he had to deal with in other days. It reminded me of an incident during one of Rockefeller's active re-election campaigns. Al was stranded up here to hold the fort in Albany while the rest of the organization moved down to New York City. We had prepared for Rockefeller's campaign use an elaborate booklet of new health programs, which we tried to show were absolutely indispensable to the future improved health of the citizens of the State. The cost of the proposals was in the tens of millions, and Rockefeller had indicated great interest. I dropped over to see Al to report our progress, saying that he'd better get busy planning for implementation. He blew up and said, "That goddamn Taj Mahal down in New York City is going to break this State!" — very similar to the words that he just used now.

During Rockefeller's first term, you may remember, he was a vocal advocate of "pay as you go." But by the beginning of his second term, the time that he appointed me to take Dr. Hilleboe's place, he was prepared to spend lavishly to improve State government. Rockefeller's interest in social policy, of course, embraced more than health, but he did not neglect the health field. During his tenure he thrust the Department into medical care in a bigger way than any other state health department anywhere in the country. Similarly, he vested the Department with huge environmental responsibilities, including the dispensing of $1.5 billion for sewage works construction, though he later took them away from us, much to my annoyance, and incorporated them in a new department.

Some measure of the changes he wrought in the health picture are evident from the other monies that were devoted to capital construction during his tenure. Within the State's Department of Health itself, capital funds expenditures amounted to $160 million. That's assuming that the laboratory in the Mall cost only $80 million. Some people think it cost well over $100 million. For hospital and nursing home construction, over $5 billion was authorized to be spent. We were able to process $3 billion of that, but considerably less than that actually went to mortgage closure before the administration changed.

We didn't handle Medicaid funds in the Department. We did recommend to the Budget Director the fees to be set for each service, and we also determined the charges to be made in hospitals and nursing homes for both Medicaid and Blue Cross. However, the maneuvering over Medicaid that Al spoke about was out of my purview; it occurred very shortly after the Governor signed Article 28 of the Public Health Law, which assigned the responsibilities for State supervision of hospital care to the Health Department, taking it away from the Welfare Department. I had been active for some time before that in the background of that transfer, and in a fit of conscience I agreed with Commissioner Wyman that we wouldn't contest his supervision of Medicaid. Later, under pressure from health groups, I recanted. In the final version, the Department did have a responsibility for the purely medical aspects of Medicaid.

Although the Department has long had responsibility for control of narcotic drugs, it was only peripherally involved in the major drug legislation. When Dr. Hilleboe was Commissioner, he and Dr. Larimore wrote a proposal for incarcerating youthful drug addicts for several year periods to areas remote from the big cities. The theory behind the suggestion was that each addict acts as a focus of infection in enlisting others to addiction and that most addicts are ill-educated and poorly prepared for the work place.

When Governor Rockefeller began to turn his attention to the drug problem, I submitted this proposal to him. He expressed interest in the idea, and I recall that shortly thereafter, on a plane ride, Ed Van Ness and I discussed the subject with him at some length. In the course of discussion with the Governor, I said that the proposal was purely a guess as to whether it would be of value or not. He replied, "Well if there isn't any better way, we'd better go along with it." He indicated that he would sponsor legislation to implement the suggestion, and asked if I would care to take the project over. I declined, saying that the purpose was primarily educational and secondarily one of detention, and not a health matter. The final legislation, incidentally, bore only a rough likeness to our proposal.

The Governor then went on to say that he also planned to introduce legislation to set very severe penalties for drug dealers. Both Ed and I expressed the view that Draconian laws would be self-defeating, but we made very little impact.

Our theme setter was intimate with the Governor and saw him day after long day. I saw him only on occasion. Hence, his assessment of Rockefeller's inner thoughts and aspirations have a far sounder basis than mine. However, from my limited vantage point, I never had any doubt that he was genuinely interested in people and very much wanted to be a benefactor. Furthermore, the suggestion that Rockefeller was not an experimenter may very well be true of him personally. But by his works he added tremendously to the medical research capabilities of New York State. Within my own department, the monies devoted to research were multiplied by a very considerable factor, and the same is true of medical schools in the State University. State aid was also made available for research in the New York City Health Department, which had a very active research organization.

The other facets of the Governor's experimentation with social policy, as noted by Al Marshall, are consistent with my observation. He delighted in attacking problems and welcomed suggestions for solutions. Once the course was set he insisted on forward movement. No one could say more effectively, "Full speed ahead and damn the torpedoes!" At the initiation of new programs he would personally involve himself in seeing them launched. After the first flush, he would call periodically for reports, preferably with charts demonstrating progress.

He appeared at times to make up his mind about big projects on the spot. Of course, since I only saw him occasionally, it was quite possible that he had been dwelling on these things for weeks and had been briefed and had discussed them with others at length. But I do recall sitting beside him at a dinner with members of a hospital association relatively early in the second term. The speaker had emphasized the need for hospital renovation throughout the State. He stated the need amounted to several billion dollars, and that there should be State loans to help the hospitals out. Rockefeller turned to me and said, "Is the figure in the ballpark, and do you think it's a good idea?" I said, "Yes" to both and he said, "All right, we'll do it." And we did.

It was also true that the worst thing was to say, "It can't be done." Once, while hosting the Public Health Council at the

Mansion, he proposed an idea he had on gonorrhea control and indicated that I should proceed with it. I demurred, saying, in essence, that it would be unproductive and impossible to implement. I was immediately and severely chastised.

It also appeared that he tried to do some things on a State basis that were only feasible nationally. One example that is very clear to me was his health insurance bill. But I must admit, I thought it was a grand idea at the time since I was to be involved in its administration.

On the other hand, several other laws he sponsored for the Department were copied shortly after by the Federal government. The Laboratory Inspection Law was made national almost word for word. The Certificate of Need legislation for hospitals and nursing homes was also taken over nationally in all essentials. With regard to the environment, Congress followed closely our legislation in the areas of both water pollution and air pollution.

Serving under Rockefeller was a heady experience. There seemed to be no end to what the State could do to improve services to the public. And I never hesitated to propose new programs because of their expense. Only after several years of Medicaid's soaring bills did it occur to me to question the State's ability to pay for even better and more expensive health services. However, it seems to me there is little doubt that Governor Rockefeller's implementation of this social policy resulted in vastly improved services for New York State citizens and left massive amounts of valuable construction of great variety. It seems incontestable that his imprint on the State exceeds that of any his predecessors since the days of the Erie Canal.

ABE LAVINE: I think everyone knows Senator Bill Smith, who is Deputy Majority Leader and, ever since I can remember, Chairman of the Temporary State Commission to Revise the Social Services Law. Malcolm referred earlier to the setting up of the Welfare Inspector General's Office. I know that Senator Smith was also very instrumental in the early reforms of the welfare system. As a matter of fact, he is known to have influenced Governor Rockefeller to appoint someone other than a social worker to the position of Commissioner of Social Services. When the Governor asked me to accept that position, I said, "I don't know anything about social welfare; I'm an expert in labor negotiations!"

SENATOR WILLIAM SMITH: I accepted, with some qualms, the invitation to discuss Nelson A. Rockefeller's legacy to New York State in the formation of social policy. My legislative record shows that, more often than not, I did not support many of the initiatives Governor Rockefeller took in the area of social welfare policy.

In Washington, with the social activism that permeated the sixties, the War on Poverty became a national priority, gaining quick endorsement by the Congress.

In New York the Governor, following suit, proposed an agenda aimed at most every social enemy in sight. Using the strength of the Executive Office, the Governor found no opposition in the State Legislature. The Democrats were eager to endorse the Governor's programs. The Republicans found them hard to refute.

Governor Rockefeller's humanitarian interests, coupled with ambition, self-confidence and imagination, ignited his determination to make New York State a highly visible showcase for the nation and to prove that money and good intentions can solve any problem. In retrospect, one now wonders whether this was a fortuitous or a cataclysmic experience for New York State.

Certainly, the altruistic motives supporting the Governor's social agenda were impeccable. Few could argue against the worthy goal of improving the quality of life, particularly for those disadvantaged citizens of our state.

But critics have pointed out that too little thought, if any, was given to the sustained ability of the State to pay the costs of the new initiatives sought by the Governor. His programs, once launched, resulted in an explosion of taxes, expenditures, and debt totally without precedent in the history of the Empire State. The reverberations of many of the Governor's actions are still causing concern today.

Even before the 1960's, there were tell-tale signs of the State's worsening economic climate which gave hint to fiscal problems which lay ahead. Reduction in growth in the State's population, employment, and per capita income gave witness to this fact. With the national economy suffering periodic recessions, New York State's position was further weakened. With the subsequent slowdown in tax receipts, expenditures outstripped State resources. This meant that the Governor needed new sources of revenue to pay the bills resulting from the expansion in social programs.

New taxes were imposed in order to meet the expanding needs of the State bureaucracy.

At the same time, State borrowing was increased to meet the costs of a massive expansion in construction. Not only was the full faith and credit debt of the State rising, but the Governor, circumventing traditional legislative and constitutional constraints, raised the level of lease-purchase agreements and moral obligation authority debts to staggering levels — certainly to heights without precedent in the history of the State, and unmatched by any other state in the union.[1]

Many feel that these unprecedented increases in taxes and debt-issuing processes have mortgaged the State's economic future to such an extent that our children's children will still feel its repercussions.

I took comfort in the fact that Chancellor Wharton's invitation to this conference referred to nine "problem" (not program) areas for discussion. This may have been a Freudian slip, but I will proceed on the premise that Rockefeller's legacy in New York State has indeed resulted in problems.

This session has been titled "Experimentation in Social Policy." The dictionary defines an experiment as "a *tentative* policy, carried out under *controlled* conditions in order to discover an *unknown* effect or law."

To call Governor Rockefeller's social programs "experiments" is stretching the point. Certainly their long-term effects were then unknown in terms of effectiveness and costs, since the programs were never really pre-tested nor evaluated. On the other hand, in no way could they be called tentative programs since they were enacted into law, setting the course so firmly for the future that any subsequent efforts to retrench became nigh impossible. Nor were they implemented under controlled conditions, but rather initiated statewide, and on a grand scale.

Even though Rockefeller's motives may have been defensible, his strategy for long-term planning was not. The major fault lay in his failure to construct his programs soundly, failure to recognize the necessity for balancing the State's projected resources against projected expenditures.

Medicaid is a case in point.

Improved health care for Americans was always an espoused cause of Rockefeller. When Congress passed Title XIX of the Social Security Act in 1965, the Governor grabbed the opportunity to launch New York into one of the most expensive and comprehensive medical assistance programs in the country.

On April 20, 1966, after a brief one-day public hearing, the Medicaid bill quickly sailed through both houses of the State Legislature.

I remember that event well. The Executive Office warned the members of the Legislature that delay in passage of the proposed Medicaid legislation would result in New York State's loss of from $6 to $7 million a month in Federal aid. When some of the more skeptical legislators, like myself, asked for confirming cost data and other pertinent information on which to base our votes, none was available.

One year later, our concern was not with the loss of a few million dollars in Federal aid, but with the exorbitant level of State and local funds needed to match program expenditures.

Our Medicaid program proved so expensive that the State's first twelve-month costs exceeded the total appropriation made for the nation. Congress became so alarmed that immediate action was taken to put more restraints on the prerogatives New York and other states could employ in designing their programs.

Our own State Legislature, realizing that the original legislation would blanket in about one-third of the State's population for Medicaid coverage, also took steps to trim the program by lowering the levels for client eligibility.

But as one authority so aptly stated, "The [Medic]aid program that was initially lavish to the point of idiocy was subsequently cut back to being merely generous."[2]

During the decade following the inception of Medicaid, despite repeated cost-containment programs, expenditures continued to skyrocket. While inflation and increased utilization certainly were contributing factors, mismanagement and abuses abounded.[3] Believe it or not, Medicaid, which almost immediately started out as a billion dollar program, was ten years old before the State installed a modern computer-based system to exert management controls over the program! By then, the expenditure level had tripled. Despite all retrenchment efforts, New York State's per capita Medicaid costs still remain the highest in the nation.[4] Today, annual Medicaid expenditures in the State are over $7 billion dollars!

During the Rockefeller years, the expansion of health service was matched by new construction of medical facilities. During his tenure as Governor, aid was provided to build or expand over one hundred voluntary and municipal hospitals and nursing homes. Hundreds of millions of dollars were also provided in long-term, low-interest loans for health facility construction financed by the State Housing Finance Agency. During this period, too, New York enriched mental health patient care by the addition of 23 new facilities.

Had the State gone into the "brick and mortar" business on a more prudent, less-typically grand scale, perhaps the fiscal fallout would not have been so great.

For example, it only took until the middle of the 1970's before it became evident that at least 20 percent of the hospital beds were excessive, adding unnecessary costs to the already high level of health care expenditures in the State. The challenge for the State was now reversed — reducing hospital bed capacity.

The paint had hardly dried on our new mental hygiene buildings when the courts made the concept of deinstitutionalization the new game plan for care of the mentally handicapped. This meant moving many of the patients out of the large psychiatric hospitals and development centers (many of them just newly built), into smaller community-based facilities.

Rockefeller's administration began this process, and during his term in office, client population in the State's institutions declined 45 percent. (While one would expect staff in the facilities would show an accompanying decrease, their numbers grew by 35 percent.)

When Federal Medicaid dollars became available for the care of the mentally handicapped in the mid-1970's, New York State once again seized the opportunity for program expansion. In fact, New York's experience in maximizing Federal dollars was so enterprising and unlike that in other states, that the U.S. Department of Health and Human Services is currently doing a special audit of New York's operations.[5]

Certainly, I am aware and pleased that national research confirms that the passage of the Medicaid (and Medicare) programs contributed measurable improvement in the health of our citizens. The issue I raise deals with cost-effectiveness of our State's programs.

Did the inordinate high level of spending result in compensatory health benefits to our State residents? Does our State's above-average health care cost make our beneficiaries that much better off than those who live in other areas of the country? Would the State have accomplished that much less in improving our State's health care system by a more prudent and restrained effort?

I think not.

In assessing Rockefeller's legacy to New York State's social policy, I do not doubt that his motives were well intended. However, I do feel that the Governor moved too ambitiously in untested and uncharted waters, unmindful of the tell-tale signs of a worsening economic climate.

I agree with the studies, made by the Advisory Commission on Intergovernmental Relations and others, which show that the most important legacy of the Rockefeller years for the average New Yorker is the State's high tax load. Even now, years after the end of the "days of wine and roses" — as his successor termed them — New Yorkers carry a governmental burden unmatched elsewhere.

At the beginning of Governor Rockefeller's term of office,

New York State's per capita tax was only 35 percent higher than the national average. When he left office, New York's taxes were the heaviest in the nation. At that time, New Yorkers were paying almost 60 percent more than the average citizen residing in other states. (Today, per capita taxes are still almost 70 percent higher.)

The Governor, too, by adopting a "spend now and pay later" policy for funding pet projects, left the State with a moral obligation debt unprecedented in the State's history. By circumventing the conventional "checks and balances" of citizen and legislative input, Rockefeller succeeded during his tenure in office in more than quadrupling the size of the public authority debt (up to $14 billion). Shortly after Rockefeller left office, the total debt of the State's public authorities was ten times higher than the average indebtedness of all the states, and even twice that of the next most indebted state in the nation (California).

Governor Rockefeller's comprehensive social agenda, which set the pattern for the State, is a major contributor to the current fiscal crisis. The State will have to deal with the consequences of Rockefeller's legacy long after this audience leaves the scene.

ABE LAVINE: We started a little late. I do want to give our last discussant an opportunity. The Chairman of the Department of Political Sciences of Union College and co-author of a book on Rockefeller which was recently published, Professor James Underwood.

JAMES UNDERWOOD: Thank you very much. I will do this briefly, I promise you, although it's not in my nature to do these things briefly. I think everyone said many things which really were very characteristic of Governor Rockefeller. However, I cannot agree with everything that was said. For example, Governor Wilson said that Rockefeller was not a liberal nor a conservative, that one really could not label him. I disagree.

In trying to put into perspective what has been said here, I would begin by arguing with any assertion that Rockefeller was not a liberal. The dominant public philosophy of the latter half of the 1950's and much of the 1960's was what is defined in our book as "pragmatic liberalism." His administration was a representation of that public philosophy. And, in fact, most political elites, and most liberal intellectuals, felt very comfortable with Rockefeller and his administration. His beliefs really were consistent with the beliefs of many other people who occupied positions similar to the one he occupied. Among Rockefeller's beliefs is something that people have talked about on this panel today — the idea that all problems can be solved. Nelson Rockefeller believed that, but he was not the only American of prominence who believed that. He believed not only that all problems could be solved, but he believed that they should be solved by the device of an activist government; not socialist government, but certainly not the sort of minimal government that some modern conservatives would advocate. He also believed that problems could be solved with determination and effort and that the effort should be led by the Chief Executive and not by the Legislature. If that meant that the Governor should sometimes manipulate the Legislature or the President should manipulate the Congress, then that should be done. That was seen as part of the task of being an activist executive.

I believe that some of these qualities that had been ascribed to Rockefeller — for example, one of the panelists cited his determination, his ambition, his self confidence — are qualities evident to many observers. (At one point in the discussion, I concluded that if one were to put the panelists together in a room, they would have said exactly the things that Bill Daniels and I say in our book. That gave me some confidence in our judgment as authors.)

I think it makes some sense to look back at Nelson Rockefeller's childhood and his experiences as an adolescent and then his experiences in Washington. He was a man who overcame a serious handicap, the learning disability of dyslexia, a man who was made self-confident by that triumph. Furthermore, he was a man who, because of his family, felt called upon to play some very significant and large role in American life. And so he rejected a career as an architect, a career that interested him. Then he adopted what we call a "life strategy": one of spending his life identifying problems which he thought were significant to the survival and well-being of his society. He would identify those problems and he would offer solutions for them. And in fact, that is what he did, beginning in his earliest days as Coordinator of Latin American Affairs, continuing into the Eisenhower administration when he became the author of various proposals, including one for the creation of the Department of Health, Education and Welfare.

Everything that Governor Rockefeller did in New York State was consistent with what he did in previous governmental service. His statements near the end of his Governorship, indicating that he had become a bit more conservative and more concerned about not spending so much money, were belied by what he did as Vice-President. For example, he made a major push for creation of an energy authority at the Federal level, an authority that could fund up to $100 billion in research and development. That authority was to look a lot like the authorities that he had established in New York State. I don't think that his proposal as Vice-President should be surprising, because I believe that Rockefeller was a man who was very self-conscious about the sort of role that he wanted to pursue.

Rockefeller represented the "ideal" combination of political beliefs, personality, and executive style. The public philosophy of pragmatic liberalism was perfectly matched to a personality which was self-confident, ambitious, and energetic, and both were perfectly matched to an executive style that minimized all possible obstacles to the generation and adoption of new programs. Almost all restraints fell before him. What happened as a consequence was that some of Rockefeller's achievements were diminished and some of his failures magnified. It is ironic that some of his worse failures were a product of the fact that in one sense he was the chief executive who best reflected the beliefs of American political elites during the era in which he was most active in public life. Knowing the difficulty of restraining Presidents Johnson and Nixon, perhaps we should be thankful that an executive as gifted as Rockefeller did not occupy the presidency during the Vietnam era.

ABE LAVINE: If you want to learn more about Dr. Underwood's observations on the Rockefeller legacy, please buy the book. I think that there is sufficient overlap in these concurrent sessions in terms of the matter covered between "Rockefeller the Builder," "Rockefeller the Manager," "Rockefeller the Experimenter in Social Policy," that you will have an ample opportunity to get into further discussion on our subject matter later in the proceedings. Thank you for being a very attentive audience.

FOOTNOTES
(to William Smith's speech)

[1] In Rockefeller's first term as Governor, there were 125 public benefit corporations in the State, with a total indebtedness of $3.3 billion. When he left office, the number of public benefit corporations was almost doubled and total debt outstanding was quadrupled. Standing at $13.3 billion, this moral obligation was almost four times the entire full faith and credit debt of the State itself.

Even though Rockefeller went on record stating that the newly-created State authorities would be self-sufficient — not costing the taxpayers anything — since he left office, nearly a half-billion dollars were appropriated from the State Treasury to shore up their financial deficits.

[2] Peter D. McClelland and Alan L. Magdovitz. *Crisis in the Making.* (New York: Cambridge University Press, 1981) p. 190.

[3] One State welfare commissioner confided that by the mid-1970's, over $1.0 million a day was wasted in fraudulent or unnecessary Medicaid payments.

[4] In Federal Fiscal Year 1979, New York State's Medicaid program spent close to 20 percent of all Title XIX funds available in the nation, while serving only 10 percent of the clients eligible in the country for these medical benefits.

[5] Federal officials noted that since 1975, New York's expenditures for Medicaid-funded ICF's (Intermediate Care Facilities) made on behalf of just the mentally retarded alone, rose more than five-fold - from just under $200 million to $930 million annually. These increases in cost rose in spite of the fact that there was a 20 percent decline in total ICF/MR (Intermediate Care Facilities for the Mentally Retarded) beds in the State during the same period.

Chapter III

Party and
Political Relations

BURDELL BIXBY: Our panel will focus on "Nelson Rockefeller: His Party and Political Relations." I would suggest that you relax and enjoy the proceedings, the personalities, and the memories.

Nelson Rockefeller was the only Governor of New York to be elected four times to four-year terms. In 1958, he was elected Governor of New York by a plurality of 573,034 votes. In 1962, he was re-elected Governor of New York by 529,169 votes. In 1966, he was re-elected by 392,263 votes. In 1970, he was re-elected by 730,006 votes. Since some of us here had a part in that enterprise, you can't blame me for mentioning some statistics!

It is now my pleasure to introduce you to the theme setter for our panel today. He is a gentleman with many roots in Albany, a few in New York City and many in Washington. He is a nationally syndicated political columnist who frequently tells the political leaders of the country where they went wrong, what they're about to do and what is going to happen. His writings may be found in the column, "Germond and Whitcover," as well as in *The Baltimore Evening Sun*. I am happy to introduce one of the great — really great — political columnists in the United States, Jack Germond.

JACK GERMOND: I am in a unique position here, or at least an unusual one, being one of the only theme setters, perhaps the only one, who never worked for Nelson Rockefeller. Indeed, Rockefeller often thought I worked against him. In the interest of truth in packaging, I have to tell you one story about our relationship. It was during the time that Rockefeller was involved in the controversy over the welfare program in Newburgh, New York (details of which mercifully escape me). We had a press conference in Binghamton and we were pursuing him on the issue but he kept changing the subject.

He went droning on about something else and I said to him "Governor, I'd like to go back to Newburgh." He said, "I wish you would!"

I want to make a few basic points about Nelson Rockefeller's political career, flesh them out a little bit, and turn it over to my betters on the panel.

At the beginning, let me make four points about Rockefeller. It seemed to me that when he first came into elective politics at the age of 50 in 1958, he was an extraordinary political phenomenon. I never saw one like it again except for Bob Kennedy in 1968. Nelson Rockefeller was a genuine celebrity totally outside the political community who became a folk figure in New York politics overnight.

The second point I would like to make is that his continued extraordinary success in New York politics, to the point that he became a kind of institution as a politician, rested I think very heavily on the perception of him as a public official who accomplished things. He accomplished things. Among the things he accomplished, of course, was angering a great many of his constituents, which was why he had all those bad polls. But when it came down to it, people wanted him. They saw him as a more vivid figure than his opposition.

The third point I would make is this: Nelson Rockefeller was a remarkably inept national politician. He was done in, time and time again, by his own misjudgments and by those of his advisors. They were misjudgments, I would submit, that were based largely on the parochialism of New York politics and New Yorkers.

The fourth point, I would make, is that he was a politician whose national ambitions were thwarted because of a basic underlying conflict between him and his party. Whatever else you could say about Nelson Rockefeller in terms of labels, he believed in an activist role for government at a time when the Republican Party was moving in just the opposite direction, a direction that's now been reached in Washington.

Any analysis of Rockefeller as a politician seems to me has to start with the fact that he was 50 years old before he got into elective politics and that he was incredibly green in his understanding of the way politics worked. He had to learn many lessons. There was a story that I was told one time (by two people who were in the room and who swear it was true) that shortly after he was elected, they had a meeting (a staff meeting) and they were talking about the problem of the budget, and the necessity to raise taxes. Someone reminded the Governor-elect that he had implied strongly during the campaign that he was going to raise

State employee salaries and that it wasn't going to be very easy to do that while you were raising taxes. Someone came up with the idea that rather than raise salaries directly, the State would pick up the employee's share of Social Security as well as the employer's share of Social Security. This, they informed the Governor, would increase the employee's take-home pay — to which Rockefeller replied, "What's take-home pay?" I find that story totally believable.

I know, from my own knowledge, that a year after he was in office, he did not know what the words "Bar Mitzvah" meant or how to pronounce them. For a New York politician it was stunning, believe me, to discover that in November 1959.

Nonetheless, Rockefeller came into politics with an enormous natural advantage. He was fresh. He was candid. He was optimistic at a time when there weren't a great many optimistic politicians — 1958 was not a very good year for optimism.

He was remarkably candid. I can remember a conversation when he was first running, standing in a corner of the Syracuse Airport with another reporter from the *New York Times*, Warren Weaver. It was everyone's dirty little secret that taxes were going to have to be raised but neither Candidate Rockefeller nor Governor Harriman really wanted to talk about it. But there was Rockefeller admitting to us quite candidly, while we wrote it down in our little notebooks, that yes, indeed, he might raise taxes if it seemed like it was unavoidable. That was the kind of politician he was in 1958; green but remarkably fresh, remarkably optimistic, remarkably straight-forward.

Malcolm Wilson has mentioned an incident. The first time I think Nelson Rockefeller went out and shook a voter's hand, as opposed to a county chairman's hand, on that quest that summer was at that Savannah, New York Potato Festival. And it was a baffling experience to those of us who covered politics and were then covering Averell Harriman, because Rockefeller really wanted to talk to these people. I can remember standing there sweltering (it was July or August) while Rockefeller stood there for 10 or 15 minutes going over the details of the problem of how you put reflector lights on a manure spreader when you drag it across a public road. Rockefeller spent the whole day — and I swear he must have talked to no more than a hundred people — because he couldn't get away from the business of finding out what they really wanted to talk to him about.

He was green, also. He made some political mistakes that were classics. The Fallout Shelter Campaign of 1959 was one of the great gems that made him the laughing stock of the State. He overcame that in the long run. He overcame that very quickly by the very persistence of his dedication to doing things and using government to solve problems. He was not a man people took lightly after they had seen him. It seemed to me he had a remarkable ability, as seen from those of us on the outside, to deal with the Legislature. He had a remarkable ability to beguile the press and he was able to convey the impression to legislators, to the public, to the press and through the press to the public that great things were just ahead. Everything he seemed to touch was going to be larger than life.

In short, it seems to me his great strength as a New York politician was the force of his personality and his ability to use that personality to convey the impression that he was doing the public good with all these programs and spending all that money. It made him a very good fit for the New York electorate. He was a little outrageous and a little brash. He was a little expensive. At that time, it didn't seem to be as difficult to spend money on public projects as it does today. But what he did do as the years went by was convince the voters that he was sincere in his efforts to make things better. The result was those successes in 1962, 1966, and 1970.

It also seems to me he was lucky in the sense that his opposition seemed to be weak at the right time. Bob Morgenthau, the man who ran against him in 1962, was not a strong candidate, or a personable candidate. In 1966, if you will recall, Franklin Roosevelt, Jr. ran on the Liberal Party line and drained away, as I recall, close to 600,000 votes. In 1970 he ran against Arthur Goldberg, who couldn't figure out which camera to look at. The red light didn't impress him. Nonetheless, in spite of the level of the opposition, I think the ability that Rockefeller showed to overcome those devastating polls — those terrible approval ratings (or disapproval ratings) was his ability to project an image of accomplishment. He was not a gray, bland, figure; he was an institution. He was a rascal perhaps, but he was our rascal. He had a natural feeling for people and they for him.

All that success in New York never translated nationally. Rockefeller's election in 1958 earned him disproportionate attention from the national news media and the national political community, because he was one of the few Republican survivors of a very bad year. Rockefeller became an instant darling of the national press. He was all over every magazine. He had, beyond that, this particular appeal as a celebrity and as a personality. It wasn't just a question of him being a Rockefeller and being a man of great wealth, it was what he brought personally to that position.

By late 1959, he was traveling the country to test the waters.

He tested them quite thoroughly and, I think, misread them. He made several forays around the country, all of which I covered, and in general, he was given pretty hostile and tough receptions by the party regulars, I must say. I remember we went to Milwaukee, Wisconsin, and they put us in the old Pfister Hotel before it was redone. And we discovered that night, while we were trying to define the meaning of all this in the bar, that the only other people staying in the hotel were members of a Polish Ballet Company. The only event they arranged for Rockefeller in Milwaukee was a luncheon. The party arranged it and they gave the tickets to city employees. We asked the Governor what he thought about all this and he said, "I would say it was a very correct occasion." He went on to Chicago and they asked him if he was President if he would raise taxes like he had in New York in late 1959, and the Governor said that he didn't know, that it would depend on what the situation was, and that he hadn't examined it. There was a political reporter, for the *Chicago Tribune*, who was notoriously hostile to the New York Eastern Establishment of Liberal Republicans, and he wrote a lead I'll never forget. He said, "Governor Nelson Rockefeller of New York, who raised the State's taxes more than any other Governor in its history, said today he would not hesitate to do the same if he were elected President." It gave him a great start.

Through it all, nonetheless, it seemed to me that that was the year Nelson Rockefeller could have won the presidency. He inspired a terrific response, an emotional response, an enthusiastic response because of his own enthusiasm, his own optimism, because he was so fresh. This was not a political technique; he was genuine.

The interest in Rockefeller was so remarkable it seemed to me then, and it seems to me now, that he could have converted it into a serious campaign by competing with Nixon in the primaries. I think the Governor himself felt that way later, felt that he was a victim of his own inexperience in making a judgment. At least that's what he used to say. I think it was also true that on some occasions he took advice on political matters from non-political people. He once told me that one of those most influential in his decision not to run, which he announced December 26, 1959, was Wally Harrison, who was a very dear friend of his and an architect. There were other occasions throughout his career in national politics when we thought he was relying on people who knew a great deal about a great many subjects but not necessarily about running for President.

It seemed to me that, too often, he thought he could persuade people who wouldn't even listen of the merits of his case. It just doesn't work that way very often. The same thing seemed to be true in 1963 and 1964 as he made that second approach.

I remember going with him in September 1963. It was the first political occasion, political trip, he had made after his remarriage. He went out to the Ogle County Corn Roast in Ogle County, Illinois, just outside of Rockford. It was a big event to which Republican politicians statewide always came. It was a lovely day and there wasn't a single Republican of any note there. John Anderson, the local Congressman, was hiding out at home when I called him and said, "What are you doing, John?" And he said he was listening to a ballgame. He was hiding out. Charles Percy was another profile in courage — he didn't show up. Everett Dirksen didn't show up. It was a monumental freeze and the Governor was puzzled by it, again, because I think he gave the party more credit than it deserved.

I'm going to say one thing about the 1963-64 campaign. It was a testament to that ability with people and all the burdens that he carried. He did manage to win that primary in Oregon. In fact, he had the primary in California in his pocket. I am one of those who subscribe to the theory that he gave the primary away by giving up all his television that final weekend. We kept having all these television film clips of Barry Goldwater looking reasonable, and seeming very reasonable rather than playing the raving maniac, which was the general thrust of the Rockefeller campaign against him. Nonetheless, it was also true that Rockefeller's position at

Governor Rockefeller conferring with Assembly Speaker Perry B. Duryea Jr. and Senate Majority Leader Warren M. Anderson after signing the "No Fault Insurance" Bill, February 13, 1973.

that point was such that even if he had won the California primary, it seems to most of us that all it would have accomplished was nominating Richard Nixon four years earlier. He would have stopped Goldwater without nominating Rockefeller because of this basic suspicion — this basic distrust — which had been built up and particularly accelerated between 1960 and 1964.

In 1968, he made those final missteps, again because I think he gave people more credit than they deserved within his party. He went through that ritual, you recall, of inviting people to encourage him to run. And then for reasons that I've never understood, and I don't think anybody in this room may really understand, he announced on March 21, 1968, that he would not run. Then on April 30, he said he was available; he started out all over again. I remember that, at the time, one of those who came and urged Nelson Rockefeller to run for President was Tom McCall, Governor of Oregon and a very funny fellow. His family is from Maine and he has a very broad New England accent, although he has lived in Oregon most of his life. And I went to see McCall, after he'd come and done this number with Rockefeller and Rockefeller chose not to run, and I said to Tom, "Governor, do you think you've been manipulated?" He said, "Manipulated? I've been fondled!"

The puzzle about 1968 was why he imagined that he could sit by for six months and allow Richard Nixon a clear path to the nomination, given the way he felt about Nixon and the way he felt about the direction of the Republican Party. And I think that the Governor himself felt, when it was over (at least he said this to me on one occasion,) that he had misjudged his own feelings. He discovered that, getting into the thing on April 30 after all the primary deadlines were past, it was too late to do anything but fly around the country and make speeches.

The final irony, it seems to me, is that he came closest to the presidency by the appointment of a conservative Republican, Jerry Ford. This was a testament both to the real regard in which Rockefeller was held as a public official and, I must say, to the remarkable self-assurance of Jerry Ford, who at no point felt threatened by Nelson Rockefeller, and who indeed felt that Rockefeller could serve him as Vice-President without being threatening but, rather, being helpful. Unfortunately, that same self-assurance did not translate itself to Ford's staff or to the party leaders. It led to Bo Callaway's famous statement, at a dinner meeting with a group of reporters one night that I attended, that it might be the time for "a younger man." And Rockefeller smiled and threw in the towel and allowed himself to be dropped from the ticket.

It seems to me that was the Governor's final misjudgment on the national political scene. As a matter of fact, Ford, with Rockefeller on the ticket, might very well have made a far, far stronger candidate than he was, as it turned out. He might very well have been re-elected. The notion of heading off Ronald Reagan in the South never had much of a shot, but everybody seemed to know that except people in the White House. In any event, it seems to me that the Governor's last gasp as a politican was as a campaigner for Jerry Ford. And even then he couldn't avoid being pursued on the possibility that he might run again if Ford faltered or if Ford were forced aside by Reagan. I looked into some old files the other day, and I found this whole bunch of stories from 1976 talking about how Nelson A. Rockefeller was acting like he was a candidate.

I'm going to make a final point here. It seems to me that on the national scene Governor Rockefeller was always the victim of mistaken perceptions. Part of it, the most obvious, was that use of the little word "liberal." This is a press word. We're not able to accommodate two-word descriptions so we use one-word descriptions — two only if we say "moderate liberal" or "moderate conservative." The fact is that the perception of Rockefeller as a liberal was founded at the time, more than anything else, on the Civil Rights issue, which you will recall was a very important issue in the Republican Party at that time.

My feeling was that Rockefeller was less a liberal than he was a Baptist; he was acting out of a personal conviction rather than out of liberal political ideology. In fact, I found him to be totally impatient with ideological notions, even impatient with constitutional questions. In 1962, when he was putting through the Scholar Incentive Program (which I thought was one of the great outrages of our time although I realize what it has done for the State,) I was riding with him one night on a plane and I said to the Governor, "It says right here in the Constitution, 'no direct or indirect aid to religious institutions' so how can you do this?" He looked at me, impatient with such a ridiculous question, and said, "It's necessary." I think that's exactly true.

But the point I'm trying to make is that if I were using a word to describe Nelson Rockefeller it would not be the word *liberal*, it would be the word *pragmatist*. I mean pragmatist in the best sense of the word — someone who wanted to get things done. He wanted to use government to do it, to accomplish social purposes by using government functions, government skills, government qualities. If there's one quality we remember about him most as a politician it is that optimism.

I want to close by recalling 1976 when he was campaigning

for Ford. I was writing a magazine article about him for the *New York Times* and I started taxing him on this business of whether he might run for President again after all, and the Governor said to me (and you'll all recognize this line): "You never know what's going to happen, it's a free country."

BURDELL BIXBY: Thank you very much, Jack. We are fortunate today to have with us five gentlemen who are going to pick up the discussion. I will introduce them to you without troubling them to rise at this time. The first I have is the Honorable Malcolm Wilson, the fiftieth governor of New York and now Chairman and Chief Executive Officer of the Manhattan Savings Bank. The second, the former Speaker of the New York State Assembly, the Honorable Stanley Steingut, who is now practicing law in New York with Baskin and Sears. I had the great pleasure of serving on the staff of Stanley's father when he was the Minority Leader of the Assembly. Next, Mr. Charles Holcomb, who for many years covered the Albany scene for Gannett News at the State Capitol, then spent a few years with Governor Carey as Chief of Communications and is now with Adams and Rinehart in New York City, having left the garden spot of the state, Columbia County. We then have the Honorable Richard Rosenbaum, the Republican National Committeeman. Mr. Rosenbaum is a former Chairman of the New York Repubican State Committee and is now a partner in Nixon, Hargrave, Devans & Doyle, a Rochester law firm. Finally, Professor Alan Chartock, joint Professor of Political Science at the State University of New York College at New Paltz and of Communications at the State University of New York at Albany.

I will first ask the Honorable Malcolm Wilson to open the panel discussions. It's all yours, Malcolm.

HONORABLE MALCOLM WILSON: First I'd like to add a few footnotes to Jack Germond's comments with respect to Nelson's several historic candidacies for the presidential nomination. As Jack says, his decision at a press conference on December 26, 1959, after he had completed this tour, was that those who would control the convention had decided that they were going to nominate Richard Nixon. Therefore, Nixon would be the candidate.

However, right up until the convention and during the convention itself, Nelson Rockefeller hoped that he would be the nominee. Indeed, there was a small group, of which I was one, which went out to Chicago four or five days before this convention and headquartered in a suite on the top floor in a hotel penthouse. The group included George Hinman, Rod Perkins, who had been the Counsel to the Governor for the first six months of his administration and an aide to the Governor previously at HEW, and Bill Ronan. This was the place where leaders came from around the country to say basically that they wished that they could support Nelson Rockefeller, but that they had made commitments and therefore the commitments were paramount.

You will recall that Dick Nixon understood the importance of Nelson Rockefeller, because they had the meeting out of which emerged the so-called Fifth Avenue Compact. That was a matter of big discussion by those of us who were around, as to whether that should be at Chicago, or whether it should be in Nelson's apartment.

Just a little footnote; it's not related to Nelson. On the Saturday after the Compact, when Dick Nixon came into town, they had an open car in a parade. As we were looking over the parapet of this penthouse, one of the male persons there saw this entourage come into sight, proceeed along the street, and disappear around the corner. He heaved a heavy sigh and said, "Well, there goes the next senior partner of a large San Franciso law firm."

I think that Jack did not mention something that had a great deal of influence in terms of the nomination of our party in 1964. The California primary was a crucial primary. I think you said, Jack, that you felt that the television should have been going. Now, back in those days, in all candor, ladies and gentlemen, — events have since changed the mores of our society, whether for better or worse, — a divorce was fatal for anyone who was seeking political office. That was one of the big problems that faced Adlai Stevenson during his candidacy. That was very much still in evidence in 1964, particularly out in the rural areas, the farm belt and in southern states. Some of us think that the fact the Rockefeller divorce was brought forcibly to the attention of the general public on the eve of the primary in California by the birth of Nelson Rockefeller Jr. was a crucial factor in Nelson's defeat. It was very much in the headlines in all of the California papers and the other media.

In 1968, there was the residual effect of the divorce itself, which our agents in the field still felt largely in the farm belt. Farm women, many of whom worked with their husbands with their hands, which got wrinkled, and did not have the chance to get to the beauty parlor and have their hair done, identified with that thirty-year marriage to Mary Rockefeller. That was a negative; that's one thing we got time and again from our people.

The other negative point, that hasn't been mentioned here, was the feeling that he had knuckled down to labor. You will recall there was a sanitation strike in the City of New York. John

Governor Rockefeller meeting representatives of the building and construction trades, 1970.

Lindsay was the Mayor; John DeLury ran the sanitation men's union. The strike went on. While it was not settled, the garbage was piling up in the streets. It was clearly a menace to public health. John DeLury had been in jail for contempt in connection with the strike. And the garbage kept piling up. In New York City, a large part of the refuse is collected not by the taxpayers but by private contractors; this is a very signficant factor that affects the whole situation. They collect about 6,000 tons a day and the Sanitation Department about 10,000 tons.

Finally, John Lindsay wrote a letter to Nelson Rockefeller and said, "I'm frustrated. I've tried. I can't do this. I ask you to please step in and settle this strike and get the men back to work." — and this is the key thing — "Call out the National Guard *if necessary*."

Nelson Rockefeller got into the matter himself and had John DeLury brought up under a court order. He came up with bailiffs and Corrections personnel and sat down in the Governor's office at 55th Street, and in four or five hours Nelson Rockefeller got John DeLury to agree, and the men went back to work, and DeLury went back to jail to serve the balance of his term.

This infuriated John Lindsay and John Lindsay's supporters, including the editorial board of the *New York Times*. They deified John Lindsay in their editorial columns and made him the hero because he stood up and he said to the Governor, "Call out the National Guard." He didn't say that, of course; he said call it out "if necessary." *The Times* ignored that. John Lindsay went all over the nation responding to invitations to tell, indeed, how he had stood up against union demands, and how he had refused to capitulate — whereas Nelson Rockefeller had done so. At that time General O'Hara was the head of the National Guard. He told Nelson Rockefeller that if the National Guard was called upon to collect the refuse in the City of New York it would fall behind by about 4,000 net tons a day. In addition, the labor union that had jurisdiction over the private carriers said, "If you call out the National Guard we'll go out on strike." And New York would have been inundated by garbage and in a really desperate situation. That "if necessary" got lost — deliberately, I'm afraid.

Now, we're talking about 1968. I remind you by the way, that while we're talking about party operations, the five living Republican national chairmen were all for Nelson Rockefeller in that year. Bix can bear this out. Our agents came in from these areas, then went out and did a "one-on-one" with the delegates and if we found a left-handed outfielder who was a delegate, we'd try to find a New York Republican who was a left-handed outfielder to go out and try to get his vote. Two problems, the divorce and "he knuckled down to labor," were insuperable obstacles.

Another thing was the impression that Nelson had approached the campaign in which Barry Goldwater was the nominee of our party with less than full enthusiasm. It was felt that he did not really go all out for Barry Goldwater in 1964.

Now, Nelson Rockefeller was a great believer in the two-party system. Many times in New York he could have gotten the endorsement of the Liberal Party, but he would not take it. Not because he was not on good terms with Alex Rose and the others, but because he believed in the two-party system. He feared, as many of us feared, the proliferation of parties which threatened to have, instead of government by a majority, government by a constantly shifting coalition of minorities — the potential threat to any parliamentary system — to which we're coming very close now in this State. So he was a two-party man, a great believer in the party system, a proud Republican. He made that clear time and again.

After his statement on December 18, 1973, when he actually resigned as Governor, he went immediately to a luncheon meeting with the Republican State Committee here in Albany at a local restaurant. If you read his 1973 Public Papers you will see what he said then about what his obligation was to the party: how he never would have been where he was except for the party, and he wanted to work with the party and for the party. It is pretty common knowledge that Hubert Humphrey, for example, had asked him if he, Nelson Rockefeller, would run as Vice-President on a ticket with Hubert Humphrey as President, and that he declined. He was a proud Republican; he never changed. He had a great respect for the organization. As we went around the State in 1958, he showed that. He operated only through the Republican structure in terms of getting to meet all the people. He took the delegates out from under the county chairmen, but nonetheless he proceeded through the county chairmen.

There was one county where the county chairman was a strong supporter of another person. I shall not mention his name; the man is still alive. I called him and said I would like to bring Nelson there just to put him before the people and he said: "He's not going to put his foot in my county." I said, "I understand." So I arranged to be invited to the Women's Republican Luncheon in that county, and I went out there and I had Nelson with me. We stayed overnight in a hotel. The next morning I called the county chairman and I said, "I know your rules. I'm here to speak to the luncheon. I have Nelson Rockefeller here and we're on a tour. Do you want him to stay here in the hotel and not to go the luncheon?" He called me a name which is not used in polite company and then said, "I'll be right over." By the time he got over to the hotel, Nelson was out on the porch, and it was like bees flocking to roses. He was surrounded by people. This man took one look, and I couldn't keep him out of the pictures. He became a convert.

On appointments, except with respect to policy-making positions and judicial appointments, Nelson was very sensitive to the political organization and wanted to keep the county leaders involved. I can testify that he was a great believer in proper political relations.

For some years he was a Republican governor with a Republican legislature. Then in 1965, he was a Republican Governor with both houses Democratic. Thereafter, for a number of years he was a Republican Governor with a Republican Senate and Democratic Assembly, and then he had the Republicans in both houses again.

There are some who say that his happiest year was 1965, when he had Democrats in control of both houses. That was great for Al Marshall, his Secretary. In all events, Nelson was able to work with the leaders of the Democratic majorities in both Houses in the public interest, and get them to support and join in approving programs. He was very friendly with some of the major leaders of the Democratic Party. He appeared one time in a beautiful silk suit which Meade Esposito, who was not without some influence in the Democratic Party, gave to him out of gratitude for the gift of a Picasso which Meade had admired on the Governor's wall and which Nelson had given to him.

BURDELL BIXBY: I'm happy at this point to bring to this microphone the Honorable Richard Rosenbaum.

RICHARD ROSENBAUM: I would want to introduce any subject on Nelson Rockefeller by quoting former Governor Harold Levander of Minnesota who said, "Once you have met him, you can no longer say this is an age without great men."

For those of you who were privileged to get inside the Governor's office, there was a little legend on his desk immediately to his right as he sat at his desk (which he rarely did). It touched my fancy very much because I believe the Governor of Minnesota was right. I thought that Governor Rockefeller had a number of very special qualities. One of them, which was most special to me, was his ability to get more out of the people around him than anybody I've ever worked with in private or in public life. They used to say that he could make you feel as though you were somebody very special even though you always knew you weren't. Most of us around him were fairly normal, came from fairly normal backgrounds, and were not much different from anybody else. But he made you feel that you were very, very special just by virtue of your association with him.

I experienced that every day, and particularly on the national scene, because, as Jack Germond pointed out, the Governor was not so popular in a lot of places in the country outside New York. But those of us who were associated with him, when we walked into a National Committee meeting or a meeting of national politicians — whether they liked the boss or not — they sort of held all of us in awe. We were considered to be a little different, and it was really because of our association with Governor Rockefeller. A few quick stories, I think, demonstrate the kind of an off-beat personalty that we're dealing with.

Governor Rockefeller was a supreme user of people. Putting it another way, anybody who wasn't used by him was disappointed. He was able to make you feel that you wanted to be used by him. We had a traveling squad that moved all over the country; that itself was to me phenomenal. The Governor, we know, would pick up and go to Oregon, or someplace like that, like most of us would go to the corner grocery store for a loaf of bread, and we would fly on the plane with him — Hugh Morrow, Ann Whitman, George Hinman, and I. (Joe Canzeri would already be there laying the groundwork.) We'd fly to someplace out west, or anyplace that we might be visiting, and always had a very unusual reception. Although in some places, people did tend to use him, when they thought it was to their benefit.

I'd like to tell a story that I know Joe Persico used in his book, *The Imperial Rockefeller,* about the time we went out to South Dakota and started back late at night. Usually we stayed overnight, but on this occasion we flew over Mt. Rushmore, and it was dark and the Governor said to me, "Have you ever seen Mt. Rushmore?" and I said, "No." (He liked to kid me about my provincial background.) He said, "Would you like to see it?" I said, "Yes." He said, "Just a minute." And he went over to the phone on the plane, dialed a number, and in two seconds the mountain lit up. It was lighter than it is in this room. You could see the faces vividly. We flew around the mountain, looked at the presidents' faces, and came home. It was at that point that I knew that we would never have a plane crash, because God was on the plane.

But this was a demonstration of the kind of, perhaps, mischievous sense of humor he had, because I often thought the Governor didn't have a sense of humor. He did not understand the kind of humor most of us trade in on a regular basis. I can think of an illustration of that. We were sitting in the Mansion with Malcolm Wilson on my left, and he said he was going to appoint Salvatore Pierro to the Parole Board. And I said, "I'm against it." He said, "Who do you think I am. What do you mean you're against it? What do you think I am, an impostor?" And I said, "No, but you told me if I became Chairman I'd make those decisions." He said, "Well, I made this decision before you became Chairman." "I don't believe that, I'm against Pierro." He said, "Why are you against Pierro?" I said, "Well, if his name was Shapiro I'd be for him." I thought that was a hilarious comment, Malcolm practically fell on the floor, which I appreciated very much because Louie Lefkowitz didn't laugh, but the Governor didn't even understand why it was funny.

That was only about a month after I became Chairman, and I think he thought he had somehow managed to get a nut — or worse — as his Chairman. He told me he was not going to ever deal with Republican County Chairmen unless I was present. And he more or less kept that promise. But he left out the Democrat County Chairmen. Meade Esposito's name was mentioned, I remember Rockefeller saying, "I want you to come up to my apartment, and I want you to meet Meade Esposito, Democratic Chairman of Kings County." I went up there, and it was quite an experience when he (Meade) said, "Oh, you're the WASP from upstate New York." That was a really confusing statement.

But, he was really an off-beat kind of a guy, you know. On his trips in his plane, when most of the normal people on the plane would be eating shrimp and caviar served to us by a couple of stewards, he munched on Oreo cookies and Fig Newtons. That's kind of an interesting thing in itself.

I think he liked to conspire. I think he was a great conspirator. There's a picture on my law office wall that was signed by him as "Your co-conspirator." I think he enjoyed that kind of thing. I think politics was a sort of special diversion to him. I like to think that I was the last person in his life to get a letter of some political substance — as Hugh Morrow knows — the letter on the vice-presidency, which he sent to me just a few days before he died. In it he said that the vice-presidency was strictly — and had to be — "standby equipment," that the vice-presidency was an office that had to be subdued, because the President had to be free to operate in any way he could.

And I think that, in a sense, sums up a side of Nelson Rockefeller that was very impressive to us all. By that I mean, he was a tremendously loyal person — a quality that's very important in politics. He was very loyal to President Ford. You know, somebody said that he withdrew as a vice-presidential candidate. Politicians like to talk like that; he didn't withdraw — he was bounced. But he was always loyal to Jerry Ford even though he knew he was forced out. In fact, I saw a quote in one of Ford's books where Ford expressed himself as being a little ashamed of what had gone on there.

When I was at the national convention as Chairman of the New York delegation in 1976 (sitting next to Nelson Rockefeller), he would not permit me to get up and, in my seconding speech for Jerry Ford, extol Governor Rockefeller's virtues. You know it's normal to get up and say you are from the great State of New York, the State where Nelson Rockefeller has been a great Governor. But he did not want me to do that, because he thought it might set off a problem in the convention which might possibly hurt Jerry Ford. I think that tells you something about Nelson Rockefeller, his greatness, his true size — larger-than-life.

This tremendously unusual, off-beat man was one the likes of which we will probably never see again, certainly in our lifetime, in politics on the State or national level. I always felt that Nelson Rockefeller was the only man I ever knew who could go to the presidency without any on-the-job training. He had broad enough vision to really handle the job the way it ought to be handled, and I still feel that way.

One other thing — during the 1976 campaign, during the primary season, there came a time when we were about a week away from six primaries occuring on one day. At that time the current President, Reagan, was out front in the delegate count, and, as you know, when the TV figures show somebody out front, there is kind of a lemming psychology to follow that candidate. And I drew up a memorandum which said essentially that New York should come out for Jerry Ford and that Rockefeller ought to also, because if he didn't, Ronald Reagan was liable to become the candidate, and it would be blamed on Nelson Rockefeller. We all knew that Governor Rockefeller, deep inside his mind, would have liked to have seen a stalemate, and perhaps pull off a miracle and become the candidate. But again, the Governor called a meeting in Washington, with Bill Ronan, Hugh Morrow and George Hinman. I brought my memo down there and had the rather odious task of informing the Governor, in a sense, that he was not going to be the candidate, unless he wanted to take the blame for Reagan beating Ford and becoming President.

On the following Monday, of course, the New York delegation met and gave almost all of its delegates to the President. On Tuesday, in those six primaries in what was normally regarded as Reagan territory, we were able to carry three out of the six states, and I think we came close to a tie in the other three. And that was the end of the Reagan candidacy for all practical purposes — led, of course, by the Governor's willingness to see the big picture.

So, to me, a kid from Oswego, New York, coming to Albany by way of Rochester, being involved with Nelson Rockefeller meant a great deal. I guess I could sum this up best by saying this: I was on the State Supreme Court by appointment of the Governor and then by virtue of an election by the people to a 14 year term. Many people have said to me, "Don't you think you made a great mistake leaving the bench to become State Chairman and do the things that you've done?" And I have said, "Mistake? I wouldn't have missed a moment of it for the world."

BURDELL BIXBY: Thank you, Dick. I'm happy to introduce now, as we cross the aisle, the Honorable Stanley Steingut, former Speaker of the Assembly.

STANLEY STEINGUT: First, let me express my appreciation to the State University for creating the Rockefeller Institute. It is my firm conviction that the Institute will be of great service to our educational process in the State, the students who go through the halls of our State University, as well as the State government. This is a marvelous endeavor and I want to express my appreciation for involving me on the advisory panel and providing me the opportunity to participate here today.

Although I am going to be brief, as our time is running out, I would like to comment on Jack Germond's description of Nelson Rockefeller as a pragmatist. This in my opinion best describes Nelson Rockefeller. Although I disagreed with him violently at times, he was a great man, as well as a great Governor. In my opinion, he joins three other great men who never made it to the Presidency, but who I believe would have made outstanding Presidents of the United States. These three: Averell Harriman, Hubert Humphrey and Robert Kennedy, together with Nelson Rockefeller,would have achieved greatness for our country and would have made great progress for the world. The people of the United States and the world have suffered a great loss because these men never made it to the Presidency.

I am not in a position to discuss the relationship between Nelson Rockefeller and his party, as I was not a member of Nelson Rockefller's party and was not privy to his activities. But, one thing for sure, he controlled his party in this State. However, as events have proven, he was not in tune with his party nationally.

Being a Democrat and a political antagonist, I can say something about Nelson Rockefeller and his political relations. I was a member of the New York State Assembly when Nelson Rockefeller became Governor in 1958. I had little contact with Nelson Rockefeller until 1965, when I was a candidate for Speaker.

In 1965, the people of the State of New York were under the impression that a Democratic majority both in the Assembly and Senate was elected. That was true in pure numbers. But in reality, it was a Nelson Rockefeller legislature. I say this, because, if you reflect and study the legislative session of 1965, you will find the minority party in both houses of the Legislature, the Republicans, joining with the minority of the Democratic majority in choosing the respective leaders in both houses under the guidance of the Governor. Of course, I was defeated for Speaker in 1965 because of that opposition. Not until the year I became Minority Leader did I really get to know Nelson Rockefeller — professionally and personally.

The first speech I made on the floor of the Legislature as Minority Leader resulted from a response that I made to a Republican member from upstate New York who complained about the adverse effect Governor Rockefeller's austerity budget would have on his district. I pointed out that the Rockefeller budget would create problems for every other member of the

Assembly, while Nelson Rockefeller was building a monument in concrete across the street. The following day, the *New York Times* bore a glaring headline: "Monument in Concrete — Steingut Charges."

I had not heard from Governor Rockefeller prior to the following morning when he called me on our hotline and said, characteristically, "Stan, how are you?" However, to make a long story short, that was the beginning of a very fruitful, educational, and invigorating relationship that lasted until he accepted the vice-presidency. We had many arguments, but as many things as we disagreed upon, there were more that we were in agreement upon.

Nelson Rockefeller was a mover, a shaker, and a shaper of his own party. As I have said earlier, it was a shame that he was never President, but in my opinion, and as I said to him, sometimes in jest and other times seriously, "Nelson, what a shame, you could have been President if only you were a Democrat." He always turned to me and remarked, "You know Harry Truman wanted me to switch parties." And I always responded, "How right Harry Truman was." I think he could have been elected President if he were a Democrat; he would have fitted the mold as a Democrat, but the mold that he did achieve in New York was the reason why he would never have been nominated by a national Republican Party for President.

He was a man of great contradictions — philosophically, programmaticlly, and developmentally — from one end of the spectrum to the other. Malcolm Wilson has referred to Nelson Rockefeller as a liberal. He was also characterized as a fiscal conservative, as a moderate, as well as a liberal, because, during his 15 years as Governor, his programs ran the gamut. As examples, consider his drug program, which I and many others in the State of New York believed to be the most reactionary in the nation; the expansion of the State University, which I and many others thought to be extremely progressive; the creation and the purpose of the Urban Development Corporation; as well as his position on abortion. I opposed the Governor's drug program, and was one of the leaders in support of his expansion of the State University, the UDC, and legalization concerning abortion. These are the best examples that I can give today concerning Nelson the man and his political relations.

Nelson Rockefeller may have been "green" when he came to Albany, but he learned awfully fast. Yes, he liked to wheel and deal and be involved with the leaders, and if we did not agree with him, he would attempt to circumvent us. As an example, on innumerable occasions, very early in the morning — as early as six A.M. — because he knew that I was an early riser, he would call me at my hotel. He said, "Stan, what is that guy Duryea doing? We have to get him today." And at times I would really try to help him. You all know that Perry Duryea at that time was the Republican Speaker of the Assembly and, although a personal friend, my political adversary.

Nelson Rockfeller was capable of being tough and rough as well as sensitive and emotional. He knew how to "touch the tender nerve." I remember, when I opposed him on an issue, out of the blue, I would get calls from people all around the state — all personal, political and good friends of mine. Then I found out that Nelson Rockefeller had Al Marshall and a whole bunch of fellows checking on who my friends were, personal as well as political. These friends would call and say, "What are you doing with this legislation?" When I got wise to Nelson's activities, I would immediately call Nelson and say, "Nelson, you know who just called me?" and he would laugh like hell.

But in sum total, as I said earlier and not to be repetitious, but rather to emphasize, Nelson was an activist; he was a mover; he was a doer; and he made tremendous contributions to the State of New York. We discussed political relations one night at a social dinner at the Mansion. My wife tried to talk about her problems in Brooklyn with a Senior Citizen Center and the problems she was having with the operations of the Center. He listened intently, made a note, and thought that what she was attempting to do was a great idea. It did not take two months before he had a bill passed that created a new concept concerning senior citizens in the State of New York.

He was a most unusual Governor. I served a year or two when Tom Dewey was Governor. I served through the entire administration of Averell Harriman, during Rockefeller's 15 years, Malcolm Wilson's one year as Governor and for four years under Hugh Carey. Of all I knew, he was, in many respects, the most unusual.

BURDELL BIXBY: Thank you, Stanley.

And now, Professor Alan Chartock, Professor of Political Science at the State University of New York College at New Paltz, and Professor of Communications at the State University of New York at Albany.

ALAN CHARTOCK: I want to thank two people on the panel: Mr. Steingut, who gave me my first consultantship, allowing me to buy my house in Great Barrington; and Mr. Bixby, who allowed me to court his temporary secretary/receptionist and marry her.

70

All this means a great deal to me. I owe a great deal to these two remarkable men.

I want to say two things and be very brief. I think that it's clear from everything that we've heard today that Nelson Rockefeller was what we call a "realigning personality." Things will never be the same because he was here. There is no question that he ruled by force of his personality. I just want to make an assessment about what is happening in the politics of New York State today. And that is that we have a very, very strong Legislature.

We did not have a strong Legislature when Nelson Rockefeller was the Governor. We didn't have a strong Legislature because it didn't have sufficient resources to compete with the Governor. And I think it's an incredible irony of Nelson Rockefeller that it was his strength which led to the situation today where we have a Legislature which is competitive with the Governor, a very good situation.

Today, for example, the Legislature is able to staff itself in such a way that it can make fiscal predictions defining the budgetary condition. In many cases the Legislature can do that better than the Governor. I think that's because of what Nelson Rockefeller did to the Legislature. He forced them to compete, and to compete on an intellectual level. I think that two things that we have heard today were, firstly, that the Legislature was not a match for Nelson Rockefeller. But it is a match for the Governor today, and that is due, in no small part, to him. And, secondly, that politics and personality, no matter what anybody says to us, have an awful lot to do with each other. James Barber wrote a book called *Presidential Character*, in which he set up a number of different typologies of what political scientists call active-positive, active-negative, passive-positive, and passive-negative. Nelson Rockefeller was clearly an 'active-positive'. He thought very well of himself; he thought there was nothing he couldn't do; and he enjoyed what he was doing. That's an 'active-positive'. And with that I'll sit down and leave this to the professionals.

BURDELL BIXBY: To conclude our panel discussions, I now present to you Mr. Charles Holcomb.

CHARLES HOLCOMB: It's always fun and interesting to hear other peoples' observations about somebody who was as compelling a personality as Nelson Rockefeller and who, in looking back, I seem to have spent a number of years watching with great fascination and interest here as a reporter. I would like to follow up on one comment, especially, that Alan Chartock just made about the Legislature having been forced to compete and that being why we have the kind of Legislature we have today. I would relate that to a remark that Al Marshall made, in which he spoke about the establishment of Program Associates and why that was done.

One of the side effects of Nelson Rockefeller's compulsion to do and achieve was an enormous proliferation of programs. I remember that the Legislature back in the early 1970's — the very early '70's — felt very frustrated because the budget was getting larger and larger, with more and more things in it, and the legislators felt less able to manage and really understand the underpinnings of it: the problem you refer to. They developed a capability of competing, but I think it's the very many things that the State government is now into and funding, which is a direct outgrowth of Rockefeller's activist approach, that has enabled them to be justifiably involved in so many areas.

Having worked for the current and outgoing Governor, Hugh Carey, I certainly was very aware of his frustrations in dealing with the Legislature and in being unable to get things through in the way Nelson Rockefeller used to. There are a lot of different personality and other differences that I won't go into, but I think that the magnitude of government these days has a lot to do with the ability of the Legislature to thwart the Governor in a way that it didn't before.

I just want to make some comments that would come under three headings: "tilt," "bear-hug," and "cork."

Nelson Rockefeller may have been green when he started in politics; he was certainly not green when I came on the scene a little bit later. He was certainly not green in knowing how to figure out what people wanted and how to turn that to his advantage in order to get what he wanted. I felt, as a long time observer of him, that he took great pains, and as a matter of principle made an effort to create a "tilt" in his direction. He did favors for people. He understood their sensitivities. He played on their egos. He knew how to reward and punish, and there was a lot more emphasis on reward than punishment, because he understood that today's beneficiary might very well be tomorrow's vote in the Assembly when you needed it. He rarely made a permanent enemy. The situation he created was like a table that is slightly tilted; the glasses all stay put until you start to shake the table — then everything tends to slide. I think he worked very hard to create a situation where, when it was necessary, he could get things to slide his way.

One of the ways he did that is what I call the "bear-hug." One of my lasting impressions of Nelson Rockefeller was of him standing at a podium or before the microphones in the Red Room with his arm around Stanley Steingut or Tony Travia or somebody else. I remember his arm around Wilbur Mills. If there was ever a weak reed to balance a budget on, it was revenue sharing. But it was a very important thing, and nobody believed he could do it. He went at it very systematically. I remember learning with interest that the Rockefeller plane was ferrying Wilbur Mills hither and yon, and some others of you can correct me, but my recollection is that he had Wilbur Mills in hand before he could bring Hugh Carey into camp. I remember his being very frustrated by Carey's lack of interest in the revenue sharing program. But the bear-hug technique was one in which he was self-confident enough in his own place, his own ability, that he was perfectly willing to share the glory and tell everybody what a great person they were for having cooperated in this and helped with that. And again that all helped him accomplish his agenda.

The final thing I would say was that, in a way, he played the role of cork in the bottle. Once he got to be Governor, we had in place a very senior political establishment that didn't change. There was Malcolm. There was Louie. There was Arthur Levitt, who was part of it but not in the Republican Party. And there was Jacob Javits. And they were in place for the duration, and the duration was really determined, in a way, by Nelson Rockefeller. That made it very frustrating for the Democrats who were trying, obviously, to capture the governorship. It also, I think, had a long term effect on the Republican Party, because it made it impossible for younger people to move into positions that would provide future leadership, or, in any event, it made it difficult because of having a fifteen year period with the same cast of characters (and I use the term with great affection) at the very top. It put everything in the deep freeze until he chose to end it by departing at the end of 1973.

It's been marvelous to sit here and have so many people who were on the inside being very candid about what went on and confirming all the worst suspicions that I used to have as a newspaperman. For example, I now know the degree to which the Rockefeller staff understood or believed in the budget figures they defended so vehemently as being accurate. Rockefeller above all was marvelous copy for newspaper people. He understood the care and feeding of the press and the importance of that in the political sense. You could always get a story out of him, because, not only was he doing interesting things, but he would tell just enough to pique your curiosity and to give you the germ of the story. And so he, I think, was very well treated overall by the press in his tenure. He was a marvel to behold for anybody who watched government.

73

Jack has spent so much of his time following political trails. I spent somewhat more time here in Albany trying to make sense out of the budget, and, you know, I think a sense of humor was always appreciated in dealing with the budget. I recall one year when there was a tight budget and there were no surprises in the budget until one came to a little footnote that established a first instance appropriation of $750 million for a sewage plant construction program: totally out of the blue, totally unsupported, totally separate from the budget. It didn't add, but there it was. That was the kind of budget-making that I suspect the Legislature rebelled against, and perhaps rightfully so.

Of course, I'm not sure that we have a better system now. I'm not entirely convinced that the present system in the Legislature — where everybody feels compelled to be in session all year round, and to have hearings, and all sorts of hot and cold running assistants — is necessarily a plus for the body politic, and I can tell you it's not a big plus for the current Governor. In any event, let me just — to the degree that I can — pull this discussion together.

I think Rockefeller was certainly a unique character in his handling of the political world, his ability to work with both sides, to go around leaders, and in the quality of excitement that he not only possessed but managed to transmit to those he worked with. It didn't always translate into electoral success, certainly not outside New York, as Jack has told us, but he was a unique figure, and I don't think we will see the like again, nor will the Empire State ever be quite the same.

Governor Rockefeller on the campaign trail in 1962 with Senator Jacob Javits, Attorney General Louis Lefkowitz, and Lieutenant Governor Malcolm Wilson.

BURDELL BIXBY: According to Dr. Hurd's note we have eight or nine minutes to go, and if someone would let me be rude by cutting him short, I invite you to make any further comment. Did I see your hand up, Sam?

ALEXANDER ALDRICH: Any discussion of Nelson Rockefeller's contribution to politics in New York State should include his impact on the various ethnic communities, especially the black and Hispanic groups in the State. I'm mindful of his relations with people like Porkchop Davis and with the extraordinary role Jackie Robinson and the mysterious Sam Singletary had at the Governor's office at West 55th Street. The Governor's impact on the Puerto Rican community was also very strong. His fractured Spanish language was so appealing to the Hispanic people with whom he dealt!

JACK GERMOND: That's an interesting point. I want to add something to what Stanley said. It's an interesting point, because, right now, you see that the National Republican Party has given up entirely on black support. You're talking about nine percent of the electorate of which they give away seven points overall. Rockefeller didn't do that and he counseled the Party against it. If the Republican Party were able to get even one-half of the vote we're talking about, we would have an entirely different makeup of the Congress today.

STANLEY STEINGUT: Nelson Rockefeller politically, not only with the minorities but with labor, co-opted the Democratic Party to a great extent. That was very, very important, the relationship to minority groups. It had a tremendous impact here in New York that could have been generated around the country if the Republican Party had adopted it.

R. BURDELL BIXBY: I would like to make an observation that may not be completely relevant in view of the subject of this panel, but I would like to observe it nonetheless. As some of you know, for many years I served as Secretary to Governor Dewey. Recently a book was published, *Thomas E. Dewey and His Times*. The emphasis in much of the book is focused on the two presidential elections in which he was defeated, not on his record as Governor of New York. Permeating our disussions has been the fact that Nelson Rockefeller was not nominated or elected President of the United States. I think that places this man's political career and political relations out of balance. He was elected Governor of the

State of New York four times to four-year terms, in a Democratic state, against overwhelming odds. No other man in the history of the State has done that.

His political legacies are the techniques he used to recruit men and women with unique professional skills, the charm and cunning he displayed to dominate the Legislature, the personal magnetism he developed to make television his secret weapon and the combination of these elements that brought him overwhelming votes of confidence from the people of our State. In my opinion, his primary legacy to the State and his party is the positive one — his precedent-breaking political achievements, not his disappointments on the national scene.

Chapter IV

The Builder

JAMES GAYNOR: We are here to discuss Nelson Rockefeller, the Builder, and that is a pretty challenging assignment. I say this from a personal sense, having been made aware of his enthusiasms and his constructive approach.

Not to be anecdotal (Norm Hurd has cautioned me), I must tell you very briefly that my wife and I had left Tennessee and decided to make our home in Denver, Colorado. There I had my own business, and in 1958 was called by an old-time associate to see if I would interview a client. I said "I'd be very happy to. I hope he has the wherewithal." He said, "I'm sure he does." "Then I'll meet him." And I came in and the client turned out to be Nelson Aldrich Rockefeller.

He suggested that I might be interested in coming with him into State government. And I assured him that I had done everything that was necessary to qualify for the hereafter, that I had worked in housing in New York City, and I had worked in various capacities in Washington, D.C., and I chose to be in the Mile High City for the rest of my mortal existence. He said, "Would you think about it?" And I said I would be very happy to think about it, and I went back to Denver.

Then I got another call and came back again. I had to call Mrs. Gaynor. Now I told her "I'm negotiating and this is not easy. This is not what I want to do." I said "I am getting convinced that in spite of everything we said, I think we ought to probably figure maybe to go back to New York." Mrs Gaynor said, "I was praying we would." So I went back to the office, saw the Governor, and said, "I'm in." But I said, "I have only one question. You're the only person I know in your administration, because I am a complete outsider now, coming from Colorado." He said, "Just a moment." He turned and said, "Meet Bill Ronan. Now you know two."

And now we may proceed with our theme on Nelson Rockefeller, the Builder. I want to introduce our theme setter, George Dudley, with whom I was personally associated at the State University Construction Fund. Beyond that, he was the Dean at my Alma Mater, RPI, at the School of Architecture, and I worked with him there. George had been with Nelson Rockefeller since about 1940. As we came into the State University Construction Fund when it was virtually established, we looked around and said, "Something's got to give." George took the initiative on his own and went to every one of our sites for the State University where we had contemplated construction. He then proceeded to set up the architecture. He is the guy who is responsible for the critical path, "the fast track." This is how we got those jobs under way so fast. It's really a pleasure for me to give you George Dudley.

GEORGE DUDLEY: Let me first respond with a scene I remember so well that takes what you just said right back to the Governor. The Governor swore us all in at 55th Street (Caroline Simon took her shoes off as she gave us the oath, which she always did so as not to appear taller than the Governor). He then said, "Let's go into the office," and we sat down. Cliff Phalen was the Chairman (he was the President then of the New York Telephone Company), Jim Gaynor was head of the Housing Finance Agency, I was head of the Office of Regional Development. The Governor said, "Now, it's a big job. Cliff, I want you to get this job done. Jim, I want you to finance it. George is going to be getting the best use of the environments of the campuses so that they're well planned, well built, and well designed." From then on we just went ahead, each knowing our areas of assignment.

He also set us up as a three-man board; any time one of us would make a motion, another would second it; that was all we had to do. No votes taken. I've always admired that.

Governor Rockefeller believed deeply in all the positive aspects of the development of mankind, the inevitability of growth and improvement and in an overriding commitment to working with those forces. He believed strongly in the upward dynamics of civilization as a whole and of its urban cultures, and societal or governmental building around the world, in the State of New York, or at home in Pocantico Hills.

Even beyond what such a passionate philosophy might have given such a leader and Governor, there are four characteristics which were uniquely his, raising him above even the normal performance of a constructive and caring Governor. These qualities were what made his legacy to the State, particularly as a builder, outstanding amongst all the great governors and the builders that this State has had. In setting a framework of themes for our discussion, I will outline briefly those four qualities and characteristics, mentioning some illustrations from my own personal experience of working for and with him throughout his public life, as Jim says, "From the year before Pearl Harbor." The framework will touch on aspects or themes of the Governor's lifetime. I realize that the discussions will fill it in for the period of his gubernatorial years with which we are particularly concerned.

First, the Governor might well be called "the complete and constant builder." He was a builder consistently through his life, and put in place during his lifetime many programs and developments which have ongoing growth built into them and which will carry far beyond his own times. As a young graduate of Dartmouth, as his first job, he elected to involve himself in renting space in Rockefeller Center. It was then being built, during the Depression, under the leadership of his father, himself a great builder who, with his mother, clearly inculcated the constructive building instincts which the Governor carried through his career.

At the same time, and thus typical of his life-long predilection for having major and minor projects proceeding simultaneously, he led a group of his fellow government graduates in forming the International Basic Economy Corporation (IBEC) and chose to start his operations in Venezuela. He realized that if IBEC was going to be successful there, there would be a need and market for modern hotel accommodations. And so he proceeded, as one of the first projects, to organize the Hotel Avila and have it designed under his new friend, Wallace Harrison.

The quality Nelson asked for was achieved to such a degree that the Avila was the prototype for many of the major new hotels built throughout the Caribbean in the post-war years. Harrison, incidentally, brought that project to the Yale Graduate School of Architecture where he was chief design critic, and it was early in 1940 that I had the first opportunity to work on a design project for Nelson Rockefeller.

I do not know of any period in his life that Nelson did not have at least one project, and usually more than one project going on simultaneously. Let me mention some of those of which you may not have thought in these terms.

As Coordinator of Inter-American Affairs during the war years, his activities ranged from supporting the efforts of the other American Republics in meeting their critical housing needs, down to the minutiae of finding a place for the office's chart room in waste space behind a classical pediment of the Commerce Department Building, which the Patent Office hadn't even been able to use as dead storage. This chart room was an early prototype for the so-called "war rooms." I helped develop this for Wally Harrison and the Governor, and the war rooms developed thereafter by the War Department and the Office of Strategic Services. (Malcolm reminded me this morning that when we went down to work with Ovetta Culp Hobby, the first Secretary of H.E.W., he again asked for a chart room to be set up, as a tool, to use his graphic approach in dealing with many of the complicated problems.)

Again as part of his activity, Rockefeller saw the need for low-cost housing in Venezuela. He saw the use of heavy equipment for road building there, and with Wally Harrison had the concept of bringing such tools to meet such needs. Thus, IBEC Housing Corporation got started.

We, with Wally Harrison as Chairman (succeeded later by Winthrop Rockefeller — I was President), built over 1,000 houses a year for ten years in Puerto Rico and helped on housing and urban development in many other countries. Nelson always took a direct personal interest in each of those activities. He and Wally saw the general need for technical assistance in these developing countries and sent teams of builders, in a large sense, to many of the countries. Not the least impressive of these was Bob Moses, another master builder, who went under the auspices of IBEC to change the highway system of Caracas, and to the city of Sao Paulo to advise on their major park and highway programs, bringing water over the mountains from the Atlantic coastal area to Sao Paulo. All of this was the prototype for the future Point Four programs of technical assistance initiated by President Truman. Nelson had fathered this program as head of Truman's task force which produced the report "Partners in Progress" the basis of Truman's Annual Message to Congress which started that program. This is also prototypical of the United Nations Technical Assistance program, which followed soon after, and for the U.N.'s continuing wide concern for technology transfer programs ever since.

The Governor was a builder in the broadest and deepest sense of the word. He never built without a clear purpose. The objectives were thoroughly and imaginatively defined. The extended impacts and ramifications of what was to be built on surrounding or related elements were always taken into consideration. This was consistently true, whether he was helping to build an international organization for peace or the physical headquarters for it (so critical as a symbol and with such an impact on urban design and development of the area around it) as Sam Bleecker has shown so well in his book, *The Politics of Architecture*. This was true whether he was working with Harrison on the design of the swimming pool in the garden of the playhouse at Pocantico or having Leger design the portico overhanging the entrance door of the many houses he built in Pocantico or Seal Harbor, Maine, or at his ranches, and so on. The articulation of functions and their implementations broadly and deeply always came before the emergence of the design of the forms.

The consistency of the Governor's building during his tenure as Governor of this State, and the stimulation and excitement he had from building for such a challenging set of needs and opportunities, made this period the most creative and productive one in his own career. In my opinion, it was the most important era of building in every sense in the history of the State. Thus, the building aspect of his administration has become a major part of his legacy, particularly as it served to establish bases for continuing growth and development. The Governor was consistently concerned, constructive, creative, comprehensive, and considerate.

I should add that he was confident. One of his great qualities was the confidence he had in himself as a builder — a practitioner of the total building process — which was legitimately based on his unusually wide experience and his ability to bring together the best practitioners of parts of the total process in the teams he knew he could assemble. He was legitimately confident of his abilities as the leader of those teams. Sometimes the Governor's consistency seemed to be almost obsessive, but we all came to realize he never brought us a building idea without a real reason or purpose or without a glint of the feasibility of accomplishing the 'built' results.

Now the second thing I would emphasize for you briefly is the fullness of the Governor's understanding and implementation of the total process of building. He knew that anything built was creating only a part of the total, evolving man-built environment, and was always an opportunity to enhance the natural environment. As indicated above, he knew that building started with the recognition and articulation of the need and opportunity to be fulfilled. How many times we all heard him speak of the great importance of sensing and then grasping the emerging forces of our society and cultures as firmly as possible so as to build with the momentum and basic dynamics of those forces. Malcolm again brought us back to that this morning, with a phrase that we often heard the Governor use, of "transforming problems into opportunities."

As we evolved the overall long-range plans for the State in the Office for Regional Development, he led us to the understanding that we needed to first know what the changes were that were already in motion — the trends, the emerging forces. But then we should not only plan to build to meet straight-line extrapolations of such changes, but should creatively find the opportunities and challenges which the dynamics of these inevitable changes gave us. And for that we should find constructive and even innovative ways to respond to those changes and the opportunities they presented.

Hence the title of the plan, which he helped select, was "Change, Challenge, Response." This was the basic philosophy followed by the Governor through his life-long building achievements. He knew the implementation of that philosophy could only be effectively and fully achieved, and thus a positive legacy left for those who came after, if all aspects of the process were considered and developed as needed throughout the process. The activation of all the parts was essential, and his intuition and thinking of all of them from the beginning was literally amazing to all of us who worked with him. He would quickly check through in his mind the interactive sequence of programming, scheduling, site and regional planning and design, financing, the governmental and political action necessary (including legislation and administrative re-organization if required) necessary to establish the infra-structure essential to support the project — often a separate project or program in its own right. Detailed architectural design was a process which he particularly loved, but which he never let get out of touch with all the other concerns. He structured the administration and funding for both the program and facilities and, finally, provided for the implementation and commissioning of the program and facilities and their future operation and growth.

The third quality which ran consistently through all the Governor's involvement in the total building process was his commitment to and his leadership in achieving excellence in everything built, in the broadest and deepest sense, throughout the State and throughout his terms of office. Malcolm's statement relating his interest in the qualitative, as well as or more than the quantitative, touched on this as well.

His personal values — his respect for excellence, his innate sense of quality, his perception of design — were his consistent standards throughout the tremendous range of his building projects, whether it was establishing the Model State Building Code, university campuses, the redecoration of the Executive Mansion in Albany or the Vice-Presidential residence in Washington, the Performing Arts Center in Saratoga, a ranch in Venezuela, a boat house in Maine, or the South Mall. All were different types, different levels, different forms, and they all had this element of quality. And these are just a few to remind us of the myriad of the projects he left behind. In all of these the quality of excellence was consistently operative, without critical compromise and with the hard personal effort required for any such achievements.

We should note that the exemplification of the use of the total process of building to achieve excellence was itself a most important part of the contribution the Governor made personally, through his leadership and the legacy he left. Mention had been made of the prototypical Hotel Avila and the pattern set by the IBEC Technical Services Corporation. Discussants will show how often innovative approaches led to new solutions being formulated (whether they were in funding of programs or new types of teaching facilities) researched, and tested on our many new university campuses.

As a part of the theme of excellence and quality, I would remind us all that we can take pride in the Governor's consistent search for the best available talent when he approached any of the new challenges he took on. One of the best examples of this was his support for drawing forth the best of the architectural firms in this State, and even outside when better expertise was available, for the creation of the network of State University facilities.

I mentioned the Governor's resistance to compromise with excellence. Unless such an adjustment was critical to accomplish greater aspects of this excellence — set as objectives of the program concerned — he was an effective pragmatist melded with an unwaivering creative idealist.

The fourth characteristic of the Governor's unique style and effectiveness as a builder was his creative and innovative approach to all programs and projects as being interactive with many others, and his realization of the possibility of maximizing the total achievement of all beyond the sum of the component elements. The Governor institutionalized this broad and productive approach when he first set up his State planning mechanism as the Planning Coordination Board, rather than as an office of State planning. That was staffed, of course, by the Office of Regional Development.

All of the key building agencies were represented on that Board. The Governor realized that the sum total of the ongoing planning in those member agencies far surpassed the sum of the individual efforts, if they could be coordinated with the others and had constructive added support from each of those related to it.

I might add another personal note. A few days after Rockefeller became Governor, Wally Harrison told me that the Governor would like me to go to Albany and talk with him about a chart room. I thought we were in for another in a sequence of chart rooms built as tools that let the Governor operate, as he preferred to, in graphic terms. I joined him at the Westchester airport and we rode up in the plane together. He would point things out that we were flying over: "That's the hospital complex such and such ... You see the highway over there ... Well, they didn't provide proper access to that hospital." He said that sometimes highways are built where other things have just been built, and they have to be torn down or moved. He said that avoiding such errors was what we needed in planning. I realized that he was talking not about a chart room as such, but of a mechanism for state planning coordination. It was his own idea, right at that time. So that everything he did was set in place, to my mind, through thinking about this interactive maximizing of the results of all the different programs.

Another example may not be covered by the discussions: no one directly involved in it, other than myself, is on the list of attendees. When the Pure Waters Bond Issue was passed, there was required the establishment of a mechanism which was initially called the Pure Waters Authority, to implement the Governor's environmental programs. He knew, for example, that a sewage treatment plant, in its siting and the land acquisition necessary for it, could represent the focus — or even catalyst — for the rebuilding of many of the urban areas of the State, providing park areas and determining urban development around it. In Harlem, for example, the Inner City State Park, one of the very first, was built largely on top of such a plant, and the land acquisition necessary for that gave it an added benefit of two areas on which high-rise housing went ahead. All of this — the park, the housing, and other amenities — was achieved because he had a Pure Waters Bond Issue. In the case of that program, he implemented this concept by the appointment as Chairman of the Pure Waters Authority not a sanitary engineer, but an architect-planner who had worked with him in just that type of integrated development (which is another personal note since that Chairman was myself).

There have been many great building leaders in our own nation's history. We think of Thomas Jefferson and Franklin Roosevelt, Eisenhower's Interstate Highway Network, and so on. Especially in our own State, we think of Bob Moses building for so many governors and mayors. The Governor's unique greatness in building, including building such a comprehensive legacy for New York, was, I believe, based on his consistent, life-long, informed interest and involvement in the total building process; his commitment to quality and excellence; and his understanding of

84

how each constructive act could contribute to over-all constructive achievement — multiplying values far beyond the value of a particular project or program itself. From all of that came the magnificent legacy of man-built and enhanced natural environments which will serve and inspire New Yorkers for generations to come.

JAMES GAYNOR: Thank you very much George. And thank you for setting the theme. As I introduce our first discussant, I think you might be interested in the genesis of the Housing Finance Agency — an agency today that's been copied by over forty states and I couldn't tell you how many counties and regions. This is a pioneer of housing financing agencies.

In 1959, as he was inaugurated, the Governor appointed a task force on middle-income housing. A very illustrious group of gentlemen came forth with a proposal, among others, that the hundred million dollars that had been approved for limited profit housing by the voters should be augmented in turn by private money. This was the concept. We spent one year on this in the Division of Housing, and I won't bore you with the number of discussions over dinners and luncheons that we had with representatives of the institutions of finance and commercial banks and savings banks and insurance companies.

It was all to little avail because the concept was wrong, as I pointed out to the Governor. I said, "We spent a year on this and it's a bomb. It won't fly, because these people are stewards of somebody else's money. They don't like risks. Housing is a very risky business." I said, "This isn't going to work. But I do have an alternative. Some years back in the New York City Housing Authority we financed a program of housing without cash subsidy. We used no subsidies, but used the credit of the City of New York. We've got a version of that that my friends on Wall Street tell me will fly. We've got revenue bonds for housing and these revenue bonds in turn will not be an obligation of the State. They don't require the full faith and credit of the State. In fact, the debt service will be paid by the rents to be charged. It is feasible. It has been done, and with public buildings in some states. And it will also enable you to sell bond anticipation notes which will permit you to proceed immediately with construction."

I thought you might be interested in that because that is the genesis of the Housing Financing Agency. It came because the proposal of the task force simply couldn't be made feasible. Now it's a pleasure for me to introduce an old colleague, Paul Belica, who was there practically from the beginning — a man who worked very hard in the vineyard of the Housing Finance Agency and today is with Smith Barney and makes his money the hard way. He earns it.

PAUL BELICA: First I want to express my appreciation to be with you again and refer to the pleasure I had, and still have today, after almost 16 years of my life spent financing public-purpose projects because of the Governor. Jim mentioned how he was contacted by the Governor and how he was talked into it. With me it was very simple. I was quite happy making money in the construction business, when the recruiting team approached me with the proposition that, as a new American, I might consider providing service to my country and agree to contribute one year of my time towards that objective. That is one of the ways the Governor was getting all the people he needed to achieve his objectives.

The greatest joy I had in joining his team was being in the company of talented professional people. You know from your own experience how pleasant it is to work with that type of people. You don't waste time. You get a response. It's constructive. Implementation reflected a top-notch professional approach, administration support came through, and the task was done.

And what happened to the New York State Housing Finance Agency? It outgrew its original concept and became a multi-purpose financing entity with so many programs and with so much volume that the housing, despite its volume, became a minor portion of its overall activity. When I left in 1976, I added up the notes and bonds. I found out that, overall, $16.0 billion worth of paper were thrown into the marketplace and sold effectively at very attractive prices during my association with the HFA and four other State agencies I had under my wing. It is amazing in retrospect to realize that we marketed forty-year bonds at as low as 4 percent interest rate compared to today's 12 percent. All together, we brought to market approximately $10 billion of short-term paper and $6.0 billion of long-term securities. All the short-term borrowing was repaid or refunded, and to date only the long-term paper, about $6.0 billion worth, is outstanding. None of it ever defaulted, all the principal and interest payments were always there on a timely basis, and it is almost 22 years since the first issue was sold.

It is very exciting to go around and see all the projects and structures you contributed to bringing into existence and to know you were involved and raised the capital to make it happen. It was a very exciting time. I don't want to waste too much time on details. I have very talented colleagues on this panel and each one of them wants to talk about the part he played in these achievements. So with your permission, I will pass the mike to somebody else.

JAMES GAYNOR: Our next discussant is Samuel Bleecker. Samuel Bleecker has written a book on the politics of architecture and the impact of Nelson Rockefeller. He's interested in communication. He's also interested in software and the uses of all those home computers. It's a pleasure for me to introduce Sam Bleecker.

SAMUEL BLEECKER: From your warm introduction, it should be evident that I come to this forum from a different route than the other distinguished panelists. Although I too worked for the State, my knowledge of Rockefeller as a builder is a bit more indirect.

I had the opportunity of meeting Nelson Rockefeller during what I like to describe as his anecdotal stage — a time when he had effectively retired from politics to pursue his interest in the arts. It was a time when he was laying to rest his past — his failed

Mrs. Rockefeller, Governor Rockefeller, Albany Mayor Erastus Corning, and Lieutenant Governor Malcolm Wilson at the laying of the cornerstone for the South Mall, June 21, 1965.

hopes for the Presidency — and had begun to analyze his contributions to State and nation.

It also was a time when he spoke candidly and at great length about his efforts in the great public building projects that will be discussed here today, as well as the construction of his private homes. And, as the author privileged to write about those recollections, I came to see him in a somewhat new and different light.

When I first came to the project — the writing of *The Politics of Architecture* — I must confess I had considerable prejudice. In fact, when I was still a college student, Nelson Rockefeller had been burned in effigy on my campus for effecting tuition in the State University system. But in truth, he was very different from what I had imagined.

I had come to learn that he wasn't a theoretician like Henry Kissinger, but much more the pragmatist. He had little use for historical discourse. He rarely read books since he suffered from dyslexia. In fact, I believe his dyslexia, in part, explains why he was an extremely visual person who gravitated toward the arts.

But above all Nelson Rockefeller was intuitive. He had a gift for seeing to the core, for acting boldly — if not occasionally a bit brashly — and for getting things done. These were his swords: imagination, courage, and doggedness. In essence, he operated on a small number of fundamental principles.

As a result, what I would like to focus on today is not his political or economic motivations, but rather his use of art in architecture — one of the concepts he cherished most.

Perhaps the best way to convey his aesthetic motivations is to relate a story about the very young Nelson Rockefeller.

It's said that when he was still a child, he preferred to walk alone along Fifth Avenue in New York rather than ride to Central Park in his father's limousine. A chauffeur would discreetly follow at some distance behind. But when young Nelson arrived at the Park's boat basin, the chauffeur would hand him an ordinary-looking toy boat. And, like all children, Nelson would proudly launch it and watch it bob in the water.

There were other children who sported more elaborate vessels with breezy sails and large brightly painted hulls. By comparison, Nelson's boat seemed somewhat frugal.

One day, as the story goes, one unkind child taunted young Rockefeller and asked why he had such a drab boat. Rockefeller answered: "Who do you think I am, a Vanderbilt?"

Although the story is no doubt apocryphal, it points up the Rockefeller family tendency to understate its wealth. It was a reticence so ingrained that it even influenced Nelson Rockefeller's architecture. For the inheritors of one of the world's greatest fortunes, the Rockefeller homes are modest indeed.

Kykuit, for instance, is the largest of the homes on the family's 3,000-acre estate at Pocantico Hills in New York. Yet it is no match for either the elaborate Biltmore mansion of George W. Vanderbilt in Asheville, North Carolina, or the magnificence of the Hearst estate in San Simeon, California.

Such displays of opulence were completely unacceptable to Rockefeller's father and grandfather, who built Kykuit and laid out its grounds on a gentle hill overlooking the Hudson River.

Until his death in 1979, Nelson lived in Kykuit and had compensated for the inherited restraint by using art as condiment, as accent. In his hands, all art — painting, sculpture, tapestries, porcelain, furniture and other collectibles — became the sauce, so to speak, that brought out the fine subtle flavors of architectural line and form.

Moore's *Family Group*, which reclines on the rolling manicured hill in front of Kykuit facing the vast Hudson Valley, continues the contours of nature while sharply contrasting the rigid lines of the stone mansion constructed from 1909 through 1913.

In all, 75 sculptures, by such artists as Lipchitz and Picasso, dot Kykuit's landscape amid the travertine gazebos and gushing fountains.

For Rockefeller, the positioning of these works of art was far from accident; in fact, it was a major preoccupation. At considerable expense, he had a helicopter move a nearly two-ton sculpture, Moore's *Knife Edge*, only a few inches, so that it best graced the landscape.

Most people would have considered the slight shift in position insignificant. However, after repositioning, the improvement was incontestable.

He did something similar with *Surfaces in Space* by Max Bill. For Rockefeller it made indisputable sense that this triangular sculpture capture the roving eye and focus it along the curve of the rose garden and the intersection of the axis of a long, narrow grass terrace and a squat arbor.

The late Carol Uht, when she was curator of his collections, noted that Rockefeller had a highly articulated sense of proportion and relationship. That observation may well have been an understatement.

His punctiliousness, in fact, even extended to the smaller art objects in his homes. Each week, the Kykuit household staff would use more than a dozen rolls of Polaroid film to photograph countless objects — ashtrays, carvings, sculptures, lamps, vases

—on every table top, mantle and bureau. Nothing could be displaced from the precise position which he established for it. Each object coexisted synergistically with others for him, and nothing escaped his eye.

Rockefeller once explained his aesthetic fastidiousness as being much more drawn to the plastic, to the three-dimensional, than to pure line and color. He was particularly interested by the problem of relating art to architecture, as it was related in the past. Hanging paintings, finding new spatial relationships for his sculpture, he said, was his only way of being creative. He also admitted to having seriously considered being an architect when he was in college and even speculated that his love of sculpture was perhaps related to his forgotten vocation.

In a deeper sense, art and architecture have a much more intimate relationship. For him, art and architecture often blurred, and there is no doubt that on one plane of consciousness, Rockefeller perceived the outer shell of buildings as sculpture.

The Mall here in Albany, for instance, can be characterized as a group of forms on a platform — sculpture on a pedestal, if you will.

The basic design of this bold new capital complex was conceived in flight aboard Governor Rockefeller's private plane with Wally Harrison, the distinguished architect and a long-time friend.

He and Rockefeller sketched out the basic design. Governor Rockefeller thought it might be done in the grand style of Brasilia, Versailles, or Chandigarh. He took his pen and sketched his ideas in black ink across the back of a postcard in awkward, scratchy lines. Harrison picked up the pen and revised the drawing. Harrison told me that together they devised a scheme which embodied the ideas which the Governor had been thinking about for a long time.

It was a tantalizing design, for Nelson Rockefeller saw in the South Mall — as it was known originally — what others only vaguely recognized: that the scale of the new capital just be enormous so that it would hold up as sculpture with distance — particularly from across the Hudson River. He understood the prominence the Mall skyline would command.

At one point, he had a model of the project placed at the foot of the old capitol stairway and illuminated with klieglights bright enough to mimic the rising and setting sun.

His strong aesthetic sense never abated. Even his summer house in Maine, the Anchorage, offers a similar aesthetic experience and another testament to his visualization of architecture as sculpture.

It was a structure of which the architect Harrison was extremely fond. The house is built above a craggy stretch of salted brown granite off the coast of Maine between Penobscot and Frenchman Bays. In many ways, the location is reminiscent of the tortured cliffs and fjords that dot Normandy and parts of France. Swept clean of soil by prehistoric glacial movements, the island site of the summer retreat is now covered with a mantle of spruce and pines that grow from moss-encrusted earth.

The house is designed as two overlapping but opposing fieldstone crescents. The upper curve connects three rooms within its 300-foot-long sweep. The floor of the lower crescent slopes downward, following the contour of the cliff. One wall curves like a wave and Harrison described the whole building as being constructed like a yacht.

The shape of the Anchorage is a consequence of the interactive design process adopted by Harrison and Rockefeller. In the 1930's, Rockefeller invited Harrison, who also was one of the architects of Rockefeller Center, to Mount Desert Island in Maine. Rockefeller's specific purpose for this visit was to admire the views from the site on which he wanted to construct his summer home. He had told Harrison that the views were unbelievable.

During his outdoor meeting at the site, Rockefeller pointed to cliffs in the distance and the sparkling water splashing against them. Rockefeller then picked up two stakes and drove them into the ground.

He said, "I want my house to have a window right here so that I can see these cliffs." And then he strode onto the ground where he wanted windows. In this manner, he proceeded around the future homestead until he determined all the best views that would be available to him. It was now left to Harrison to make a topographical map of the property and to accommodate the design of the structure to his client's needs. He created two sweeping crescents which allowed Rockefeller in one room a view of a natural pool cut deep into the rocks, and in another of the crashing waves of the Atlantic Ocean.

Rockefeller also worked with Harrison on the design of a quiet retreat called The Lodge, in the woods at the Pocantico Hills estate. Again the architect exploited unusual form prompted by Nelson Rockefeller's aesthetic sense.

The Lodge is constructed with a sculpted roof derived from a sketch by Leger, another favorite artist of Rockefeller's. Harrison also designed a guest house on the estate, a unique fieldstone building with a large circular living room with electrically operated floor-to-ceiling windows that permit the landscape to be part of the interior.

These buildings, taken together with a Japanese-style house and formal gardens designed for Nelson Rockefeller by Junzo Yoshimura, are the exceptions on the family estate.

The Japanese House is sculpted to fit the landscape. The pebbles in the mini-garden fronting each floor-to-ceiling window are raked in appealing patterns. The placement of rocks and stones, of brushes and shrubbery, of sculpture and fountains is inseparable from the architecture.

The Lodge, the Guest House and the Japanese House are contemporary, bold in form and quietly aesthetic. They are quite distinct from the estate's generally New England formality and respectability and, thus, are suited more to his mother's time than to his grandfather's. These buildings carry the light touch of his mother, Abby Aldrich Rockefeller. She, of course, was a devotee of contemporary art and a founder of the Museum of Modern Art in New York City.

It was she who aided Nelson in persuading his father to commission artists for Rockefeller Center. The Center was conceived as a daring experiment for marrying culture and commerce, and it was to have a unified artistic theme.

Originally Rockefeller Center was to incorporate the new home for the Metropolitan Opera House with a commercial enterprise that would help offset the Opera Company's consistent deficit programs. The Depression of the 1930's, however, took the wind out of such a plan, and the Metropolitan Opera was forced to withdraw from Rockefeller Center. Nevertheless, John D. Rockefeller, Jr. maintained the ideal of a new type of commercial venture whose goals were not solely financial. Instead, he envisioned an enterprise of broad commercial and aesthetic scope — a cultural center that would display the arts.

To select and commission the best art, John D. Rockefeller, Jr. convened a blue-ribbon art panel composed of five leaders in the academic art world. Nelson Rockefeller assumed the delicate task of providing the art committee with a more modern outlook than it perhaps had or wished.

With maternal imprimatur, the young Rockefeller persuaded the art committee to bring Leger, Matisse, Picasso, Rivera and others to Rockefeller Center. He told me that he tried to get modern artists who were reflective of our times. And the only two he was successful in getting were: Diego Rivera, a Marxist; and Isamu Noguchi, who did the bas-relief aluminum plaque commemorating the Associated Press Building.

Rockefeller and his mother had to be very persuasive to get John D. to accept an artist like Rivera. But Nelson could not be dissuaded. He championed modern art because he strongly believed that "we must come to know and understand the best of our time in order that it may be fully utilized." And for him, art was the means for this self-enlightenment.

Eventually, scandal surrounded the work of the Mexican socialist painter who decorated the main lobby of the RCA building in Rockefeller Center with an anti-capitalistic mural. But Nelson Rockefeller was undaunted. He continued to support the arts at Rockefeller Center throughout his early decade-long tenure there, first as key manager and then as president.

The source of his concern for art in architecture has deep roots stretching to his childhood. Constantly surrounded by the efforts of his father in undertaking architectural restorations and of his mother in popularizing the avant garde, Rockefeller had promoted the arts unceasingly — even to the extent of forming a mail-order company to reproduce pieces of his vast collection for sale to the public. It was his hope that everyone could share in his pleasure of art.

This desire was characteristic of him. He used the arts to create aesthetic environments for both himself and for the public. And no matter what the source of his aesthetic motivations, it is evident that Nelson Rockefeller took pride in his art and his architecture and merged them into a whole that surpassed the sum of its parts.

In his own words, he saw architecture not just as bricks and mortar, steel and glass, but as an expression of economic needs, cultural aspirations, political life and international relations.

If we simply look around us, we can see that Nelson Rockefeller not only built extensively, but he also built well.

In fact, as George Dudley has indicated, Nelson Rockefeller built more than any other 20th century New York governor. As Governor from 1959 through 1973, he launched the State University Construction Fund, a massive effort to build not only new campus buildings but entire new campuses throughout the State. He built public and state office buildings, launched 90,000 low-to-middle income housing units, and created public outdoor spaces around collections of art. And, in each case, he was as concerned with the quality of the architecture and its cultural implications as he was with its political and social consequences.

It was Governor Rockefeller who put his finger on the map and said we needed a park, an office complex, a university campus, a hospital, a low-cost housing project. It was Rockefeller who campaigned for the construction of quality architecture, who introduced a new era establishing the New York State Council on the Arts and the Council on Architecture. It was Nelson Rockefeller who secured the funds, organized the projects, and, in many cases, directed the architects. It was he who had a vision for the State's future and used buildings to give form to that future.

In the end, not all that he worked for has come to pass. Not all of what he set out to do was doable — or perhaps should have been done. But he tried.

Much of what he attempted, he could be proud of and we are glad to have. If there is any fitting testament to Nelson Rockefeller, the builder, it is the landscape of the State of New York which he helped shape as few others have.

JAMES GAYNOR: Thank you, Sam. Our next discussant is a little contraire. She is very experienced in Housing and Finance and though not a lawyer, is probably the finest lawyer that I've ever retained. I respected her counsel far more than many of the legal staff that I've been exposed to. She should have Esq. following her name, but that's not the case. I can merely tell you, in introducing Lee Goodwin, that she was a superb craftsman and when she wrote a report it was a considerable one.

Again we had one of these unfortunate circumstances where housing had to be voted by the electorate and "housing" was a nasty word. And in this instance Lee came up with a proposal and we decided to present it to the Governor. It was practically Lee's proposal and the Governor went through it pretty tediously. He was always a quick study. When he got to the fifth page where Lee had written that this recommendation required only the approval of the Legislature, it did not require a referendum to be approved at a general election, the Governor turned to her and said, "Why didn't you say that in the first place?"

LEE GOODWIN: Thank you very much, Jim. I'm really delighted to have the opportunity to join in this tribute to Nelson Rockefeller. I cannot think of a more fitting gesture than to have the State University of New York, which he deeply loved, honor him by creating the Rockefeller Institute of Government.

I came to the Rockefeller administration out of the State Legislature where I worked for a chap by the name of McNeil Mitchell who was the author of the Mitchell-Lama Law. As a very junior member of Mac's staff, I went to the Republican Convention in Rochester in 1958. It was my first introduction to Republican politics at the State level. Nelson Rockefeller's name was placed in nomination for Governor and Malcolm Wilson's for Lieutenant Governor. The floor went wild. A wonderful lady from New York County, who was leading our delegation, turned to me and suggested that it would be appropriate for me to join the floor demonstration for "our next governor." This was the beginning.

During the campaign, a group was put together to form a task force on housing. It was headed by Roswell Perkins, who subsequently became the first counsel to Governor Rockefeller. At the end of that campaign I received one of those wonderful Rockefeller letters saying, "I hope I'll continue to have the benefit of your views in the field of housing." And in fact he did. In 1962, I left Mac's staff to join the administration as Executive Assistant to Jim Gaynor. I went on vacation a little while later on an island off the coast of Massachusetts where there was no phone. I came back and found I was named Assistant Director of the New York State Housing Finance Agency.

Several things stand out in my mind about Nelson the Builder. One was the very wealth of the programs that he created. As Malcolm said, Rockefeller's building program was far from a single purpose approach. We had programs for the construction of family housing, cooperative housing, rental housing, and special purpose housing for senior citizens. We went forward and provided for the construction and financing of non-profit nursing homes, hospitals, even day-care centers and senior citizen centers — an amazing array, during the years where virtually no other state was beyond a rather traditional approach to public works. In the public works sector, his approach was startlingly different — as exemplified by the State University Construction Financing Program and the Public Health Facilities Program. Nelson Rockefeller's hallmark was the creation of totally new entities to provide mechanisms that would bring to government a level of productivity, achievement, creativity and design quality that, if we look back to the early days of the sixties when this was happening, was startlingly different from the horizon of activities being undertaken either by the Federal government or any other state government.

In my mind, Governor Rockefeller had a very deep concern for harnessing the creativity and sensitivity of the private sector for the benefit of New York's public programs through the use of outstanding architectural and construction teams, as George Dudley discussed, in the creation of new facilities for the State University and the Department of Mental Hygiene. He also placed great emphasis on enlisting the private sector in fields such as housing by providing mechanisms that served to attract the quality builder and developer.

As Jim said, we also recognized during these years that we had to be prepared to accept certain risks beyond those associated with conventionally financed real estate. We had to look at traditional mortgage instruments, recognizing that we were getting into the field of multi-million dollar construction loans. We needed a much higher loan-to-value ratio than private lenders had been prepared to put in place, first 90 percent and then 95 percent of development costs. We needed to develop means to encourage builders to build and own properties as a long-range equity investment through equity syndication. When we passed the legislation in 1968, New York was the forerunner in what has become the primary vehicle for encouraging investment in residential real estate on a nationwide basis.

Rockefeller was also concerned with the quality of life in the buildings that he built. Jim told the story, when he introduced me, of what was to become the Capital Grant Low-Rent Assistance Program. The program takes its name from the fact that we had come up with a device to convert a periodic subsidy into a one-time grant program, a device for which the Governor was famous. The capital grant program provides a means to aid low-income families to live in middle-income housing with the goal of both economic and racial integration. It was a very new concept at the time.

Rockefeller was a forerunner and a leader in civil rights. He was concerned long before it became a popular thing. I think one of the first actions he took was to spell out an affirmative action program for State-aided urban renewal areas. He took the initiative in the development of a very creative loan program to enable low-income families to purchase their own co-ops. The program has the acronym of HOPE — Home Owners Purchase Endorsement. It was extremely successful.

Rockefeller was truly a renaissance man. Malcolm Wilson cited in his opening statement the epitaph inscribed on a tablet over the inner north doorway of St. Paul's, where Sir Christopher Wren is buried — "If a monument is required, look around you." In every corridor of New York City and in virtually every part of upper New York State, his administration left a lasting imprint. This is the Nelson Rockefeller whom I knew.

JAMES GAYNOR: Thank you, Lee. One thing George Dudley and I were concerned about with the State University Construction Fund (SUCF) was how, eventually, that Fund would be integrated within the State University. Because right then we had to have, separately, the SUCF to get what the Governor wanted done, and there was no choice about it. We had to go on a fast track. We had to get these things done.

I won't bore you with this business that Lee happened to mention concerning the single contract. The brickbats were being thrown by my good friends, "the mechanical subs," as we call them; those contractors who felt that I was a traitor to the cause.

Governor Rockefeller poses before a housing project.

And all I could do was smile and say, "I'm sorry but that's the legislation, and of course, we must follow the legislation." Of course, we had written the legislation.

But now, as I introduce our next speaker, Oscar Lanford, who has been with the State University since its creation, I see that the State University Construction Fund is well integrated. He is Vice-Chancellor of the University, representing the State University Construction Fund.

DR. OSCAR E. LANFORD: I have been asked to describe in a few minutes the achievements of the Rockefeller administration in the building of the State University of New York (SUNY). To do so in that time is not only difficult, it is impossible! Thus, my remarks will be limited to summarizing the Rockefeller administration's overall achievements in building the University and mentioning some of the important elements which made the achievements possible.

As is well known, New York was the last of the 50 states in the nation to establish a state university. It was not until 1948, during the administration of Governor Dewey, that SUNY came into being. Between 1948 and 1961, very little occurred insofar as the capital development of SUNY was concerned.

During the same period, the babies born after World War II were growing toward college age. Their parents, in many cases, had attended college under the GI Bill, many as the first generation of their families to have this opportunity. Consequently, both these parents and their children were determined that the "baby boom" children would receive a college education.

But there were not enough places in the State's colleges or universities for these rapidly increasing numbers of college-aspiring high school graduates. When Nelson Rockefeller assumed the governorship of New York, he immediately recognized the gap that existed in higher education in this state and the fact that, because of this gap, a great many of the State's most able young adults were migrating to other states to attend college. New York was faced with the necessity of greatly increasing the number of places available for students in SUNY as well as increasing the number, diversity and quality of the academic programs available. In short, New York State at the beginning of the Rockefeller administration faced the need to accomplish in a period of a few years what most other states had required a century to accomplish — namely, to build a system of public higher education adequate to meet the needs of our society in this latter half of the 20th century.

It is apparent to all who lived through that period (as I did) that Governor Rockefeller undertook this challenge not only with a great deal of political and managerial skill, but also with a great deal of pizzazz. (I parenthetically would say that in one of the few private conversations I had with the Governor, he said, "My father came out of upstate New York and he had only a basic education. He taught his children and grandchildren to appreciate the virtues of education and I hope that when my administration is done, I will be known best of all for what I did for education.")

First, the extent of need — for example, the definition of what needed to be done — was undertaken by a special commission headed by Henry Heald. The Heald Commission report, together with the SUNY Master Plan of 1961, provided a blueprint for the statewide system of public higher education which is strikingly similar to that which in fact exists today.

But how was this university to be constructed? Many said it could not be done in time to accommodate the large number of high school graduates who would be knocking on the door. The fact is that it was done in spite of the obstacles that at the time seemed overwhelming. It was done so rapidly and successfully that, near the end of the Rockefeller administration, it was said that SUNY was then graduating, each year, more students than it had enrolled in its entirety when the Rockefeller administration took office.

I will mention three of the actions which made this rapid growth possible:

1) Rockefeller worked together with Frank C. Moore (who was at that time Chairman of the Board of Trustees of the State University) and T. Norman Hurd, then Director of the Budget, to eliminate many of the regulatory restrictions which, up to that time, had hindered the growth of the university.

2) The establishment of the State University Construction Fund - a unique public benefit corporation with the single purpose of providing the expertise for planning, designing and constructing the university's capital plant.

3) An ingenuous financing plan whereby bonds sold by the New York State Housing Finance Agency provided the capital funding for all of SUNY's academic facilities with University revenue pledged to the debt service on the bonds.

Both the Fund itself and the University's capital financing plan have become the envy of many other states.

As a result of these actions, and the passage of legislation to implement them, the State University Construction Fund has constructed about $2.6 billion of SUNY academic facilities since it was established in 1962 — so that SUNY now has more than 2,200 buildings with a total of approximately 66 million square feet of space on its 34 State-operated campuses. This constitutes both the largest and one of the finest university capital plants in the world. Incidentally, it now has an estimated replacement value of about $6.6 billion — which makes it look like a very great investment.

The Construction Fund, as a single purpose organization, has carried out this impressive program with a) timeliness, b) concern about fitting each facility to the academic need it is to serve, c) high quality of architecture, d) minimum cost consistent with academic requirements, and e) a great deal of user satisfaction.

a) *Timeliness*: In spite of the rapid increase in demand for admission, I have not found one case in which a would-be student was denied admission to SUNY because the facilities were not there to accommodate him or her.

b) *Concern about fitting the facility to its academic need*: The fund has exercised great care to the end that the buildings accommodate the University's academic programs, not vice-versa. For example, SUCF buildings are carefully designed to fit the academic requirements of those who will use them. This has been possible because the Fund, being a single-purpose agency, is staffed with professionals who understand thoroughly the unique requirements of university buildings. Through Governor Rockefeller's leadership, the Fund was encouraged to design and construct wholly new types of facilities to permit new and creative teaching methods. Thus, facilities which have come to be known as Instructional Resource Centers and Instructional Communications Buildings were constructed on most campuses to provide the physical facilities with which the faculty could carry out the most modern teaching-learning processes.

c) *High quality of architecture*: From the beginning, Governor Rockefeller made it clear he wanted the best architects in the country to design SUNY buildings. In fact, he convened a meeting of State University officials and Trustees, Construction Fund officials, and private architects in the fall of 1962 at the Governor's Mansion, at which time he stated that he wanted the University to represent the best architecture in the world. His wishes in this regard have been faithfully followed. As a result, State University buildings have won more than forty awards for architectural excellence.

d) *Minimum costs consistent with academic requirements*: Several studies have shown that Construction Fund buildings are put in place at a lower cost per square foot than comparable buildings done by independent universities or by public universities in other states.

e) *User satisfaction*: The general reaction to our buildings by both faculty and students has been very positive.

It should be stated that this very large capital development program has been carried out by the Construction Fund without even a suggestion of improper or unethical action on the part of its staff. To put it bluntly, there has been no scandal.

In some cases, the University's construction program has involved major additions to existing campuses — for example: Albany, Stony Brook, Binghamton, Amherst (said to be the largest single-campus construction program ever undertaken), Old Westbury, Purchase, Utica/Rome, Canton and Alfred.

Time does not permit discussion of the enormous influence the Rockefeller administration had in the development of the statewide system of community colleges, but it should be noted that the system which exists today is the result of Rockefeller's leadership and legislative and managerial skill. There have been a total of twenty-two new community college campuses established since 1958.

Finally, we all recognize that these great university buildings, on sixty-four campuses (including community colleges) stretching across the state from Long Island to Fredonia, do indeed constitute a great legacy of a great governor. They are seen daily by all of us as we travel about the State. It is well to remember, however, that Governor Rockefeller's legacy is more than just the buildings — his real legacy is what is occurring in the buildings: the shaping of the intellect of our youth, the new ideas that are being formulated, the new understandings of man and his environment that are being developed. And although the buildings themselves will last into the 21st Century, the activities that occur within these buildings will influence this state and nation for as long as man inhabits the earth.

JAMES GAYNOR: Thank you, Oscar. And now we will consider any questions.

JOSEPH F. ZIMMERMAN: I was the first staff director of the Joint Legislative Committee on Mass Transportation. Transportation is a topic that has not been covered. As most of you are well aware, the Rockefeller-initiated Transportation Construction Program is still the largest single construction program of a public nature in the history of the United States. A general question: "Does anyone on the panel have comments on Rockefeller's role in bringing about what could be called a transportation revolution?"

GEORGE DUDLEY: I can only say from my perspective as one involved in the overall planning that the Governor participated particularly in the setting up of the Tri-State Transportation Commission as a broad mechanism for joint efforts in that revolution. This again illustrated his realization that it wasn't simply a matter of building, it was a matter of commissioning, it was a matter of financing, it was a matter of integrating the neighboring states. It was a matter of integrating a program for transportation to conform to and support the existing and proposed port authority's activities, the airports and all the other elements. They all were tied together.

JOSEPH F. ZIMMERMAN: My concern was simply that some recognition should be accorded the Governor's role in transportation, not only in terms of building, but also in terms of organizational innovations. A key example of the latter is use of one of his grandfather's favorite devices — the interlocking directorate.

GERALD BENJAMIN: Some of the matters that you discuss are not without controversy. I thought that I might ask, for example, if the financing mechanisms, although sound for these purposes, were stretched too far and used in other areas in which they were less sound and contributed to the crisis in the 1970's. I was wondering if Mr. Belica could talk about that. Another point of criticism is that, in fact, the building for each particular purpose was appropriate but the net effect was too much, that there was just too much done. I am an employee of the State University and as a consequence am loyal to it. Yet there has been some thought that the State University was overbuilt as an institution. Perhaps Mr. Lanford would want to comment on that. With regard to Mr. Dudley's point about the Governor's sensitivity to the relationship between the environment and his construction projects, some have said that the Albany Mall was built to overcome and overcame the barriers provided by the physical setting, that the Albany Mall was built not to fit into the environment but sort of in spite of the environment in the city and the immediate location.

PAUL BELICA: I'd like to respond to the financing question that has just been mentioned. Nobody questioned the securities which at one time had higher ratings than the State of New York itself. Consider, too, the fact that they were accepted in volume, in billions, in the marketplace and accepted originally at prices that today cannot be achieved. Now that's quite an achievement. It was user financed, backed up only in a contingency by the commitment of the State to make up a deficiency of a reserve fund, if invaded. It was never invaded, or it was invaded later on because of political problems not financial or feasibility problems.

Every issue you run into, whether it is housing, State University, mental hygiene or hospitals, was initiated on the basis of a very tight structure and determination of feasibility which (in-house) the Commissioner had to certify before I could sell any paper in the marketplace. So it was very carefully put together.

One thing that you could criticize, and which I criticized myself is the great volume of activity, a great volume of construction which required a great volume of financing and bonds and loans sold in the marketplace that at one time we

102

thought exceeded the capacity of the market to absorb it all. So, we could have done it at a slower pace, but a lifetime is short, and I guess the Governor wanted to do everything he could.

MILTON MUSICUS: You have not given adequate attention to the Mental Hygiene Facilities Improvement Corporation's operations. Their program had somewhat of a different context. First of all, we did not have the privilege and pleasure of having the Governor tell us how to design our facilities. As a matter of fact, I don't think that we ever saw the Governor in our facilities. I want to say something about how we ran our operation. It's quite different from the State University Construction Fund.

I was interested to note in the discussions, how these directors were chosen by the Governor. I used to work for the Governor in the Governor's office and left him to go back to the more serene job of being the Assistant Commissioner in the Education Department. Then, one day I got a call saying that probably, by this time, I must have gotten tired of living in the ivory tower and better come out and begin to do some work. So I became Director, and I was not a construction man, I was not an engineer.

But, the important thing was not how our directors were chosen, but the authority that they were given. That is extremely important, because I was given complete freedom of operation. And Jim Gaynor, who was head of the Trustees, gave full support to what we were doing. However, there was accountability. The quality of work had to be high, the architect used had to meet high standards, the costs had to be within reasonable figures set by the Budget Director, and above all, work had to proceed with speed.

We did not have the single contract; we had to have multiple contracts for each project. The question was how we could work with multiple contracts and get our job done. We started the idea of having a construction manager. Instead of getting a single construction contract to build a facility, we hired a construction firm as a consultant and they managed the multiple contracts.

We had freedom of staff. We had freedom to select architects. We did not use Phillip Johnson or I.M. Pei; rather we selected architects with a tremendous amount of potential who were emerging in the field.

Our projects were quite different from State University projects. We had to have facilities in urban centers so people could get to them conveniently and obtain out-patient assistance as quickly as possible. We had to overcome local objections. We had the facility designed to fit in with the environment. If you see the Capital District Psychiatric Center here in Albany you could pass

103

it and I don't think you'd view it as an institution.

In addition to that, we also developed the concept of lease-purchase arrangements for health care institutions. We went to the municipalities to build for them, and then leased the properties to them.

Here was a case where the Governor had delegated a great deal of responsibility and authority with the hope that we would pursue his philosophy with respect to high quality of architecture in everything we built, and had a group of trustees that were most supportive and certainly kept a good eye on things.

While I was in the Governor's office, I was in charge of administration. In that position I was faced with the proposal of having a chart room over and over again, but we were so strapped for space that I don't know where we could have put it!

I do know that when we did the State reorganization study, we did not give Governor Rockefeller a report. He refused to read a report. Every part of the reorganization had to be shown on a chart. He read the charts, and thereafter he was the one who explained the reorganization to all concerned.

As far as coordinated planning goes, I recall being in the New York City 55th Street office and I saw Dr. Ronan, greatly disturbed, rushing out of a meeting with the Governor. Evidently the State University Construction Fund was planning construction of a university and another State agency was planning a highway right through the middle of the University. That's why we had to set up an Office of Planning Coordination. With all this construction going on, we might have been building projects on top of each other.

OSCAR LANFORD: I just want to say one thing about the University being overbuilt. It wasn't overbuilt!

GEORGE DUDLEY: I'll give you a short minute on the South Mall. The Special Commission on the Capital District selected areas which might be the new capital, with the planners and the environmentalists assisting. Environmental considerations were amongst the more important ones, along with the others in their deliberations. The relationship with the environment of the Hudson Valley was fully considered.

PAUL BELICA: Consider the replacement cost of the volume of construction that has taken place! How fortunate that we did all this stuff in the years when it was feasible. We were fighting inflation of 8 percent or more. Every time we delayed a project it cost us millions of dollars.

Chapter V

"Revolution" in
Higher Education

PAUL VEILLETTE: I'm Paul Veillette from the State Division of the Budget. I assume I was selected to moderate this panel because I was responsible for the State's higher education budgeting for 12 years and, as a result, am acquainted with the people in the field. My role here today is as a traffic cop. The panelists will do the talking.

Our theme setter for tonight is Jim Lawrence, who I first met when he was an Assistant Chief Budget Examiner in the Division of the Budget, charged with the overseeing of the State University of New York (SUNY) and City University of New York (CUNY) budgets. He has since gone on to the City University of New York, where for several years he was its budget director. He is now the Vice-President for Finance and Administration of the City College of CUNY, which is considered by many to be the flagship institution of City University. Earlier, he served as staff director of the Keppel Task Force on Higher Education during the Rockefeller administration. His intimate association with both the public and private sectors of higher education throughout most of the Rockefeller era eminently qualified him to be our theme setter today. It is my pleasure to present Jim Lawrence.

JIM LAWRENCE: Governor Rockefeller's contribution to higher education in the State ranks among his most significant achievements, perhaps the one with the most important long-range impact. To talk about the Rockefeller legacy, one might well begin with higher education.

My initial thought was to discuss the Governor's contributions by "sector" — that is, State University, City University, and the private colleges and universities. I quickly decided that this was the wrong approach — that it was important symbolically *not* to do this. One of the Governor's many vital contributions was to see higher education in its totality, not as separate sectors to be dealt with independently.

Four themes will run through this analysis:

1. Higher education was a major priority of the Governor and an area of enormous accomplishments. He devoted a high level of attention to it throughout his administration, and New York gained national prominence for his successful efforts.

2. One of the Governor's major higher education objectives was to expand opportunities for college attendance. He succeeded. Higher education enrollments more than doubled during his administration, rising from 380,000 students in 1958 to 842,000 in 1972:
   - SUNY rose from 43,000 to 169,000
   - CUNY rose from 70,000 to 153,000
   - The community colleges went from 31,000 to 196,000
   - The private colleges went from 238,000 to 324,000

3. While this expansion of educational opportunities took place primarily in the public institutions, the Governor believed strongly in a balanced system of public and private institutions in which students would have the opportunity to attend the State's many excellent private colleges and universities.

4. The Governor believed strongly in educational excellence and quality. A unique Rockefeller contribution was the State's policy of developing excellence at all levels of education - from two-year colleges through doctoral programs. Many other states adopted the view that educational excellence should be limited to a few "flagship" institutions, to the detriment of tens of thousands of students attending the non-flagship institutions. This latter view was decidedly not Rockefeller's.

I. Historical Context

Higher education in New York State had always been dominated by the private institutions. Higher education meant Columbia, Cornell, Colgate, Hamilton, Vassar, Barnard, and other prominent private colleges and universities. Public institutions had been established as early as 1844 (City College of New York), and several small teacher training institutions were established in the 19th century, primarily in rural areas of the State. When Governor Rockefeller assumed office, the public institutions played a relatively minor statewide role. These institutions offered limited graduate work, and the State University had only one liberal arts college. Their role seemed to be viewed primarily as one of providing teacher education and two-year programs. The State's Board of Regents was strongly supportive of the private institutions. The State had even used its Federal land-grant funds to support schools and programs through a private institution (Cornell University) rather than establishing a strong public university, as happened in other states.

The State University had been established in 1948 to coordinate the several upstate public institutions, but it was extremely weak. It was located within the State Education Department (SED), an organizational relationship not designed to strengthen the public institutions. In the ten-year period from 1949 through 1959, SUNY's budget rose only from $29 million to $44 million and enrollments rose only from 26,000 to 39,000. The University suffered from a lack of direction and support, and quality was not discussed. The somewhat larger and stronger City University colleges were little better off than their SUNY counterparts.

The Governor came to office at a time of major national strains that strongly affected higher education. In particular, the post-World War II baby boom meant that in the 1960's there would be a tremendous expansion in demand for college opportunities. New York State clearly was not prepared for this event. Neither the private nor the public sectors had facilities for such expansion, and many of the private institutions had no desire to grow in any case. New York already was a major exporter of students. Some 25 percent of the State's high school graduates, who attended college, went out of the State, making New York second only to New Jersey as a net exporter of students.

In addition to this major issue, other forces were at work. The Russian Sputnik had spurred national interest in improving higher education quality and access. Other states, including such competitors of New York as California and Illinois, had developed nationally prominent public universities and extensive community college systems. In New York, pressures to expand public higher education had grown as a result of perceived discrimination against minority groups by private institutions. The climate, therefore, seemed ripe for major changes in the State's management of higher education.

II. The Heald Commission

Governor Rockefeller was known for his expert use of external study groups to prepare the ground for his actions. In higher education he used this technique with outstanding results. The most important of the several prestigious task forces he established to review higher education was the Heald Commission, chaired by Henry Heald, President of the Ford Foundation. John Gardner, President of the Carnegie Corporation, and Marion Folsom, former Secretary of the Federal Department of Health,

Education and Welfare, were the other two members. The Commission, which was appointed in 1959 and reported in 1960, laid the groundwork for the structure of higher education and much of the legislation and major developments for at least the next decade. In fact, the Commission's report even today could be considered the State's only master plan for higher education.

The Heald Commission projected that higher education enrollments would double from 1959 to 1970 and rise another 50 percent by 1980, going from 401,000 to 1,270,000 over this period. The report noted the State's large student out-migration and found it unlikely that the private institutions could begin to meet the projected demand. As a result, the public sector's share of total enrollment would have to rise from 40 percent of the total to 60 percent in 1985.

The State's higher education goals, the Commission recommended, should be threefold:
1. Wide availability of higher education to all income classes and for students with varied talents and interests;
2. A strong public system of higher education, including major universities, as well as a strong private sector;
3. Attainment of excellence in all institutions.

The Commission made several recommendations:
1. The Board of Regents should play a limited role in higher education, with primary emphasis on reviewing institutional master plans under a new planning process recommended by the Commission.
2. SUNY should be given extensive independent powers; authorized to develop its own master plans; and freed from detailed budgeting, personnel, purchasing, and other State requirements. The Commission reports noted that, "the State University appears to have less administrative and management freedom of operation than almost any other public system in the United States."
3. SUNY should be empowered to carry out a needed capital expansion program without fear of bureaucratic delays.
4. The City University's Board of Higher Education should be given powers similar to SUNY's trustees and the University unified. SUNY's trustees would be represented on the CUNY Board.
5. The private institutions had been the bulwarks of the State's higher education system and had to be preserved. A $10 million program of State aid to these institutions, based on the number of degrees granted, was recommended.

6. SUNY's teachers' colleges should be converted to liberal arts colleges.
7. SUNY should establish two new graduate institutions, one at Stony Brook and one upstate.
8. To help finance the needed rapid expansion in the community colleges, the State should pay a larger share of college operating costs. The then current 33 1/3 percent State aid might rise to 50 percent.
9. SUNY and CUNY should charge tuition, perhaps at $300 a year, but with rebates to needy students with satisfactory grades.
10. The Regents Scholarships should be doubled in number and the maximum award raised to $1,500 a year with the amount based on need.
11. A special task force should be established to review health and medical education.

As a sidelight, the Commission report emphasized how badly New York was faring in higher education compared with our key competitor, California.

III. Results of the Heald Report

The Governor wasted little time in developing a program to implement the Heald Report's major recommendations. In 1961, legislation was adopted which:
1. established the master plan process proposed in the report, with SUNY and CUNY submitting quadrennial plans to the Regents and then the Governor;
2. removed SUNY from the Education Department and gave it independent powers;
3. established CUNY as a unified University system;
4. established a new Scholar Incentive Program for needy students (Grants of from $100 to $300 would be awarded to needy full-time undergraduates — somewhat more to graduate students.);
5. doubled the number of Regents Scholarships;
6. raised the ceiling on State-guaranteed loans from $1,000 to $1,500 a year; and
7. authorized SUNY and CUNY to charge tuition - statutory language requiring CUNY to maintain free tuition was repealed.

In 1962, complex but highly important legislation was enacted which established a mechanism to finance and build the needed expansion of State University's facilities. The State University Construction Fund was created to build the facilities with financing from the State Housing Finance Agency and

Dormitory Authority. The initial goal was a $700 million construction program.

This legislation package can readily be characterized as a "revolution" in higher education in New York State, in that it substantially reversed about two hundred years of historical development. The Governor had brilliantly set the stage for his package with the Heald Report which, in turn, was building on the public's recognition of a critical need in the State. He then worked closely with the Board of Regents, the private institutions, and the SUNY and CUNY leadership to develop a comprehensive, balanced package. In a classic case of executive leadership, the Governor had established the agenda and worked effectively with the various parties to see a program erected. Nor were administrative aspects ignored. For example, the Division of the Budget worked out a budget flexibility program with State University that gave the University some of the powers found in other states.

IV. Muir Report

The Governor also adopted the Heald Report recommendation on health and medical education and in 1961 he established a small commission to review higher education for the health professions. The commission, chaired by Dr. Malcolm Muir, reported in 1963 that the State should:

1. expand health manpower training in all fields;
2. develop a new, major health education center with medical, dental, and nursing schools and a teaching hospital at SUNY at Stony Brook;
3. expand enrollments in SUNY's three other medical centers; and
4. provide State support for private medical and dental schools to help them expand.

The Muir Report's recommendations became the basis for the Governor's program in the health sciences, which radically transformed the State's approach and sharply increased health education opportunities.

V. City University

The State's role in funding the City University senior colleges had grown slowly over the years. An important change occurred in 1966, however, when the Governor agreed to:

1. provide a 50-50 State matching of all city funds provided by the senior colleges;
2. establish a City University Construction Fund, similar to the SUNY Fund, to accelerate construction of desperately needed

facilities (the State would pay one-half of the debt service for construction); and

3. establish a State-funded program for disadvantaged students (SEEK) which became the forerunner of CUNY's Open Admission Program.

City University appeared to be viewed by the executive branch as something of a legislative prerogative, particularly of the Assembly Democrats, and the Governor's role in CUNY developments was far less clear than in the case of State University. The 1966 legislation was frequently attributed to the leadership of Assembly Speaker Anthony Travia. Nevertheless, the State's role in supporting CUNY grew remarkably during the Rockefeller era and expanded substantially. It is unlikely that much of this would have occurred without the Governor's support.

VI. Bundy Report - Support for the Private Colleges

The public institutions began to grow quickly under the new Rockefeller legislation, and the private institutions, some of which had developed fiscal problems, began to request State support. In 1967-68, enrollments in the public universities exceeded those in the private sector for the first time. The Governor had provided strong leadership for SUNY with Frank Moore as Chairman of the Board of Trustees and Samuel Gould as Chancellor, and the University was rapidly transforming itself both quantitatively and qualitatively.

The Governor, working with the Regents, in 1967 appointed another prestigious commission, chaired by McGeorge Bundy, to determine how the State might aid the private institutions. Four of the country's most distinguished University Presidents — James Conant, John Hannah, Father Hesburgh and Abram Sacker — served on the commission. The group reported in early 1968. Although critical of the private sector's inability to generate data that would help determine whether the institutions actually had fiscal problems, they felt that real problems existed. They recommended a program of State aid per degree granted ($400 for each baccalaureate and master's degree and $2,400 for a doctorate) at a total cost of $25 million. This was, of course, quite similar to the proposal made earlier in the Heald Report.

The Governor prepared legislation to implement this program and it was enacted in the 1968 session. The bill did require the private institutions to submit appropriate data and reports to the Regents.

This was landmark legislation. For the first time, direct governmental support was to be given to private higher education institutions. Once again the Governor had, based on the report of a prestigious study group, provided strong leadership on behalf of higher education.

VII. Full Opportunity Program - Community Colleges

The community colleges became the State's fastest growing sector of higher education. Each year found at least one two-year college opening, until residents of almost every county had access to such an institution.

Under political pressure from supporters of the City University, which had begun a massive enrollment increase under a new "open admission" policy, the State in 1970 enacted a "Full Opportunity Program" designed to increase college access, particularly for the disadvantaged. The legislation's major feature was an increase in State operating assistance to the community colleges (recommended by the Heald Commission) to 40 percent of costs if the college agreed to enroll all qualified applicants. The State had provided one-third of costs from the start of the community college program in 1948, and the new legislation was symbolically important in that the State now would pay a larger share of costs than did the counties or other local sponsors.

In exchange, the State gained for the first time an element of cost control over community college budgets (one which in recent years has been used to bring the State share of costs back down to the old one-third level).

The last major action of the Governor in higher education was his appointment in 1972 of a committee to review all aspects of higher education finance and related issues. This committee was chaired by former United States Commissioner of Education, Francis Keppel, and included such other distinguished leaders as Sol Linowitz, Harold Howe, and Clifton Phalen. The State's fiscal problems had come into conflict with the rapid expansion in higher education and, after a decade of remarkable growth and change, a comprehensive review was needed.

The committee reported in early 1973. The report focused on student access and funding and on the need to pull together all the various Federal and State programs that aided students into a rational package. To maximize student access while maintaining healthy competition among institutions, the committee recommended an expanded State program of student aid based on need. Middle-income students were eligible for grants, although at lesser amounts than lower-income students.

Among other recommendations, the committee suggested: that the State increase support to CUNY, but that the Governor should appoint a majority of the CUNY trustees; that CUNY should charge tuition and directly operate its community colleges; and that the CUNY construction program should be accelerated to relieve overcrowding.

The major legislative result of this report occurred in 1974 with the enactment of the TAP (Tuition Assistance Program), which provided aid to students of up to $1,500 a year based on their need. The CUNY recommendations all were implemented later, primarily as a result of New York City's fiscal crisis and its resulting inability to fund the University.

VIII. In Retrospect

What was the Rockefeller legacy to higher education? When the Governor assumed office in 1959, New York's public colleges, with some exceptions, were of marginal importance and quality, and New York high school graduates, particularly if they had low incomes, had very limited options within the State. The Governor provided the leadership that altered this situation beyond recognition, making New York a national leader in higher education. The best statistical measure of this growth is seen in the expansion of enrollments during his tenure from 380,000 students to 842,000, with increases in all sectors.

The most remarkable achievement, of course, and one which ranks among the Governor's most important contributions, is the remarkable expansion and the qualitative improvement in the State University system. To give some idea of the growth, the amount of university space rose from 14 million square feet when the Governor took office to 65 million when he left, and much more was being planned or constructed. New campuses had been built at Albany, Stony Brook, Buffalo, Old Westbury, Purchase, and Canton, and expansion occurred everywhere else. The country's leading architects were brought in to design these facilities, and many award-winning projects resulted.

Institutional quality was improved in many ways. SUNY's competitive salary scales and increasing budgets enabled it to attract an excellent faculty, and students competed vigorously to enroll in SUNY institutions. The graduate and liberal arts programs expanded dramatically.

SUNY also developed a far-flung system of community colleges with open-door policies, good facilities, comprehensive programs, and qualified faculty. Almost every State resident could commute to nearby colleges as a result of this expansion.

While best known for his development of SUNY, the Governor strongly supported a balanced system of higher education. He sponsored a radically new institutional support plan for the private institutions, and (although enacted after he left office) a large, new need-based student aid program. When combined with an expanded student loan program, State Dormitory Authority construction, and various specialized programs of assistance (aid to medical and dental schools, and so forth), New York was providing more direct and indirect support for private institutions than all the other states together.

During the Governor's tenure, the State also substantially increased its support to the City University system and enabled it to support a major new mission of serving the disadvantaged.

It's true, of course, that higher education was expanding across the country in the 1950's and 1960's, but New York's growth was phenomenal during this period. This was primarily attributable to the vision and leadership of Governor Rockefeller. From this higher education experience, one can see several ways in which he successfully transformed his vision into reality. First, he made higher education a major priority. He knew, and everyone else knew, that higher education was important and had to be supported. He then exerted determined and persistent leadership in its behalf. Higher education was not at the top of the agenda for one year only to disappear the next. It was there to stay. He had recognized a public mood that would support higher education — always the mark of a good politician — but he built on that public mood to support his programs — the mark of a good leader.

His negotiating skills were frequently in evidence as he obtained approval for his programs. He worked carefully to ensure that his legislation was enacted and his programs executed.

He used prestigious outside study groups with great effectiveness to establish a basis for his programs. The Heald Report, for example, laid the groundwork for the entire Rockefeller higher education program.

He appointed strong leaders in State University and then supported them fully as they implemented the University's expansion. His study groups also had outstanding chairpersons.

His demonstrated concern for balance between the public and private sectors minimized conflicts between the sectors. This enabled him to achieve his goals more easily.

And, last but not least, he put his budget behind his goals. State spending for higher education rose from $88 million in 1959 to $972 million in 1973.

Postscript - Higher Education Today

In closing, it might be asked whether the Rockefeller legacy was a lasting one. Now, about a decade after he left office, how has higher education fared?

Higher education certainly has become a lower State priority in the post-Rockefeller years. The crash of the City University system, in which in one year 70,000 students left the system and thousands of faculty and staff were terminated, was the most dramatic evidence of this lower priority. The State University had no such single traumatic experience, but annual budget reductions have gradually eroded the University's strength. State support for the community colleges also has been limited and expansion slowed. Tuition first was imposed on CUNY, and annual increases have brought tuition levels in all sectors to high levels. Politically, much of the leadership in behalf of higher education has passed from the executive branch to the Legislature, with governors appearing to view public universities as legislative items, much as they do support for the public schools.

This reversal partially reflects factors beyond the State's control, or localized aspects of national trends. The State's economy has not been strong and, in view of the widespread opposition to tax increases, budget limitations have been applied to most State programs. States throughout the country have been taking fiscal actions similar to New York's. This new attitude recognizes not just fiscal realities, but a public and political attitude that programs other than higher education merit priority. Funds that formerly might have gone to colleges and universities have been allocated in recent years to prisons and the criminal

Governor Rockefeller at ground breaking ceremonies for the State University of New York at Stony Brook.

justice system, to mental health programs, and to health and social services efforts. Facilities expansion became much less necessary in the 1970's as college enrollments stabilized or, in some cases, declined. Finally, an increasingly conservative public began to question the value of almost universal higher education.

In New York, at least two special factors were at work. One was that considerable fiscal growth was built into the higher education system, particularly as a result of the implementation of the TAP student aid program, the State's assumption of funding for CUNY, opening of new facilities planned during the Rockefeller years, and payment of salary and fringe benefit increases required by inflationary conditions. As a result, State support for higher education continued to expand, but little or no funding was available for programmatic expansion or improvement. It also is possible that, given Governor Rockefeller's dominance of higher education issues, new governors felt it important to establish their own priorities.

Despite this loss of priority and funding, higher education remains strong because of the programs Governor Rockefeller established and the plans he put in motion. As a general matter, all three sectors are in satisfactory fiscal health, academic quality is strong, and opportunities for college attendance remain high. The Rockefeller legacy for higher education is a lasting one.

PAUL VEILLETTE: Thank you, Jim. That amazing record of growth and expansion during the Rockefeller years deserves to be described as "revolutionary." I recall, in 1973, when SUNY was twenty-five years old, that Governor Rockefeller commented in a talk at SUNY-Albany that little was done to expand the State University from 1948-1958 — unlike the situation in other states —because of an informal understanding between the State government and the private sector of higher education. That understanding stipulated that there would be a minimal expansion of SUNY for the first decade of its existence. A man who must have heard some of this first hand is our next speaker, Robert MacCrate, who was was Counsel to Governor Rockefeller from 1959 to 1962 and is currently a partner in Sullivan and Cromwell. Mr. MacCrate.

ROBERT MACCRATE: The subject of higher education is a particularly appropriate one for consideration of the Nelson A. Rockefeller legacy. I suggest that it provides a classic study of effective governing which I perceive as having five essential steps.

First, Nelson Rockefeller, looking ahead, identified a major problem area for attention — the State's role in public and private higher education;

Second, he enlisted the best talent to provide an authoritative study of the problem and to make recommendations;

Third, he took those recommendations and integrated them into the political process in the form of a comprehensive legislative program;

Fourth, he mustered the political and public support to enact the program;

Fifth, he saw to it that the program was effectively executed.

My personal participation in this sequence of events between 1959 and 1962 was the high water mark in my experience as Counsel to the Governor. He made me acutely aware that we were engaged in a matter of great significance to the people of New York State and that higher education, both public and private, would be shaped for years to come by the actions taken at that time. I believe they have been.

Let me take each step of Rockefeller's approach to governing in turn.

First, *identifying the problem area.*

Right from the beginning of his first administration in 1959, Nelson Rockefeller identified the problems in meeting the burgeoning demand for higher education as a matter of the greatest concern and one to which he was assigning the highest priority. At the 1959 session of the Legislature, he took note of the "seemingly staggering problems in the decade which lies ahead" for colleges and universities in New York State, and supported as an initial step in addressing the problems an expansion in the powers of the State Dormitory Authority to construct buildings other than dormitories, including libraries, laboratories, and classrooms.

Second, *enlisting authorities to make recommendations.*

Having thus at the beginning of his term as Governor identified and broadly defined the problem area to be addressed, the next step that he took — in what became a familiar Rockefeller pattern — was to enlist acknowledged leaders in the area of concern to provide a thorough analysis of the subject and authoritative recommendations. For this particular project, in December 1959, he enrolled Henry T. Heald, John W. Gardner, and Marion B. Folsom to review the needs of higher education and its facilities. Mindful of the special role in higher education of the Board of Regents in New York, he asked the Regents to join with him in appointing the Heald Committee. On December 21, 1959, a joint announcement was made of the committee's appointment. Dr. Sidney G. Tickton of the Ford Foundation was enlisted as Director of Studies.

Eleven months later, on November 15, 1960, the Heald Comittee issued its report. It predicted that college enrollments would double by 1970 and triple by 1985. It pointed to the historic predominance in New York of private higher education over public higher education and suggested that the percentages would have to be reversed by 1985 if the need were to be met; that by then more than 60 percent of the college students in the State would have to be enrolled in public higher education.

To meet this challenge the committee called for a realignment of responsibilities, with the State University being given far greater administrative and management freedom and the full responsibility for planning public higher education throughout the State. To strengthen the private colleges and universities, the committee called for a program of per capita grants to each institution in the State for each student graduated with a degree approved by the Board of Regents. The committee noted that its program of per capita aid to private colleges and universities would probably require a constitutional amendment to implement it fully in view of the so-called "Blaine Amendment" of Article XI (now Section 3) of the State Constitution, barring aid to (1) any institution under the control of any religious denomination and (2) any institution in which any denominational tenet or doctrine is taught.

Students who could not afford college training were to be encouraged to attend by increased scholarships and loans.

While the broad message of the Heald Committee was widely supported, the proposal for per capita grants to private colleges and universities drew an increasing storm of criticism. The proposed constitutional amendment was seen both as a breach in the wall between church and state and as an invitation to a three-year delay in effective action.

Third, *integrating reform proposals into the political process.*

The third step, in effectively addressing this major problem area, was to integrate the Heald Committee's proposals into the political process and to develop a program for State action capable of winning wide support. During the final six weeks of 1960 and the first two months of 1961, the proposals were the subject of wide public comment. During this period the Heald Committee's report was exposed to all interested constituencies and was the subject of extensive discussion between representatives of the Governor, the legislative leaders, the State Education Department, and representatives of the host of groups concerned with the future of higher education in New York.

Meanwhile, within the Governor's staff, there was an intensive analysis of the Heald proposals, the budgetary implications of various alternative modes of implementation, and the legal issues presented by these alternatives. The Governor's Annual Message to the Legislature on January 4, 1961, emphasized the dimension of the problems, referring to the Heald Committee's observation that the problems "will be so large as to make everything we have been doing in higher education until now seem insignificant in retrospect." Noting that the Board of Regents, the State University, and the combined body of public and private institutions (represented in the Association of Colleges and Universities of the State of New York) were all making an effective contribution to public understanding of this problem and its solution, the Governor undertook to submit detailed recommendations in a special message, which would follow completion by the State University of its master plan and include the benefit of further consultation with the legislative leaders and committees, and with interested groups. As to the content of the program, the Governor at that time was prepared to say only that it would include a doubling of State scholarships and an endorsement of the proposed constitutional amendment sponsored by the Temporary President of the Senate to make $500 million available through the State Dormitory Authority. In fact, the program, at that time, was still in the process of being formulated.

The Heald Committee had called for a flat grant, pursuant to a contract with each institution, for each student from the State graduated by the institution. The Association of Private Colleges and Universities called, instead, for a tuition supplement, while the counsel for the New York State Catholic Welfare Committee was urging a "maintenance allowance" for each student resident in New York.

It was in these circumstances of conflicting counsel on how to achieve a balance in the program that the Governor's staff turned their attentions to the possibility of "tuition-grants-in-aid" to all students who were residents of New York and attending institutions of higher learning in the State. Sometime around the middle of January 1961 the descriptive term "State Scholar Incentive Program" was coined in Counsel's Office and the drafts of the special message began to refer by these words to what earlier had been described as the "College Tuition Program." During this period, the Governor's office maintained virtually daily contact with the Commissioner of Education, and the thinking regarding the program developed along parallel lines within the Executive Chamber and the State Education Department.

On January 26, 1961 the Board of Regents issued a statement proposing to add to the existing program of Regents Scholarships a system of "Student Tuition Awards" payable to full-time students in a degree program in the State. Five days later, in his Special Message on Higher Education, the Governor first proposed the "Scholar Incentive Program". As then defined, it would have provided an annual grant of up to $200 to help full-time undergraduates to pay their tuition in excess of $500 annually, a similar grant of up to $400 for graduate students to the master's degree level, and up to $800 for students in graduate work above the master's into the doctoral level.

The Special Message recommended that the new program of scholar incentives be supplemented by doubling the number of Regents' College Scholarships — to a number equal to 10 percent of the 1961 high school graduate class — and providing 300 additional nursing scholarships, together with an expansion in the student loan program of the Higher Education Assistance Corporation, which was created in 1957.

For campus construction, the Governor endorsed the State's guarantee by constitutional amendment of up to $500 million of bonds of the Dormitory Authority and a change in its name to the New York State College Building Authority, to reflect more accurately its expanded role, as then visualized, in college and university construction.

Alert to the continuing concerns of the private colleges and universities in the State in announcing the program for expansion of the State University (which had been founded only in 1948), the Governor took note of the special nature of the institutions then comprising the State University. He noted that they had been directly related to the great and rich role of private higher education in the State. He stated that the primary emphasis would continue to be upon developing, in the State University, facilities which would not otherwise be available, or in filling gaps in the State's educational pattern.

Drawing upon the State University's recently proposed Master Plan, the Governor recommended:
— two comprehensive graduate centers, one on Long Island and one upstate;
— a substantial broadening of the liberal arts and sciences curricula in the State colleges of education; and
— the local expansion of the two-year community colleges.

In addition, the Governor's program called for the development of coordinated long-range plans for public higher education in New York City (with that of the State University), for the grant of authority to the State University trustees and the City Board of Higher Education (each to determine its own tuition policy), and for improved educational techniques (college and university management and utilization of facilities.)

The message closed with a call for a master plan of medical education and a regular quadrennial review by the Board of Regents of all higher education in the State.

Fourth, *mustering the political support.*

With a comprehensive program thus formulated, the Governor turned to the next step of mustering the political and public support to enact the program. At the Governor's staff meeting on February 6, 1961, some eleven separate pieces of legislation were identified as being in the drafting stage with target dates — with the longest lead time assigned to what was referred to as the State University Autonomy Bill. Successive agendas of staff meetings reflect a pushing back of the date for the introduction of legislation as the extensive round of meetings with interested groups continued and their varied concerns were addressed.

The most difficult issues to be addressed were those presented by the debate as to the purposes for which public funds must be used. Some argued that public tax funds should be used only to support public institutions of learning, and that the scholar incentives were indirect aid to private colleges and universities. More widespread was the opposition invoking the Blaine Amendment and the historic position of Jewish and Protestant groups opposing any public assistance to church-related education.

Prior to the Governor's Special Message on January 31, 1961, the *New York Times* had voiced editorial opposition to any program of tuition grants whose underlying purpose was to provide indirect support to private institutions. In the week following the Special Message, more than a score of substantial organizations registered their opposition to the Scholar Incentive Program as it had been enunciated in the Message.

From discussions with the opponents, it became apparent that a "merit and means" test was the basis upon which the opposition distinguished scholarships, which were acceptable, from the proposed program. Accordingly, we fixed on more closely linking the Scholar Incentives to this test. Various formulations were considered during the first half of February by the Governor's staff and by representatives of the Education Department. A means test was written into the draft bill which varied the sum payable to a student with family means (in the same manner as for Regents' Scholarships). The tuition requirement to qualify for the payment was reduced by $100 per semester (thus extending the program to students in public institutions) and a merit test, to be defined by a Regents' rule, was provided for (based on the statutory requirement that a recipient "give promise of satisfactory completion of the degree program" in which he or she was enrolled). So revised, the bill for the Scholar Incentive Program was introduced on February 20 and promptly endorsed by the Board of Regents.

As of February 28, 1961, the agenda for the Governor's meeting with the legislative leaders indicated that there remained for resolution five substantial questions pertaining to the higher education program:

— Were additional resources to be allocated to Speaker Carlino's version of an expanded student loan program?
— What action should be taken on the Education Department's proposal to increase its role in higher education and the role of the New York City Board of Higher Education at the expense of the State University?
— What action should be taken on the competing proposal, based on the Heald Committee's recommendations, to give the State University greater autonomy?
— When should further action be taken on the bill to establish a unified City University for New York City (which bill had already passed the State Senate)?
— Finally, should the legislation be framed to implement the proposed constitutional amendment to guarantee the bonds of the Dormitory Authority, so as to address the concern of various groups, that if the amendment were adopted by the people, it might be construed as repealing the "Blaine Amendment" for purposes of the Authority's operation?

In the ensuing weeks these matters were addressed and resolved with a pragmatic recognition of the interdependence of the various parts of the Governor's program and the importance to the enactment of the basic program of each of its component parts.

The program was ultimately embraced in seven bills which, after passage by the two houses, were signed into law by Governor Rockefeller on April 11, 1961. Thus the comprehensive program for higher education was enacted, including both the Scholar Incentive Program and the grant of substantial autonomy to the State University.

Fifth, *assuring the effective execution of the program.*

The fifth and final phase in this saga of effective governing relates to the action taken to implement the program and to see that its objectives were accomplished. The Governor's direct responsibility for the implementation of educational programs in New York is, of course, limited. Having initiated this large commitment of State resources to this program initially, Governor Rockefeller actively monitored the action taken and stood ready to pursue (and did pursue) further initiatives as circumstances suggested.

Dedication ceremonies at the State University Plaza in Albany. Left to Right: Beth Moore (Chairperson of the State University Board of Trustees), Education Commissioner Gordon Ambach, Nelson A. Rockefeller, Governor Hugh L. Carey, and State University Chancellor Clifton R. Wharton, Jr.

It soon appeared that the existing procedures and organization for State University construction were wholly inadequate to carry forward, on the proposed timetable, the massive building program for the State University. There was also the need to develop financing techniques to fund the substantial capital requirements of the program. In the *Governor's Annual Message to the Legislature* the following year, on January 3, 1962, after reciting the results of the higher education initiatives of the 1961 session, he stated:

> "The immediate problems are to expedite construction already in progress or in the planning stages, to reduce the time lag between determination of need for new facilities and student occupancy, and to finance the large additional capital expenditures which are required...."

He went on to say that he would shortly present an important proposal to meet this problem. Actually, the task of detailing that proposal for the creation of the State University Construction Fund consumed some two and a half months, and it was only in the third week of March 1962 that the complex of legislation for the construction fund was ready for submission to the legislature.

However, the bill creating the State University Construction Fund became law by the end of March, and the Governor immediately designated the three trustees to operate this unusual agency, which had as its stated purpose achieving on-time completion of the $700 million construction program required by the ten-year master plan for the rapidly growing State University.

The trustees were granted the authority, as agents for the State University, to design, construct, acquire, and improve all necessary facilities and to utilize a wide variety of public and private resources in order to carry out the Fund's assignment. In addition to being able to call upon the Dormitory Authority and Department of Public Works for various parts of its program, the Fund was authorized to call upon the State Housing Finance Agency to issue bonds and notes for the Fund and a variety of other funding sources were authorized to be used. The record University building program which followed appears to have confirmed the utility and effectiveness of the agency.

By the end of the 1962 legislative session the general contours of the Rockefeller program had been firmly established, and a wholly new course had been fixed for higher education in New York State.

It remained for later years to revisit the question of direct aid to privately financed colleges and universities, with the appointment of the Bundy Select Committee, in 1967, and to consider further the financing of higher education, with the creation of the Keppel Task Force, in 1972.

PAUL VEILLETTE: Bob is the kind of person with whom I'd really love to spend a day talking on the history of all these problems. Very clearly, the genesis of some of the philosophical issues of today rests in 1959. It would be very instructive for those who came a little bit later to have the full transcript of Bob's comments for the conference proceedings.

Our next speaker, John Morris, currently President of Union College, was holding a succession of posts at Colgate University during the Rockefeller era, ranging from Assistant Professor of philosophy and religion, to Dean of Faculty, to President. I look forward to his views from the vantage point of the private sector.

JOHN S. MORRIS: I'd like to make some observations with respect to the system that you might say Governor Rockefeller created. First of all, I want to state my understanding that the higher education system in New York includes all the institutions which derive their degree-granting authority through the Board of Regents. That obviously comprises the so-called three sectors. Like many others, I tend to use the term "State system" as a kind of shorthand for the State University of New York. But I have an even more particular reason for using the term "State system" this afternoon, because the State University of New York *is* a — "system", a point to which I want to return presently.

Let me begin with some observations regarding that State system, so closely identified with the Rockefeller era. First, the growth of the State system came at a time of enormous expansion in higher education in the United States. The State University of New York is a creature of its time. It has expansionist tastes and because of its creation during this period of expansion, those tastes are somewhat difficult to shake. The result is that one aspect of the Rockefeller vision appears as somewhat of a threat to the balance between the private and public sectors. This is not any Machiavellian theory. It is simply a fact of the clash of two periods — the clash of two times.

The second point I want to make is that the State University system has become a *system*. Because it is a system it has strengths and weaknesses. It can have, because it is a system, central control and therefore the strengths of central development. Also, it can realize the savings that comes from having a central administration. It can move with some sense of structure and with a sense of planning towards the future.

The weakness, of course, that comes with this system is that it reflects a "dinosaur syndrome". Size is not necessarily a condition of quality and this is sometimes forgotten. Further, central control can lead to the dampening of initiative at the local level. The point I'm making, is not that our State University of New York is a dinosaur, but that one has to remember that in the system itself there is the potential danger of there being too great a size.

As the SUNY system was founded in a political arena, one has to become aware sometimes of the political presence. And the dangers of the political game are something that an organization, which lives on a political wisdom, needs to be aware of constantly. The need for the political wisdom of the central administration in Albany is necessary for survival for the State University of New York. But the extent to which such political wisdom becomes a political game will depend very much upon the controllers of that SUNY system. Are they willing to understand that the politicians' help comes with a price in these days, and that the price could indeed be political control? (And I stress *political*, not governmental control.)

This is a danger to the whole of higher education in this State, because the work of one sector pulls all the sectors into a political posture. There needs to be a recognition that some of this is indeed a necessity, but does it follow that the competitive mode is therefore necessary? That is the central question that I would pose when we look at the question of balance between the independent public institutions in higher education.

125

The genius of Rockefeller was that he recognized this as a problem, and therefore his first foray into the creation of a State system found its corrective in the Bundy Report, with its emphasis on funding of so-called *institutional* aid for the independent sector. There was, in the Bundy Report, the fundamental recognition that the balance of institutional sectors would preserve the elements of excellence in higher education in the State. The Heald Commission Report before it, the report that stated so strongly the need for the expansion and administrative freeing of the State University system, spoke strongly also of the absolute necessity of strengthening independent higher education. Was all this mere political rhetoric, or did some believe that in fact both could and must be done? I believe that people really meant it. Political reality in Albany should be to recognize this, today, still as a fundamental need for the State, so that higher education is not simply a part of a political game that is played for immediate short-term gain in specific districts within the State. I am not suggesting that higher education should or can be "above politics;" I am suggesting that it is our history in New York to strive to keep our educational system in the delicate position of being both part of and critic of how we meet our public responsibility.

Where then can we look for the leadership to understand how important that need is today? The role of the Governor as a strong force in educational policy in the State was clearly perceived as an important element within the Bundy Report and is an important element in the legacy that Governor Rockefeller has given to us.

In summary, this perception gave recognition to Rockefeller's strong executive function in the creation of higher education policy in the State. The genius of Rockefeller's vision was that he recognized that the interest of the State was for a strong educational system. This implies that the basic tenet of the Bundy Report was its perception that, in institutional support for the independent sector, there was a State interest. Thus, there was not merely a balancing of interests within the Bundy Report, but rather a perception in State higher education policy of the necessity for excellence.

We need to reaffirm in a time of stasis (or even of retrenchment) the broad outlines for an educational policy which is coherent, and which clearly looks to the future — where the choices leading from present budgetary concerns can decimate excellence. We need to make the three sectors recognize that their tasks are ultimately a common task — a common effort in which the State balance amongst the sectors furthers the maintenance of excellence in higher education in the State. This would be a reaffirmation of the Bundy approach.

There needs to be a recognition of the national significance of the independent sector. And this is something that the new Governor could perceive as being of such great importance — that nothing would be done to diminish this significance in the eyes of the Nation. We need to remember that New York State does not follow California. We have our own ways of doing things. And the bold strike for today would be to state a clear policy which would commit the State to the three sectors, unequivocally — to set out a formula which does reflect the political reality, but which also reflects the ideals of excellence and national reputation. The Governor, the Regents, and the organization in which the three sectors combine (ACUSNY) should grasp this moment to do this bold thing. Indeed, it might be a point at which a new Governor would consider a new select committee, a task force or a commission. This would be in the spirit of the Rockefeller governorship, but it would also reflect the realities of a different kind of time.

The danger that faces us is the danger of timidity. Better for us to be bold in our vision and expectation for what is now in place, rather than, in weakness, to fritter away our collective resources — resources in each sector which have been built up over many years.

This is a time, it seems to me, for clear-sightedness for us all, not vision clouded by local issues and a simple scoring off of each other. We must all recognize the integrity of the independent colleges, the need for independence from political stress of the State University of New York system, and the peculiar demands of the City University of New York system. This is going to demand an all-embracing degree of leadership from the Governor's office, clear-sighted policies from the Regents, and irenic consideration from the leaders of all the sectors. Support is essential to each one of the sectors. But support is not all the answer — it is support which arises out of the recognition that each plays an important part in the overall needs of the State. And these roles must be seen above all political maneuverings. This is the time for that focus of action which accepts the problem and helps define our cooperative future.

It's not enough to ask for cooperation between the sectors, however, for that can come only if there is some sense of security present among them. The present sniping is, as much as anything else, due to a radical feeling of insecurity on all sides. If there is a time that calls for leadership, this is it. Just as Rockefeller grasped the moment in a time of expansion (the time of clear transition in the 1960's), such a grasp of the moment of transition to the time of stability and economic stress is needed now. Our leadership must provide the sense of stability which is needed by all the sectors to plan for the problems of a dangerous age which lies ahead — a stability which sets limits but which also sets the stage for cooperation.

PAUL VEILLETE: Thank you, John. Our next speaker, and also the last one this afternoon, is John Kirkpatrick, who is currently a private consultant with a beautiful record of accomplishment in higher education.

JOHN KIRKPATRICK: A discussion of Rockefeller's impact on public higher education would be incomplete without a discussion of his impact on independent higher education, given the State's long tradition of strength in that sector. From what has been argued by others in this volume, three questions stand out. First, as Mr. MacCrate reported, the Heald Commission was very concerned that the skyrocketing of enrollments would require that the then ratio of private institutions bearing 60 percent and the public bearing 40 percent would need to be reversed. The public would need to bear 60 percent and the private institutions 40 percent. That assumption has turned out to be true. The full-time undergraduate enrollment has risen tremendously from 205,500, in 1961, to a huge 567,700, in 1981, (an increase of 176 percent.) The division in 1961 was 60 percent private and 40 percent public; in 1981 the ratios were reversed: 58 percent public and 42 percent private. Heald's prognosticating was right on the button.

Secondly, Mr. Lawrence has referred to the huge increase in student financial aid and the question is: How large an increase? Let me quantify the enormous growth in twenty years by saying that Scholar Incentive and Regents Scholarships in 1961-62 were $23 million (for 120,000 recipients) compared with TAP and Regents Scholarships of $305 million in 1981-82 (for 360,000 recipients) — a twelve-fold increase. Interestingly, and surprising to me, the 1981-82 TAP figures included $44 million (15 percent) for students at proprietary institutions. TAP eligibility is determined by family income, full-time enrollment and state residency. Sixty-one percent of full-time undergraduate residents enrolled in independent institutions currently receive TAP, fifty-three percent in SUNY, and seventy-eight percent in CUNY.

The third question is: What did it cost to build the public system? Several references have been made to the SUNY Construction Fund established in April 1962. As of November 1975, SUNY construction completed since 1962 was $1.5 billion and construction projected, $1.3 billion — for a total of $2.8 billion, *excluding* dormitories and community colleges. The community colleges under construction or projected at that time were $221.8 million (of which the State's share was $110.9 million). The 14 projects were financed 50 percent or 100 percent by the Dormitory Authority. Incidentally, Nassau and Suffolk Community colleges alone accounted for $222 million (75 percent).

It should be said that several powerful presidents of private institutions (including James Perkins of Cornell and James Hester of New York University, among others) strongly supported the establishment of the SUNY Construction Fund, because they realized that increased autonomy for SUNY was a necessary condition for the attraction of first-class leadership, and that the Governor's commitment was to make SUNY a reality in fact rather than only in name.

Without repeating the overall aspects of the three most important studies commissioned by the Governor and the Regents: the Heald Report of November 1960; the Bundy Report of January 1968; the Keppel Report of March 1973 — all monumental and mentioned previously — let me refer to three other studies for the sake of completeness and for their worthwhile accomplishments.

1. The Herman B. Wells Report of December 1964 studied the activities of SUNY, its master plan, and made a dozen recommendations.
2. The College Board's "The Opening Door" of March 1967 (in which I actively participated) helped to reconstruct the State's student financial aid.
3. The Hurd Task Force on the Financing of Higher Education in New York State, February 1972, identified fundamental problems and listed possible alternative solutions — some eighty-three of them covering ten areas. It recommended the formation of a Temporary State Commission to Study the Financing of Higher Education in New York State — which led to the Governor's appointing the Keppel Task Force eight months later.

I. Bundy Aid — Constitutionality and SED administration

Article 11, Section 3 of the New York State Constitution (Blaine Amendment), which forbade public financing for religious institutions, became effective (at least) by 1821. Efforts in the early 1970's to amend the Constitution on behalf of parochial elementary and secondary education were not successful. But the efforts of the Governor and Legislature did result in a mandated-services law, one of the very few in the country, permitting the reimbursing of parochial schools for some expenditures required by the State.

The Bundy Law was enacted in 1968. The State Education Department proceeded to set criteria and a process for the applying institution to answer. Then followed the Commissioner's preliminary finding, joint meetings, rewriting of catalogs, restructuring of Boards of Trustees, visitation by distinguished clerics and educators, and the Commissioner's final binding decision. The SED believed what applying institutions told them. They saw no need for full-fledged oath-taking hearings.

Some others disagreed with the administrative process of SED Canisius sued — all the way to the Court of Appeals — and lost. The College of New Rochelle also sued to the Appellate Division — and lost, but won the right to receive Bundy Aid.

In anticipation of the enactment of the Bundy Law, Fordham University commissioned a study by Columbia Law professors Walter Gellhorn and R. Kent Greenwait. The study was conducted in 1967-68 and published in 1970 — "The Sectarian College and the Public Purse: Fordham — A Case Study."

There were more than ninety potentially eligible four-year private institutions in 1969. Fifty-two of these were immediately declared eligible in July 1969. In that first year of payments, 1969-70, Hartwick, a Lutheran-related college, became eligible in mid-July and was followed by Manhattanville, Fordham, St. John Fisher, and Mercy College. And so, fifty-seven colleges received $25.5 million in 1969-70.

As 22 two-year colleges awarding the associate degree became potentially eligible in 1973, the total number of two-year and four-year potentials rose to 115. Of that number, 92 received $93 million last year. Among the top recipients, N.Y.U. received $10 million; Columbia, $6.8 million; Syracuse, $5.4 million.

The original amounts of grants were $400 for bachelor's degrees, and $400 for master's, $2,400 for doctoral, and then $300 for associate's. Last year, these grants were $1,200 for bachelor's, $900 for master's, $4,500 for doctoral, and $450 for associate's.

Of the seven four-year institutions which have never applied, St. John's, in Queens, is by far the largest. Concordia, Lutheran-related, has not applied; its church support was very large, relatively speaking — for example, as of a half-dozen years ago to my knowledge.

In recent years, one of the huge professional unions-I think it was CUNY's-has gone public in its opposition to Bundy Aid grants being given for degrees awarded to out-of-state students.

Let me repeat the reasons why the Bundy Select Committee strongly justified including students from out-of-state in the degree count for aid purposes. It did not wish to discourage the desirable cosmopolitanism of its most distinguished institutions, thought that many graduates will stay in New York, and hoped to encourage reciprocation by other states — especially in view of New York's "exporting" many more students to other states than it "imports." In addition, as a matter of equity, SUNY subsidizes its out-of-state students through tuition rates which do not cover education costs, and the amount of the proposed grants was a very small proportion of the total cost of education. Finally, and most importantly, Bundy aid is for the health of the independent institutions, not for the students.

The SED is to be congratulated for its handling of a vast, very important, very delicate program. It should be said also that the Roman Catholic Church — with perhaps about 45 related institutions at the time — did not oppose the Bundy Law. Several of its presidents, led by Father Lavery of St. John Fisher and Brother Nugent of Manhattan College, went to Albany to actively support Bundy.

Another final word: It has been said, from the usual authoritative sources, that, at the time of legislative action on the proposed Bundy Law, the independent institutions gave up their exemption from unemployment insurance and their exemption from compulsory collective bargaining in return for the Bundy Aid.

And still another final word: SUNY Chancellor Sam Gould publicly supported the Bundy Law.

II. Statewide Master Planning

In 1961, *statewide master planning* every four years was required of SUNY and CUNY (which was established in 1961). In 1971, the independent institutions were required to prepare quadrennially statewide master plans, with the Commission on Independent Colleges and Universities named as the responsible agent. I came aboard as President of CICU on September 1, 1971, with the assignment, one of many, to produce a statewide master plan for our 106 independent institutions by June, 1972. The mission was accomplished.

III. Regional Planning Councils

The Governor's Executive Order No. 44 on February 1, 1971 set up 11 official regions — corresponding to SUNY's regions — to more efficiently use facilities, public and private, to minimize duplication of programs, and so on.

a. *Hudson-Mohawk*, which started as an independent consortium in 1969, invited public institutions to join in 1974. It has been effective in coordinating some efforts of 15 institutions: 4 publics (Hudson Valley Community College, SUNY at Albany, Schenectady County Community College, Empire State) and 11 independents (including RPI, Union, Skidmore, Russell Sage.) It has been effective in cross-registrations, central purchasing, continuing education, and cooperative use of television.

b. *The Rochester Area Council* started as a consortium in 1964. There are 13 members (5 public: SUNY at Brockport, Geneseo, Monroe Community College, Finger Lakes Community College, and Empire State). Any new programs are discussed and reacted upon before going to SED for a decision. Effective cooperation! Good stuff! Father Lavery was largely responsible for its good start and continuation.

c. *The New York City Regional Council* had a few good years. CUNY and the independents regularly submitted new programs for analysis and "approval" before sending to SED. I attended several meetings with Bob Kibbee, William Magill, Jim Hester, and Father Finlay. There was a good staff — funded by the Regents (through Federal 1972 planning appropriations), the Ford Foundation, and members. Unfortunately, it died as it could no longer support staff.

d. A few other consortia existed: Northwest (Clarkson, St. Lawrence and two publics), Finger Lakes and Westchester — now pretty much luncheon groups.

The problems were funding, staffing, and SUNY central office's lack of enthusiasm about regional planning.

I regret very much that the Legislature did not appropriate $1 million for planning councils, as recommended by the Bundy Report. After all, communication must be the key in minimizing duplication of programs between public and private at the more local level. The State Education Department needs this help.

IV. Federal Education Amendments of 1972 — Characterized as the most significant higher education law since the Morrill Act of 1862, it provided for:

1. State Post-secondary Education Commissions (1202 Commissions — after July 1, 1973, such commissions were to have sole responsibility for administration of State plans under Titles VI and VII);
2. Grants to 1202 Commissions for comprehensive statewide planning;
3. Authorization for the appropriation of $100 million for Fiscal Year 1973, $250 million for Fiscal Year 1974, and $500 million for Fiscal Year 1975; and
4. Promotion and encouragement of occupational education

(authorized for fiscal year 1974: $622 million for Basic Equal Opportunity Grant — BEOG; $200 million for Supplemental Equal Opportunity Grant — SEOG; and $390 million for College Work-Study — CW-S).

Governor Rockefeller, as a powerful figure, was not too fond of the constitutional separation and power of the Regents. As time came for appointment of New York's 1202 Commission, there seemed no doubt that the Regents were eminently eligible under the Federal law to become New York's 1202 Commission. There was considerable discussion, however, about setting up a separate 1202 Commission but nothing came of it. Rocky retired in December, 1973, and his successor, Malcolm Wilson, took no steps in that direction. The Regents were named as the 1202 Commission.

The Keppel Report of March 1973 recommended the establishment of a State planning council for postsecondary education — appointed by the Governor — to prepare a statewide master plan for postsecondary education for submission to the Regents and to the Governor, and to have an executive director and adequate staff. Nothing happened.

V. Opportunity Programs for Postsecondary Education

To make postsecondary education available and possible for the *financially* disadvantaged *and* the *educationally* disadvantaged, CUNY started SEEK in 1966, SUNY started EOP in 1967, and a number of independents started HEOP in 1969. All of these programs were financed by special State appropriations along with individual campus support funds. By 1982, the State had appropriated for all of these opportunity programs almost $400 million to benefit 160,000 students — 25,500 of whom were graduates.

In summary, under the leadership of Governor Rockefeller (generally with the full support of the Regents and the Legislature) his fifteen-year Administration was chock-full of substantial and important things for higher education in New York State. I think it is probably unmatched by any other period in New York's higher educational history and unmatched by any other state in the nation.

The development of SUNY will always be a monument to Rocky. At the same time, however, he fully appreciated and aided the long-time strength and reputation of the independent sector.

Chapter VI

Elementary and Secondary Education

STANLEY RAUB: Let me begin with a story about the Governor. He was consistently accessible to school district officials. Each year, for example, he would invite a group of metropolitan New York City area superintendents to meet with him, Lieutenant Governor Malcolm Wilson, and Budget Director T. Norman Hurd. The main subject never changed. It was always more State aid for the public schools. Never hurrying, he would spend several hours listening to our concerns, suggestions, and ideas for improving State aid.

His charm and warmth always came through. After the meeting he would take time to have an individual picture taken with each of us. In each case, relying upon his phenomenal memory, he would have something personal to say that made one feel at least ten feet tall. Even when he could not promise additional State aid, we knew he cared about us personally and that he was truly concerned about the young people of New York State. His concern and his accessibility help to explain why the superintendents of the 1950's and 1960's viewed Governor Rockefeller with deep respect and affection.

Whether measured in terms of programs and services, enrollment and staffing or dollars received and spent, the years of Governor Rockefeller's administration represent a massive expansion of public education in New York State. Many regard this period as a golden age for public schools, a time when rapidly growing enrollments created unprecedented educational needs. Among other ways, those needs were met by new school construction, innovative support services, expanded staffing, and the implementation of new school management techniques.

It is no wonder that those of us involved in school administration look back upon those years fondly. Just as the 1960's can be viewed as a time of educational birth and growth, so the decade which followed has been aptly called a time of giving birth in reverse. In retrospect, the Rockefeller governorship created an aura of strong, positive commitment to the public schools. Over the years, that aura has indeed grown brighter because of the difficult trends and decisions faced by our schools during the following decade.

Historians of the Rockefeller years who are interested in the public schools must ask themselves this question: "Given all of the new and dramatic developments for the schools during the 15 years of his administration, to what extent can change be attributed directly to the Governor and his policies, or, by the same token, to what extent would those changes have occurred anyway, regardless of who held the governorship?" The answer, of course, is not clear-cut. But I must tell you, I subscribe to the theory that Rockefeller's educational philosophy and vision; his political savvy; his willingness to listen to all points of view, sort out the facts, build a consensus, and act forthrightly on the basis of that consensus, all benefited the schools immeasurably during his tenure.

The Rockefeller climate was both ambitious and inspiring. It convinced people that good things could happen for the schools on a big scale. I would identify three key ingredients for the nourishment of that climate. First, Nelson Rockefeller brought to his office a deep-seated belief that State government could solve major social, economic, and education problems if the Governor served as an aggressive guide and facilitator. Toward the end of his administration Rockefeller turned more directly to the Federal government as the State's financial problems intensified, but as political scientists have emphasized, his strong beliefs about what State government can do never wavered. He has been rightly called an "active-positive" Governor.

Second, Governor Rockefeller was deeply aware of New York State's position of national leadership. Where public education was concerned he was very proud that we ranked first in many categories, from test scores to innovative programs of assistance, such as the State Breakfast Program for needy city children, to expenditures. He wanted to preserve New York's leading position and to build upon it.

Third, while the Governor made sure he had access to many different outside sources of information, the fact is that he surrounded himself with an unusually competent and able staff. These were and still are good people, totally professional people, who shared Rockefeller's vision and knew how to get things done. Many, I am pleased to say, are here today. They certainly had much to do with establishing the Rockefeller climate.

Plenty of startling statistics are available to tell us what happened to the public schools during the Rockefeller tenure of office. Many are records that will not soon be exceeded. Rockefeller was elected in 1958 for a four-year term and was re-elected in 1962, 1966, and 1970. Resigning from office in 1973, the Governor served for 15 years, a record exceeded only by George Clinton in the late 18th and early 19th centuries.

Using 1959-60 and 1972-73 as comparative reference points, here are some of the more significant public school statistical trends. Fall enrollment in the public schools increased nearly 30 percent overall, reaching a record high point of just over 3.5 million during the 1971-72 school year. At the same time, professional staffing increased 64 percent, thus explaining why there was substantial improvement in staff/student ratios throughout the 1960's. This meant more individualized student attention, more specialized support services, and a general elevation of the diversity and quality of instruction. It is no surprise, therefore, that the schools' student holding power improved throughout the period under consideration. As illustrations of expanding related services, consider that from the beginning to the end of Rockefeller's tenure, the number of school psychologists increased 219 percent, social workers increased 618 percent, and guidance counselors approximately 200 percent.

School district consolidation continued throughout the 1960's, with the number of districts declining from 1,369 in 1959 to 757 in 1972. At the same time, as older facilities became inadequate, and as larger student populations had to be grouped together, many new school construction programs were undertaken. Between 1960 and 1972, close to 1,200 new school buildings appeared. This represented well over a quarter of all school buildings in use during that era.

Such figures help to explain why total public school expenditures rose nearly 274 percent during the Rockefeller years, reaching almost $6 billion by 1972-73. Significantly, the growth of State aid to the public schools during the Rockefeller governorship outpaced the growth in total school expenditures. In 1959-60, it reached $2.4 billion — an increase of 283.5 percent. As a percent of total school expenditures, State aid started at 39.9 percent in 1959-60 and rose to an as yet unsurpassed high mark of 48.1 percent in 1968-69. Unfortunately, the proportion dropped back to the level we currently have before Rockefeller left office. But we continue to believe that the elevation of the State's financial partnership realized during the Rockefeller administration can and must occur again if public education is to be the State's top policy priority, as it should be.

Were the Governor with us today, I believe he would support that priority. As he pointed out to the membership of the State School Boards Association at one of its two annual conventions he addressed:

> The only way we can keep local government[s] strong is by helping them meet their financial responsibilities with the broader tax base of the State... To any of those cold and glassy-eyed, and concerned only with money, let me say that it is cheaper to educate people than it is to carry them on relief for the rest of their lives."

The impact of increased State aid for the public schools during the 1960's should be viewed not just in terms of product, that is, dollars received, but rather in terms of process — the method of distribution, which underwent fundamental change as a result of the Joint Legislative Committee on School Financing, known as the Diefendorf Committee, established in 1960. As Rockfeller noted in his 1963 Budget Message, the recommendations of that committee, enacted into legislation, meant that the State shared local school district operating expenses rather than underwriting a minimum program, as had formerly been the case. The patchwork aid pattern than had grown through the years was greatly simplified. The new formulas, which included building construction and transportation aid as permanent provisions for the first time, recognized financing problems caused by sudden shifts in population from urban to suburban areas, the continued increase in the number of children to be educated, and the necessity for improving the effectiveness of the system.

Financial innovations indeed continued throughout the Rockefeller tenure. As just one illustration, the 1970-71 State Budget included high tax aid for school districts — this had been developed over the two preceding years — and special urban education aid for the disadvantaged. Also introduced by Rockefeller was a major expansion of the State Breakfast Program, the first of its kind in the nation for underprivileged inner city children. The problems of our city school districts were always a strong concern for the governor. Remember, it was during his terms of office that significant legislative steps were taken to alleviate the problem of city districts' constitutional tax limits by means of exclusions. Unfortunately, a permanent solution to that problem is still wanting; but, the concern was and still is compellingly valid.

Certainly it should be noted that the Governor sought to reinforce the programs and financial underpinnings of the nonpublic elementary and secondary schools during his years of office. One accomplishment was enactment of legislation in 1966 which provided reimbursement to public schools for textbooks to be provided free to all children in grades 7-12 in both public and nonpublic schools. Another State aid program commencing in 1970-71 provided support to nonpublic schools for administering State-mandated tests and maintaining certain kinds of pupil personnel records.

As the decade of the 1960's moved toward a close, the Governor became increasingly concerned about the steadily rising costs of public schooling. In response, and to his credit, the Governor appointed the Commission on the Quality, Cost, and Financing of Elementary and Secondary Education. Under the leadership of Manly Fleischmann, the Commission developed recommendations which, especially in the area of educating the handicapped, have helped us set standards recognized nationwide in the 1980's. The Governor clearly recognized the importance of using study groups — much more so than his predecessors — relying upon temporary commissions, task forces, and Governor's conferences. During his term of office, the Governor named some 70 task forces, appointed 5 temporary commissions, and convened 16 governor's conferences. These vehicles gave him fresh perspectives, enabled new elements in the forces of decision-making to be combined, and created new types of policy-making flexibility.

Of course, I have barely scratched the surface of the Governor's accomplishments. What I would have you remember from this panel introduction is that the Governor surely had a sympathetic ear for public education's problems, and he designed his gubernatorial powers so that he could play a direct role in helping to solve many of those problems. In 1974, just after the Governor left office, Columbia University political scientist Robert Connery eloquently defined the nature of Rockefeller's lasting influence on New York State government. He wrote:

> "Perhaps Rockefeller's greatest legacy to New York will prove to be his redefinition of the scope of the Office of the Governor. During his tenure, the responsibilities of State Government were greatly increased, and the capacity of the Governor to get things done increased with them. Future governors of New York will be acting in an institution defined by Rockefeller, and his expansive interpretation of the gubernatorial role provides a model of 'what might be' for chief executives of other states as well."

What I would like to do at this time is introduce my colleagues up here, some of them very dear friends. I think most of you probably know Ken Buhrmaster, President of Scotia Bank, who has been in the school business as a school board member since 1948 and up through the middle 1970's, and I guess maybe a little later than that. Ken was the President of the New York State School Board Association. He's still active in education; he's now Chairman of the Board of the New York State Teachers' Retirement System. And here on my left, your right, is one of our dear friends, Max Rubin, distinguished attorney and President of the School Board of Great Neck, probably one of our greatest school districts, and also many years ago the President of the largest school district in the United States, New York City. More recently, of course, he's been the chairman of a task force for another Governor, trying to solve some of our financial problems by giving recommendations as they relate to the Levittown case. Over here on my right, our clean-up hitter, Donna Shalala, President of Hunter College and a very accomplished student of public school finance in New York State. Our theme setter is a close colleague of mine and probably a colleague of yours too, Lois Wilson. I knew Lois when she was working for the New York Teachers Association. She worked for that Association and did most of the research and represented them on the conference floor. In fact, if I'm not mistaken, that's how the Governor found her. Lois then worked for the Governor to help him put together our State aid formulas in order to help our public schools. Truly, it's a privilege for me to introduce our theme setter, Lois Wilson.

LOIS WILSON: During the 15 years in which Nelson Aldrich Rockefeller served as Governor of New York, the State had a strong leader whose personality strongly affected the lives of those with whom he came in contact. Although only a relatively limited number of educators were directly involved in meetings with the Governor, the reports of such meetings circulated throughout the school community. For public school leaders, both his style of leadership and the goals and objectives he sought helped to create the feeling among educators that they had a friend in the Governor's Mansion during the Rockefeller era.

Today, I'd like to talk about:
— Some of the specific accomplishments of the Rockefeller era,
— Governor Rockefeller's style of leadership within the educational community, and
— The continuing impact of his contributions.

In the Rockefeller Public Papers of 1959 the subtitle of the first address listed in the volume is, "Education is the most important program in our State today." This address was delivered in the annual meeting of the Westchester County Republican Committee. Here are a few excerpts from his speech:

"Education is not only the most important program in our State today, it is also the costliest. It accounts for almost one-third of our total State budget....

"The localities, meanwhile, have risen to this... responsibility by steadily increasing local taxes to help carry the burden.": (1959 Public Papers of Governor Rockefeller, p. 1034).

The rest of the speech becomes a strong plea for support for his education budget recommendation. A key paragraph says:

"[If] education is to do what the people of this State and Nation want it to do, it cannot stand still. Both its quality and extent must be improved. Schools can and should do more in discovering and cultivating talent and unusual abilities, in developing among young people a high sense of purpose and moral responsibility. They should be doing more to remedy physical and mental handicaps and to equip people generally to perform at higher economic and social levels."

This January 1959 speech illustrates the effort which Governor Rockefeller made to increase State aid to public schools during his administration. State aid for public schools equaled $594 million when he took office in January 1959, and ten years after he took office the State was providing $2.55 billion for school aid. However, even as early as 1959, the Governor posed a series of penetrating questions related to possible changes in the State's school funding formula.

I. Specific Accomplishments of the Rockefeller Era

The 1973 Public Papers of Governor Rockefeller has a 10-page section on "Legacy of Leadership — the Rockefeller Record" which includes a "General Summary of Major Programs." Elementary and secondary education is specifically mentioned four times in a fourteen-point summary of major education programs:

"- more than quadrupled State aid to primary and secondary schools, from $594 million to $2.5 billion, to improve education and help relieve pressure for further additional local school taxes;

"- provided State text-book aid and certain other assistance to private primary and secondary schools;

"- provided the first financial support for educational television;

"- required special education for mentally retarded children in public schools." (*1973 Public Papers of Governor Rockfeller*, page 1380)

After skimming the Rockfeller papers, I would suggest the addition of a fifth contribution:
— initiated programs to identify and develop the talents of the underprivileged.

Let's look at each of these contributions.

A. "More than Quadrupled State Aid to Primary and Secondary Schools"

This achievement meant:

1. Highest level for State aid as a percent of General Fund expense in the post World War II era: 48.1 percent in the 1968-69 school year. The 1968-69 State aid increase of $360 million is the second highest in the State's history — exceeded only by the increase in 1974-75. The 22 percentage point increase for 1968-69 has not been surpassed since then. (Governor Malcolm Wilson, however, currently holds the New York State record for signing the highest annual public school aid increase into law — $371 million for the 1974-75 school year.)

2. Aid as a percentage of total General Fund expense has been 42.6 percent or higher in only ten school years since World War II; all of these school years occurred during the fifteen-year Rockefeller administration.

3. In the 13 years from 1945-46 to 1958-59, State aid increased from $121 million to $594 million — an increase of $473 million, or $36 million per year. From 1958-59 to 1971-72 (the first 13 years of the Rockefeller era), State aid for public elementary and secondary schools increased $1,780 million, an average change of $137 million per year.

How did these changes come about? One should point first to Governor Rockefeller's ability to work with the Legislature. The Joint Legislative Committee (JLC) on School Financing (Diefendorf Committee) was a creature of the Legislature, but Governor Rockefeller worked with the Legislature on the 1962 aid changes which resulted from the JLC recommendations. In his Public

Papers, the "new" formula is described in very complimentary terms. The Diefendorf Committee made it possible for the State to achieve significant changes, such as the elimination of preferential treatment for central school districts. The Governor was also able to gain support in the 1962 legislation for one of his own recommendations — increasing aid for city school districts through a 10 percent density/size correction.

By 1969 it was apparent that the Governor felt that additional changes were necessary in the State system for supporting public schools. From 1969 through 1973 there are repeated references to his desire to see a new funding system developed. In his October 1969 charge to the Fleischmann Commission, he said:

> "...while quality education has been New York's tradition, wide educational disparities continue to exist throughout the State. Public school expenditures per pupil range from less than $500 in some districts to over $1,500 in others. Large numbers of children of disadvantaged backgrounds are still being deprived of full access to educational opportunity. Enormously complex problems evolving from the effects of years of discrimination, segregation and economic handicaps are placing a great strain upon the structural and fiscal framework of the school system....The situation is particularly acute in the cities.
>
> "...in confronting these massive problems, the State is equipped with an outdated system of supporting education..." (*1969 Public Papers of Governor Rockefeller*, pages 1411-12)

His specific seven-point charge to the Fleischmann Commission posed questions which are relevant today.

B. "Provided State Textbook Aid and Other Assistance to Non-Public Schools"

The 1967 New York State Constitutional Convention recommended that the voters of the State repeal the so-called Blaine Amendment which had limited aid to private schools. The defeat of the convention package (for which Nelson A. Rockefeller announced he would vote) triggered a focus on constitutional ways to assist private schools, as statements in the Rockefeller public papers indicate.

It is interesting to note in Governor Rockefeller's Executive Budget for 1973-74 that the State:

"...assisted nonpublic schools by providing them, through the public school system, with pupil transportation, health service, textbooks, and other services, and by paying a large share of the cost of private and sectarian schools for the handicapped. The cost for such services and subsidies is now approaching $100 million a year." (*1973-74 Executive Budget*, page 155)

In the 1981-82 school year, the State Education Department has estimated that State and local expenditures for nonpublic schools, including nonpublic schools for the handicapped, will total $160 million - a continuing Rockefeller legacy.

C. Provided the First Financial Support for Educational Television

In his 1966 Annual Message, Nelson A. Rockefeller spoke as follows about educational television:

"Educational Television. Under a program of assistance initiated in 1961 (c. 724), the State has provided support for the establishment of educational television projects, thus far for 23 participating school districts. In 1965-66, $800,000 was appropriated for this program" (*1966 Public Papers of Governor Rockefeller*, p. 25)

However, in 1971, the Rockfeller administration proposed to cap this program. By the 1982-83 State fiscal year, support for school district educational television projects had fallen to $162,000.

The decade of the 1980's is producing new approaches to the introduction of technology into school districts.

D. Assistance for the Handicapped

There are references throughout the Rockefeller public papers to State assistance for public school children with handicapping conditions, but it is difficult to document precise costs in that era because of the number of different formulas used prior to the 1980-81 school year to provide aid for the handicapped. (Many of these formulas were consolidated in 1980.)

If Governor Rockefeller were alive today, he would be interested to learn that the latest Education Department projections show that local, State, and Federal expenditures for children with handicapping conditions in New York will be approximately $1.5 billion in the 1982-83 school year.

E. Concern for the Disadvantaged or "Underprivileged".
A number of programs which were initiated by the Rockefeller administration during the 1960's for disadvantaged pupils are still funded by the State today.

In his 1961 Annual Message, Governor Rockefeller said:
> "No waste is more tragic than the waste of human talent which occurs because the possessors of such talent are held back by accident of birth or other social circumstances for which they have no responsibility." (*1961 Public Papers of Governor Rockefeller*, page 11)

At a time when reducing racial imbalance wasn't always a popular concern, Governor Rockefeller repeatedly asked the Legislature for funds for programs designed to correct racial imbalance in the public schools. In 1966-67 for example, he requested an appropriation increase of $1.5 million (up to $1.7 million) for racial imbalance programs and $5 million for an experimental pre-kindergarten program for culturally deprived children. (The 1966 Legislature approved $489,000 for the racial balance program and $4.86 million for pre-kindergarten).

Another related program which he recommended during the 1960's and which has been continued through the 1982-83 State fiscal year is a $90,000 appropriation to provide schools for migrant workers.

The 1982-83 State Budget provides $9.46 million for districts which have participated in the pre-kindergarten program since the 1960's. Racial balance is not a term which political officials use too openly today. I would note, however, that State appropriations for 1982-83 provide $500,000 for Urban-Suburban Transfer Programs for pupils in the Buffalo and Rochester public schools.

II. Style of Leadership Exhibited to the Educational Community

Several aspects of Governor Rockefeller's personality, approach to leadership, and management style seemed to have contributed to his rapport with educational leaders. The love of people, about which Governor Wilson has spoken, was repeatedly communicated to members of the school community — even though only a limited number had direct contact with the Governor.

A. Establishing Rapport with an Individual or Group

Examples of his style in meeting individuals are legendary, both in campaign appearances and small group meetings.

1. *Fall 1958 Campaign Appearance.* I don't think that I'll ever forget one Rockefeller campaign appearance when I was a student at Cornell University in the fall of 1958. I was walking up the hill in front of Myron Taylor Hall (for those who know Cornell) and around the corner came Governor Rockefeller in an antique car with a few other people, heading for a rally at Willard Straight Hall. Although I was the only student in sight, I was still the beneficiary of the moving car version of the "half-Nelson" — wave, full-faced smile, and a big "Hi".

2. *Meetings with New York State Educational Conference Board.*

On two occasions, I participated in Educational Conference Board meetings with Governor Rockefeller. The first of these two meetings (which probably took place during the 1972 session) was a perfect example of how a busy executive can use ten minutes to make all participants feel that the meeting was worthwhile. Time had been allocated for a longer meeting, but it turned out to be a very busy day for the Governor. We were ushered into a second floor conference room and a staff member arrived to explain the delay. When Governor Rockefeller and one or two aides first entered the room, the Governor greeted Conference Board Chairman Hugh Davies very warmly and went around the room to speak to all participants and to make appropriate comments. He then settled down at the head of the table. The Governor candidly explained why his presence was required elsewhere (a development which turned out to be the State headline story of the day.) Mr. Davies made an abbreviated presentation to which Governor Rockefeller devoted full attention. The Governor designated a staff member to remain for a few more minutes and get more details, assuring the group he would be fully briefed. After another round of handshakes, the Governor left, and I believe that everyone in the Conference Board delegation felt that the Governor was concerned about their views — even though the total meeting had only lasted about ten minutes. The second Educational Conference Board meeting in which I participated took place in January 1973 in the Red Room. Both Governor Rockefeller and Lieutenant Governor Malcolm Wilson participated in the meeting which lasted about one and a half hours.

To prepare for the 1973 meeting, Conference Board Chairman Hugh Davies had asked staff at the State Teachers' Association to prepare a series of charts to document the Board's State aid recommendations. During a briefing session held on the morning of the Red Room meeting, Chairman Davies asked me to make the chart presentation to the Governor. During this presentation, Governor Rockefeller asked several questions and quoted from

145

some statistics prepared for his use. I remember that I had occasion to look frequently at my back-up notes. One portion of the dialogue went something like this:

NAR: Education is one of my priorities, but the State doesn't have the resources for an increase of the magnitude requested by the Conference Board.

LW: Sir, the Fleischmann Commission recommended an overall State aid increase of more than $1 billion. When you add up the cost of the recommendations in the 1972 report, including the main State aid plan and the other aid proposals, the Educational Conference Board program is not as costly.

NAR: [The governor put his sheets of paper down on the table before he spoke.] It is too bad we don't have people like you in State government.

Right then, I realized that Governor Rockefeller did not know that Dr. T. Norman Hurd had arranged for him to interview me for a job in the Executive Chamber immediately after the Conference Board meeting. Toward the end of the meeting, Lieutenant Governor Wilson was slipped a note which I later learned asked him to make certain that I met with Governor Rockefeller. Governor Rockefeller's first words to me as we walked to his private office off the Red Room were something like this: "All during the meeting, I kept thinking that I'd rather be interviewing you than the person I was supposed to interview." As we arrived in his office, he paced up and down and said, "I can't believe it. I'll have to tell Happy!"

B. Public Communication Style

Another factor in Governor Rockefeller's rapport with the school community was the style presented in public documents.

1. *Printed recognition of the views of the Regents and of the major educational organizations.* For example, in his 1965 Annual Message, he said:

"Despite the magnitude of past and proposed new school aid, I agree with the Regents, the State Educational Conference Board, and other representative spokesmen for education who point out that increases are essential to keep pace with rising school operating costs." (*1965 Public Papers of Governor Rockefeller*, page 22.)

Some of the veto messages signed by Governor Rockefeller noted the views of the State School Boards Association, the State Teachers Association, and other educational organizations. I even found one 1971 veto message in which he quoted extensively from a New York State School Boards Association memorandum. Several education groups were listed as recommending veto of a 1966 hazardous zone transportation aid bill.

2. *Public recognition of individual school districts and educators.*

In a 1966 speech in conjunction with the dedication of Corning Community College, he referred to the Corning Painted Post School District, noting with approval that "fourteen new elementary schools have replaced forty-two one-room schools in rural areas."

On another occasion he appeared on a television program with Education Commissioner James Allen and several school district representatives.

3. *Careful choice of language to reflect geographic balance within New York State.* In a February 17, 1960 television program (WRCA-TV, New York City) with Speaker Joseph F. Carlino, Governor Rockefeller spoke as follows concerning his 1960 school aid program:

> "There are three phases to it: we want to
> take care of cities' needs, the suburban needs,
> and the rural needs." (*1960 Public Papers of
> Governor Rockefeller*, page 1432.)

4. *Desire to balance conflicting interests.* For example, in his 1969 Annual Message, he sought to include all of the interests with concerns related to the establishment of a New York City school decentralization policy. He said:

> "The subject of decentralization of the New
> York City school system will be a matter of the
> highest priority for your consideration this year.
> It is my hope that the New York City Board of
> Education, the teachers and the community
> groups involved, together with the Mayor and the
> State Board of Regents will be able to unite
> behind a workable program that will assure the
> best possible educational opportunity for the
> children.

D. Management Style of Rockefeller Administration

The management style and general modus operandi of the Rockefeller administration helped to create the feeling among school people that they had a friend in the Governor's Mansion.

1. Periodic meetings with large educational groups. He spoke at conventions of the State School Boards Association, the New York State Congress of Parents and Teachers, and other educational groups.

Governor Rockefeller meets members of the younger generation in a classroom visit.

2. Prompt response to invitations inviting him to speak allowed education groups to make definite plans in terms of whether or not the Governor would be present.

3. Annual meetings with the Regents. Such meetings were usually held in conjunction with the November Regents meeting in New York City. Since Dr. Ronan has spoken about the Governor's focus on details, it may be relevant to mention that at the November 1973 meeting (the only such meeting I ever attended), Governor Rockefeller intensely questioned individual Regents on progress being made with exhibits planned for the new State Museum in the Empire State Plaza. (I happened to know that this item had not been highlighted in the staff briefing paper.)

4. Vetoes of school aid bills designed to benefit one district or a very small group of districts. Such actions served in my view to help keep the focus of the school community upon aid programs which had more general application.

III. Impact of Governor Rockefeller's Contributions

The Governor's record of achievement in education is hard to digest, let alone summarize in a short period of time. Some aspects of his continuing legacy are highlighted below.

A. Identification of Basic School Finance Problems

One sign of his impact is that many of the school finance problems identified during the Rockefeller era remain, but his proposals in several cases could be useful to the transition team of the incoming Governor. Let me cite just a few examples of fundamental problems identified in his administration that still await resolution in the decade of the 1980's.

1. Need for Larger School District Units. In 1960, Governor Rockefeller vetoed a bill which would have given independent taxing powers to supervisory districts. The language of the veto message clearly suggests, however, that although the Governor had been advised about substantial constitutional questions, he would have preferred to sign the measure into law. He said:

"The basic constitutional defect in the instant bill is apparently that provision which permits taxation and the incurring of debt by all the qualified voters of the proposed new district. It might be advisable to alter this constitutionally-defective procedure so as to provide for the approval of such expenditures and taxes by a majority of the qualified voters in each of the constituent districts. This would appear to meet the fundamental objectives raised against the instant bill." (Memorandum of April 30, 1960 on S.I. 847, S.P. 4266, *1960 Public Papers of Governor Rockefeller*, page 400.)

I was particularly interested in the language in this gubernatorial veto message, because recent commentators have assumed regional funding was not discussed with regard to school finance in New York until around 1982.

2. Use of More Equalizing Aid Formulas. In a 1969 message, Governor Rockefeller called for a series of "primary and secondary state aid formula revisions," some of which are remarkably similar to those found in the 1983 legislative program recently adopted by the State Board of Regents. The Governor called upon the Legislature to:

— "reduce flat grant operating aid and the minimum apportionment;

— "place aid to Boards of Cooperative Educational Services on an aid ratio formula similar to the regular aid formula for school districts;

— "reduce transportation aid by placing it on an aid ratio formula basis."

149

Other interesting legislative recommendations in that 1969 message are calls to:

— "limit the expenditures for professional salaries which may be included in computing allowable expenses for school aid purposes;...

— "reduce operating aid to school districts scheduled for reorganization which have not taken steps to reorganize; ...

— "limit capital aid for school construction to the cost of building under standard State school plans."

3. Relationship Between State Revenues and State's Ability to Aid School Districts. If the figures used in a Rockefeller speech in October 1969 were updated, the basic message could be repeated today by the Governor of New York. Governor Rockefeller said:

"No state is doing near what we are doing for education.

"But we have been approaching a financial crisis.

"Prior to this year, our aid formulas for education,welfare and per capita aid reached a point where State aid was increasing automatically at a rate of $700,000,000 a year. But our revenues were growing at a rate of only $350,000,000 a year.

"It doesn't take a genius to figure out that we've reached a point where we'll be faced with an automatic annual State tax increase. And, as of last year, we had also reached a point where we were the state with the highest tax effort in the Country. ...

"We have to come to grips not only with the problem of school financing but the whole range of educational problems. ...

"This year I've had the pleasure of approving legislation that relieved the pressure of some of your city school districts that are nearing the constitutional taxing limit.

"But maybe these limits ought to be removed from the Constitution, as your Association

recommends, and be handled by legislation."
(October 28, 1969 Address at Annual Convention
of the New York State School Boards Association,
1969 Public Papers of Governor Rockefeller, pp.
1615-1616)

IV. Conclusion

The legacy of the Rockefeller administration is clearly set
forth in the 15 brown volumes which contain the *Public Papers of
Governor Rockefeller* and the 15 Executive Budgets which he
submitted to the Legislature.

As I reviewed the published statements in preparation for
this conference, I was repeatedly struck by how current some of
the educational ideas still are. I'm really grateful that this
conference provided me with a reason to review the Rockefeller
record.

MAX RUBIN: I have two threshold observations to make. I was
asked to recollect some personal anecdotes involving Nelson
Rockefeller. All I can say in response to this is to tell you a story
about Justice Oliver Wendell Holmes. When he was about my age,
he went aboard a train. The conductor came around to collect the
tickets. The judge could not find his but the conductor recognized
him and said, "Don't let that worry you, Judge. When you get
back to your office, just mail it in." Holmes replied, "That isn't
what is worrying me. Unless I find my ticket, I won't remember
where I'm going." This explains why I can't comply with the
request for anecdotes.

The other thing I would say is that in connection with
whatever I say about Nelson Rockefeller, you have every right to
take it with a discount. Governor Rockfeller never hesitated to
remind me that on the last day of the extended session of the 1965
Legislature, he signed into law the bill that increased the size of
the Board of Regents by one and on that day I was elected a
Regent. The Governor had a mortgage on my conscience.

In thinking about Nelson Rockefeller and elementary and
secondary education, it is clear that the relationship cannot
possibly be as dramatic as his involvement with higher education.
(I have always resented the term "higher education" apparently
as distinguished from "lower education"). In the field of higher
education, almost a vacuum existed in that the State University
had never been developed adequately. Governor Rockefeller filled
that vacuum with his outstanding contribution to the development
of the State University of New York.

At the elementary and secondary level, New York always was a strong state with a fine program. There could not possibly be the kind of dramatic impact that he could give to the State University.

He was responsible for the creation of the Fleischmann Commission. I believe that the Fleischmann study is the most undervalued study I have known about. I do not believe any other state has ever had so complete an analysis of a system of elementary and secondary education. It analyzed all aspects of the subject and suggested reforms. I suppose the reason it is undervalued is that its recommendations did not receive legislative implementation. Because of several of its recommendations, it became very controversial. But that was inevitable because there are very few issues in the area that are not controversial. The Fleischmann report was so large in its scope that there had to be people who would disagree on one or several or more of the Fleischmann recommendations. It was politically a very difficult document to implement.

The fact is that anybody undertaking any study of an aspect of elementary and secondary education in this state would do well to go back to the Fleischmann report because one will find the problems identified and the analysis careful. Fleischmann recommended full State assumption of funding of elementary and secondary education. Politically this had no chance. Recently the Court of Appeals in the Levittown case indicated that it would consider full State funding as illegal.

Fleischmann recognized that the most likely unit for improvement and reform of public education is the individual school — not the State, nor even the district. Fleischmann emphasized that educational philosophy is less important than actual educational practice. Parents are concerned with what is going on in the school which their child attends. They are much less concerned about school district policy.

I believe the Governor made a major contribution when he created the Fleischmann Commission and saw to it that it was adequately financed.

There was something else of which I was very aware during my service on the Board of Regents. That was the Governor's respect for the jurisdiction of the Regents. He met with the Board periodically and would always respond to a request for a meeting by even an individual member of the Board. What was impressive about his meetings with the Regents was his preparation. He knew the problems that were bothering him and he was prepared to discuss them with the Board. He was equally prepared to discuss all the issues raised by the Regents. It was gratifying and reassuring to all of us to be able to sit and talk out questions in that fashion.

I remember a personal meeting I had with Governor Rockefeller in which we discussed the difficulties faced by the Commissioner of Education. He is a member of the Governor's cabinet. However, he is employed by the Board of Regents and is the "executive director" to carry out the policies of the Board. Whenever the Board and Governor disagree on an issue, the Commissioner is in a very difficult position. I was impressed with the Governor's sensitivity to this fact. It reflected still another aspect of the Governor's understanding of the governance of elementary and secondary education.

I also remember that before I went on the Board of Education in New York City, I had a meeting with him and with Senator Earl Brydges. It had to do with the New York State Committee for the Public Schools. Roy Larsen stimulated such a committee on the national level. Nelson Rockefeller expressed his high regard for what Mr. Larsen was accomplishing, and in the discussion, he showed his awareness of the importance of involving the public, and that portion of the public which is made up of parents, in the actions and achievements of their schools.

I also recall being impressed with the Governor's recommendation of the need for adequate State aid for the schools. I recall that when I came to Albany on behalf of the New York City schools, I was invited to a meeting attended by the Governor, Commissioner Allen, Senator Mahoney, and several others. This was during the time of the Diefendorf Commission. That Commission had come into being at Governor Rockefeller's initiative and it was studying the problems of State aid. The Governor was keenly interested in what we were attempting to do in New York City to improve efficiency in operation. I told him of our engagement of the Cresap-McCormick firm to make a study and recommendations respecting operating procedures. For example, the practice of the Superintendent's Office to send over even minor bills for approval by the Controller caused enormous delays, with the result that bids were higher because of delay in payment. He was obviously interested and approving of our effort. He wanted to know what we were doing to institute reforms in the office responsible for school building construction and repair. In fact, he asked about a number of operations to satisfy himself that we were making every effort to reduce, if not eliminate, waste.

We discussed the particular problems of the urban communities. At that time, in 1962, the matter of municipal overburden was already being discussed. The problem then, as now, was to design a formula that could, with reasonable accuracy, measure overburden. It also was difficult to design a formula that would allow the State rather than the municipal government to compute the aid. There was understandable fear that the formulas then under discussion would simply encourage municipal extravagance.

The result was the inclusion of a density factor in the State aid formula, which factor remained in being for a number of years. This meant a great deal to me because it produced a substantial sum for the City.

In 1963, there was a threatened teachers' strike in our city. Governor Rockefeller involved himself in the problem. In fact, he called a conference at his 55th Street office which was attended by Mayor Wagner, Charles Cogen, who was then the head of the UFT, and others. Nelson Rockefeller, along with the Mayor, worked very hard to avoid a strike, and I suppose the best test of the kind of settlement that was reached was that both sides were unhappy.

I remember the Governor's tremendous impact in the decentralization of the New York City system. Finally, he designated Al Marshall to be the one who would meet with all the parties in the drafting of the legislation.

Nelson Rockefeller's concern for elementary and secondary education was deep and great. He made sure to know the problems and be able to help in finding solutions.

I believe that I have one of the last letters that Nelson Rockefeller ever wrote. It arrived the day after his death. At that time, I was chairman of a task force studying the possible responses to the Levittown decision. In his letter he assured me of his support for the work of our task force. I was deeply touched.

Perhaps all this will explain why I am delighted that I was invited to participate in this meeting. I have every confidence that the Rockefeller Institute will be worthy of the name it bears.

KENNETH BUHRMASTER: I'm delighted that I've been asked to be here. It was a great pleasure to work with Lois Wilson. Lois has covered many of the things that took place during the Rockefeller regime.

The relationship that I had with the Governor was one that caused me to understand this field. The statement has been made that he had a love of people. He had a special love of children. It just so happened, that we had sons born about the same time. We used to talk, from time to time, as to what happens to children of their age.

He was a supporter of financial aid to schools. Over his period of time, support for education increased 400 percent. He supported more money for education. He was sure that we had great need. He was not always sure that we were getting our dollar's worth, but he was sure if we reduced support, we would reduce the quality of education we had in this State. He spoke to me of the need to get the rest of the United States up to par as far as education was concerned.

I was involved in this during the time that Max Rubin came in to take over the New York City School Board operation. About that time the support of education that came from the Federal government was under six percent. The Governor talked with me about emphasizing the need to develop the understanding of the people at the national level of what New York State was doing.

At that time it seems there were about 220,000 Puerto Rican children and about 270,000 black children in New York City schools; the two groups, together, were still a minority. I was President of the National School Boards Association, and was attacked for being a Northerner. The Governor asked me to emphasize that we had a greater population of foreign children in this State than any other state in the nation. We had more black children in the New York *City* schools than any other *state* had in their total public school system. The point he asked me to make was about the migration of Puerto Ricans and blacks into New York City and Buffalo. We had to take children, whether they were six years of age or sixteen years of age, with no formal education. This was costly to the City of New York.

These were not only New York City problems, they were New York State problems. More importantly, as the Governor would say, they were national problems. We needed to work hard to bring these children's education up to par. These children, as they got some sort of education, often moved to the Midwest and to the West. For that reason, we thought that we ought to have 40 percent support from the Federal government, 40 percent from the State government, and 20 percent local support.

I recall being at a meeting of New York State University Trustees, both public and private. Somebody asked that I repeat this point. Immediately, up came the people who said, "You're going to lose all kinds of local control." I was questioned by a man who turned out to be a Trustee of Cornell University. He attacked me, stating that this was a terrible request to make of the Federal government and State government; he told how private universities could handle themselves without any such aid from the Federal government. I asked him if he thought that the Federal government had hurt his control as he had administered Cornell University. He said Cornell University had no trouble with the

155

Federal government because the Federal government did not support Cornell University with even one cent. I told him I was not so sure about that; it seemed to me that Cornell was a land-grant college, and that land-grant colleges have had a considerable amount of Federal support. The fact of the matter was that Cornell did have Federal support. He as a Trustee didn't know it, and the Federal government had not interfered with their control.

I bring up this point about support because only a few years ago New York State had 9 percent of the population and we were paying 11 percent of the cost of the Federal government and the total Federal support of education was less than 6 percent of the National budget. It seemed that we should have more Federal dollars sent back to us.

Most recently, I find that, since we are a wealthy State, we are still receiving a very low percentage of Federal aid — about 6 percent — but some of the other states receive up to 16 percent. The Governor's vision of what we needed to do was way ahead of his time.

The name Earl Brydges was mentioned earlier. I would be remiss if I did not speak of how much Governor Rockefeller and Earl Brydges did for the handicapped children. Earl Brydges and Max Rubin were working on the Committee of Educational Leadership at that time and those fellows did much for support of the handicapped child. With all due respect for the State of California, if you had a blind or handicapped child, you received no special support. In this State, you have education for that handicapped child. New York State is a leader in this. It would not have happened without the vision of Nelson Rockefeller.

I keep thinking of the times I met with Governor Rockefeller, Norman Hurd, Alan Marshall, and Lois Wilson, to discuss public education and the need of financial aid for children in the State of New York and to develop support for the arts as well. The Governor, understanding all of the State's needs, would come back with an answer to our requests. If he said, "We can do this or we can't do this," "It can be in the budget," or "It can't be in the budget," you could depend on him all the way through. His integrity was not to be questioned. If he said you can't do it this year, but you can do it next year, it would happen that way.

The Governor was a friendly person; he wanted to do much for education in New York State. As Lois Wilson said, many of the things he did back in those days are alive and doing well today and are things that we can be extremely proud of. The Governor always gave a lot of support to public education. He believed if we didn't do a good job in the area of education — elementary, secondary, and higher education — the State of New York would not continue to be the "great" State of New York. He believed in New York State and we can all be thankful for that. Much of the good that was done in education came from either Governor Rockefeller or his "idea" men and women.

DONNA SHALALA: I actually probably have had the least experience with Governor Rockefeller. I only had one face-to-face meeting, about 15 years ago, when I was a new graduate student at Syracuse. For one reason or another, Scotty Campbell sent me down to Albany and asked me to see Al Marshall. We stopped to see Al, and he introduced me to the Governor. The Governor was very polite and shook my hand and said to Al, "When she grows up, bring her back and we'll hire her."

My second experience with Governor Rockefeller was really special. I love this story and will remember it forever. I had moved down to New York City and was teaching at the City University. I had written a little monograph called "New York City Statehood: An Idea Whose Time Was Past." It was essentially an attack on the Norman Mailer proposal that New York City become a state, and, remembering I had had this wonderful meeting with the Governor, I sent him a copy of my monograph. He sent me back a letter that clearly was drafted by staff, but at the bottom was penned a little note that read, "If New York City was dumb enough to become a state, it would go bankrupt." A wiser man we never had in State government.

Let me summarize and give you some impressions as a political scientist about elementary and secondary education. I have reviewed State aid under Nelson Rockefeller and I remember one significant finding: If you look at local assistance during the years he was Governor, over one-half of the increase went to education. That is remarkable considering that during that period we saw the expansion of social service programs. And yet he maintained a very high commitment to elementary and secondary education.

The second point I'd make was his willingness to modernize educational finance — the movement from a foundation system to an equalization system is not to be underestimated. And in fact, New York State was far ahead of most of the other states in the country in that proposal.

A third point I'd make is that Nelson Rockefeller made education a multi-billion dollar business. It was a relatively small half-billion dollar operation until he became Governor. We moved into the multi-billion dollar era with major sums going to elementary and secondary education.

And the fourth point I would make is that he really changed the nature of school politics at the State level. We saw powerful interest groups, but at the same time we reduced the number of programs in school finance by pushing everything into a formula. If something was going to break out of that formula then it really had to have a strong justification; it had to be a very specialized program. And, for a long time, that kind of discipline meant that when funds were put out they would go directly to the school district. There was a lot more flexibility, I believe, on the part of the school districts in the State because of this general approach. I would argue that if you put all these changes together they represent a major commitment to education. And that was really Nelson Rockefeller's contribution to elementary and secondary education.

I agree with both the strength and the creative aspects as well as the depth of the Fleischmann report, and there were really first class policy and political pieces done during this period. In addition, the wonderful thing about Rockefeller is that he actually got things done. You saw substantive change.

Finally, what I really liked about Nelson Rockefeller is that he wasn't afraid. He really was bold and there were no issues that he wasn't willing to challenge. That is a memory and a leadership model, in addition to my short meetings with him, that I will always cherish.

AL MARSHALL: A session about elementary and secondary education and Rockefeller wouldn't be complete without putting something in the record about his terrible frustration in the area. He probably was more frustrated in the area of elementary and secondary education than in any other area that he worked in, with the possible exception of drug abuse. He hated to talk about the increase in the State aid to local groups. He didn't really like that. The truth of it was we used to understate that, and then Norman had to carry the heavy load, because we knew that was a legislative plum that they had to have. Earl Brydges had to come in with a higher amount.

I can remember the times he would sit with Jim Allen and Joe Nyquist and would say, "Look, you've got to find a way for us to do what we're doing, better, in education." It was a concern for money, not in the normal sense of just cutting the price, but as Malcolm said, "The bang for the buck". He oscillated between the handiness at times of having the Board of Regents, on which he could blame certain things that were necessary (putting it in my words, not his — he could hide behind the Regents) and other times he almost "nagged" the Regents. He wanted to have education as much under his control, as responsive, as he liked the community health program or one of the others to be. And time after time, as things got to the level which we all mentioned, he would sit with me and say, "My God, what are we going to do?"

What the record really should show is that this man agonized over this area. He knew how to deal with $1,800 million worth of buildings in eight years with the State University. Education was one or two steps away from him, and drove him nuts as a doer, as an innovator, someone who wanted to get his hands on a thing. This was also reflected in his willingness — eagerness — when somebody could come up to with the School Breakfast Program or a special program. He thought: Good, we're doing something. He just could not get his hands on that, like he could other functions of government.

GORDON AMBACH: I'd really like to expand on a few points that have been made. My first contacts with Nelson Rockefeller were in 1967 when I was involved in the sessions with the Board of Regents, Jim Allen, and Joe Nyquist. In 1970, I represented the State Education Department in the Governor's town meetings on drug abuse. As Executive Deputy Commissioner, I joined other commissioners and the Governor on the platform to deal with the issue. Lois provided us with a very comprehensive look at the Rockefeller legacy as we come into the 1980's. I would like just to add a couple of points to that by expanding on what Al and Donna have said.

It's interesting to speculate that the move to equalization of school funding already established in New York in the 1960's was responsible for the fact that the Court of Appeals denied the Levittown Case in the 1980's. You won't see that circumstance in another state. Even though we had a considerable gap in the level of expenditures between the high spending and low spending districts, the fact of the matter is that in New York, by the 1980's, all the techniques to equalize had already been tried here, going back into the 1960's.

Al made points about the Governor's frustrations over education spending. I can remember that. It certainly came through in those sessions. He did, however, have a keen interest in some aspects of education. Lois Wilson mentioned educational television. The Governor had a fascination with instructional technology and with visual learning. We sold him a program in the early 1970's. It was a technique for using television in the classroom along with teachers. We called it "The Place of Doors." That program no longer exists, but the age for more instructional technology, certainly with computers, has now come along, and we should note the connection with his earlier interest.

The other recollection is with the problem of youthful drug abuse. That was a key issue in 1969 and 1970. The act that passed put $75 million into treatment. Then the Governor went to the town meetings and heard from almost everybody: "Treatment won't work. What you really have to do is prevent." The Governor then directed more than half of that money to education programs. The direct practical outcome was a change of what was in the statute. The Governor, very much involved in this area, moved almost 60 percent of this program into the area of education.

The legacy is one of connecting education with other services, that couldn't work alone. He saw these connections and promoted them.

STANLEY RAUB: We knew the Governor as a builder, especially in higher education, but I don't think most people realize that a quarter of all the elementary and secondary schools built today were new schools during his administration. The Governor had commissioned stock plans. There were five models!

The other story, that I remember, is when Jim Allen went across the street, and this was the late 1960's. This was just before Fleischmann and Jim knew that we were in economic turmoil in the State. He wanted to go over and ask the Governor for more money for the schools. That meant, of course, a study, and that was not unusual. (The Governor had 70 task forces during his administration.) Jim came back to report to the cabinet at that time, that the Governor expanded upon this proposal. He wanted to look into all aspects of education — a very ambitious program — and of course he was concerned at that time, too, about capability and efficiency.

The Governor's sensitivity to youngsters, as mentioned by Ken Buhrmaster, was demonstrated on a day that I will never forget. I attended one of his "town meetings" with industrialists, labor leaders, educators, the press, and the general public. We went to an elementary school in Schenectady, and at 10:00 A.M. he was to have a meeting with the industrial leaders in this area. But the pupils had prevailed upon their teachers to line them up in the corridors to see the Governor. I'll never forget how Nelson walked in and looked to the right and the left and saw all these youngsters lined up along the wall. He kept the industrialists waiting for twenty minutes, while he shook the hands of all those little youngsters through sixth grade. Some argued that this was a matter of political reality. But I think we would all agree that his interest was real and reflected his genuine sensitivity to people.

The Governor's ability to empathize with people, especially the disadvantaged, was also illustrated on the day I went with him to Brooklyn to open a new office. It was in the Bedford Stuyvesant section, and we had a host of black teenagers and other young people, many of whom were unemployed and disadvantaged. Nelson stood up at the desk and started off by saying, "I want you to know that I'm disadvantaged," and he talked about dyslexia — about how it was difficult for him to read a speech because he read things backwards. He told them how he got assistance and soon had those youngsters eating out of the palm of his hand.

Chapter VII

Transformation
of the Workplace

LOUIS LEVINE: For nine years, starting in 1966, as Commissioner for Labor Affairs and as Industrial Commissioner, I had the challenge and privilege of working with Governor Rockefeller. Some of my most vivid memories of those years are of the personal qualities that contributed so greatly to his unusual ability as a leader: innovative, intelligent, humorous, with an enviable energy and a boundless willingness to respond to challenge. Paradoxically, given the great personal wealth into which he was born, Nelson Rockefeller had a deep understanding of and respect for the needs of working people; and that understanding helped to bring forth his labor philosophy during his first gubernatorial campaign. His words are as meaningful now as they were in 1958 — perhaps more so. "We not only must have employment, but full employment. Every person who is willing and able to work should have a good job at good wages, under good working conditions, and with reasonable security. Until that is accomplished, we shall have failed to achieve the full potential of our economy and the full benefits of our democratic society."

For Nelson Rockefeller, talk was not cheap. It was a valued, respected means to understanding. He believed in exchanging views and negotiating differences. And although he brought a global, idealistic view to the State environment, he was not an "idealogue". He was a man committed to practical improvement. His sense of purpose, of what could and could not be done, was developed over a period of 25 years of activity at the local, State and Federal levels — well before his election as Governor. With his rare ability to get along with all sorts of people, he was able to create a coalition for productive action. The democratic principle was, for him, very close to a religious principle, and he felt that our political structure was, or should be, rooted in the concept of human brotherhood. This he sincerely believed.

Governor Rockefeller was also a man of great personal charm who could, and indeed did, "...walk with kings nor lose the common touch." With his easy manner and infectious grin, he largely won over the press and the public — and because of this, it was a while before many political analysts gave serious thought to what he really stood for. This oversight was more than remedied in the long years of his public service. Part of our purpose at this conference — which addresses nine important areas of his public service — is to put into perspective those considerable accomplishments, while not hesitating to consider also the limitations and setbacks that accompany all achievement.

In his book, *Persons and Persuasions*, Oren Root observes, "There are few greater liabilities that a person can carry in life than too much money, too much good looks, or too much personal charm." Those of us not so burdened may or may not agree, but in any case, he adds (and I think you'll agree) that history is full of people who put too much reliance on one or another of those gifts —and as a result, "...came a cropper in the end." But Nelson Rockefeller rose above not one or two but all three of these potential liabilities. His personal success became a success story for the State of New York as well, which he led to a position of national pre-eminence.

Since my activities in the Department of Labor were directed more to the private sector than to the public sector, and since at least two of the discussants with us this afternoon have dealt with the public employment area, I'd like to make some general comments about the private sector. It's interesting to note that it was the private sector unions which felt strongly about Nelson Rockefeller's leadership and were among his most obvious supporters. They were interested in things like the minimum wage, social insurance legislation, workmen's compensation, and disability. For the most part, in my judgment, outside of the minimum wage in New York State (which for many years was ahead of the Federal minimum wage), the benefits that accrued to the trade union movement in the private sector were not as great as those enjoyed by the public employees.

If you take a look at what has happened to the public employees in New York State — collective bargaining and the growth of the public employee unions — one finds it hard to understand why that group of unions, those leaders, the teachers, and the Civil Service Employees Association (CSEA), have been so critical of Nelson Rockefeller and the Rockefeller administration. You sit and talk today to many of them, and they constantly carp on the negative aspects of the Rockefeller years. Yet, quite frankly, without him they would not be here.

The private sector enjoyed a boom, but only a very small aspect of the private sector, and even that was spotty across the State. It was always assumed that Nelson Rockefeller was a great savior of the private sector and the trade union movement. I always thought the private sector lost many jobs in New York State, not only due to high taxes, which was used as an excuse, but due to aging industries. Even in the 1960's and 70's they were beginning to die: textile mills in middle and upper New York State and steel plants were aging and closing down, electrical plants were moving south and moving to the Midwest. And jobs were lost.

But yet the private sector — the private unions (and I knew many of the leaders, people like David Dubinsky, in those days, and Stuhlberg in the International Ladies Garment Workers' Union [ILGWU] and Petofsky of Amalgamated Clothing Workers' Union) had a fond recollection any time you talked to them about the meetings they had with Nelson Rockefeller, and how he convinced them about the things that they had in common. Those of you who read anything about Dubinsky would find it hard to figure out what he had in common with Nelson Rockefeller, or what Petofsky had in common with Nelson Rockefeller, and yet he could in fact charm those people.

It was a charm which wasn't all one way. He didn't just over-whelm them. He gave freely of himself and his time, which was very important, and he had an open door. This was very important to labor union movement leadership and their member-ship. A lot of people, who don't understand the labor movement and the politics of the movement, don't realize this. You don't always have to deliver for your members, but you have to give the impression of being able to deliver. If you don't have the strength to get in the front door and be a spokesperson and be able to get a commitment — at least publicly — to look at the problem (even if nothing ever gets done), you are a poor labor leader. Nelson Rockefeller recognized that fact and he kept that door open.

There were comments made in the other session about the sanitation strike and what it did to Nelson Rockefeller's chances to be President. I admit that might have hurt him nationally, but, in terms of the labor movement in New York State, he was a giant. And he really didn't do very much outside of having an open door, a willingness to listen and a willingness to conciliate.

Rockefeller was not just a taker, he was always a giver. He had an ability to talk not only with Dubinsky and Petofsky, but also with George Meany, Peter Brennan, and sometimes with Ray Corbett. But Meany was the most difficult in terms of what he

164

wanted and when he wanted it. And Meany never forgot.

You talked to George Meany and he'd say, "Nelson Rockefeller, now there was man who stood to protect the interests of the working people." And if you ask Meany what Nelson Rockefeller did, the first thing he would say was, "He protected my bill." (For those of you who don't know what Meany's bill was, it concerned the right of strikers to collect unemployment insurance in New York State. That was a Meany bill when Meany was Secretary-Treasurer of the New York State AFL). Meany felt jealous about his bill, and nobody dared do violence to it. The mere fact that Nelson never recommended this bill be amended in any way was enough for George Meany to say, "He understood the problems of workers."

This afternoon, we have with us the gentleman who took on the very awesome responsibility of dealing with the public employee unions in New York. I can tell you that our theme setter made history in his own right. He had to structure and re—structure an operation from the very beginning. Nobody could quite believe that you could have an "independent, non-governmental interferred-with" entity in New York State to deal with unions. The Governor wouldn't tell him what to do, the unions wouldn't tell him what to do. Bob Helsby had that awesome responsibility, and he performed it magnificently.

ROBERT HELSBY: As I contemplated the contributions of Nelson Rockefeller, particularly in the area we're talking about today, no incident emphasizes and illustrates Nelson's qualifications for what he did, better, than when I was with George Taylor about two weeks before he died. George, as you remember, was with the Wharton School in Pennsylvania. He had worked for five Presidents, had been given the Medal of Freedom: nominated by John F. Kennedy; given the medal by Lyndon Johnson. George took me around his apartment and showed me his memorabilia. In the process he told me this story: One night about three o'clock in the morning the telephone rang. George went to the phone, and it was Nelson Rockefeller saying that the Taylor Law had been passed and he wanted George to be the first to know it.

It is interesting that they called it the Taylor Law. George says the reason was that, unlike all the other labor legislation both Federal and State (the Wagner Act, or Taft-Hartley or Landrum-Griffin), all named after legislators, no legislator would put his name on the bill. He said that the reason they named it after him was because they knew he would never run for public office!

Governor Wilson has talked about leadership and how

Governor Rockefeller got what he wanted. I thought back to the days when I took on the chairmanship of the Public Employment Relations Board (PERB). I had gone back from the Labor Department to the State University, when Robert Stone of the Governor's Office called me and asked me if I would be interested in chairing the Public Employment Relations Board. He said they had just passed the Taylor Law , and I said, "What's the Taylor Law?" I said, "I'll get a copy of the Law and take a look at it." I got the Law and I learned that I wanted no part of administering it! I also learned that within a very few weeks after the Law was passed some 18,000 unionists gathered in Madison Square Garden and vowed to repeal the Law. They called it every name in the books, including the "Slave Labor Act" and a lot of other derogatory names. Having returned to the University only about a year and a half earlier, I called Bob Stone and said, "Thanks but no thanks."

Sam Gould, the Chancellor of the University, and I were then at Alfred University. I got a call from Ann Whitman of the Governor's Office at about ten o'clock in the morning. She said, "The Governor would like to see you and Sam Gould in his office at four this afternoon."

We drove in and we met the Governor as planned. There were the three of us at the meeting: the Chancellor, the Governor, and myself. The Governor opened up the conversation by saying to Sam Gould, "I'd like to borrow this guy for a year and a half." Of course I knew pretty well what was going to happen, so I had developed two lines of strategy. Number one, I would tell the Governor why I was not qualified, and I really felt that I was not. And secondly, I would be prepared with a list of at least five or six people whom I considered qualified. So when he said to Sam Gould, "I'd like to borrow him," I started with the strategy I had developed. I had said about two sentences, when the Governor stopped me and said, "Rightly or wrongly, we've decided you are the person to chair this board. Are you going to help us or aren't you?" I looked at Sam Gould and he looked at me. He shrugged his shoulders and I did too. Without saying it we were saying, "What can you do?"

Governor Rockefeller also had another technique which I think some of us may want to use sometime. I don't think I've ever had the chance to use it, but I will never forget it. I tried to tick off a few other names of people who I felt were better qualified. I had gotten through one of the names, when he stopped me and said, "I have already talked with him but he hasn't got any guts." Now you know what that says. It simply implies, although it doesn't say it directly, that if you don't take on this job, you don't have any guts either. I looked at him and I said, "Nelson, not even the

Governor of the great State of New York is going to sit there and call me gutless."

As I walked out of the Capitol and got into my car, I felt a very heavy load descending on my shoulders, because I had been handed the Taylor Law to try to make it work. He said, "Here's $250,000; if you need more come back." I did in a couple of months. At any rate, this was the beginning of public sector labor relations, as it is now known, in the State of New York.

Now I would simply like to drop back for a minute to remind all of us where we were at the time Nelson Rockefeller became Governor. I refer to the field of public employment labor relations. Even though I speak largely about public employment, this has had, and it is even now having, a tremendous impact on the private sector. When the so-called "Magna Carta of Labor," the Wagner Act, was passed in 1935 (giving collective bargaining rights to private sector employees), public sector employees were excluded from that Law, because it was the almost universal notion of that day that any kind of collective bargaining in the public sector simply had no place. It didn't belong; it didn't fit. There was no more powerful advocate of this position than Franklin D. Roosevelt. It didn't make any difference whether you were Franklin Roosevelt or Calvin Coolidge, liberal or conservative, Republican or Democrat; this was the position of the United States until after World War II. After all, you can't strike against government; if you do, you have an anarchy, because government must remain sovereign.

After the war, some things began to happen, largely led by teachers. I used to kid Joe Manch, at Buffalo, who led the strike of teachers there in 1946. Joe later became Superintendent of Schools there. The Buffalo teachers went out on strike because they didn't like the conditions of employment that the school board was providing. The State Legislature was incensed by this so-called act of anarchy. They passed the Condon-Wadlin Law. It was not a labor relations law, but simply served notice to public employees of the State of New York that, if they struck, they would be fired and could not be re-hired except under certain stringent conditions. The Condon-Wadlin Law was on the books for roughly twenty years and, increasingly, became less and less enforceable. Public employees struck and they struck with increasing impunity. As powerful blocks of public employees would go on strike, they would say something like this to their employer: "Let's be sure, Mr. Employer, that we understand each other. If you try to enforce the Condon-Wadlin Law, we don't come back to work."

That is precisely what happened in 1966, when the subway workers went on strike in New York City and tied New York City up in knots for roughly fourteen days. Mike Quill was the leader, and when he said that very kind of thing to John Lindsay, the incoming Mayor, the Mayor said, "I have to enforce the penalties of the Condon-Wadlin Law." Then Mike Quill said, "Well then, we don't come back to work." It was then that the Legislature wound up giving the transit workers amnesty from their own law.

Then we come to Nelson Rockefeller, who was by that time Governor. He said, "Maybe we had better take another look. Maybe this whole notion, that public sector collective bargaining is not appropriate, needs re-examination." And so he appointed the Taylor Committee.

When we talk about all the task forces he had, I think that this one was typical of the kind of expertise with which he surrounded himself. The Taylor Committee was composed of five men with a combination of 184 years of the best labor relations experience in this Nation. The Chairman of course was George Taylor, as I've mentioned. The only living member is John Dunlop. Later, he went on to become Secretary of Labor — truly one of the giants of the field. David Cole, who died a couple of years ago, was an internationally known arbitrator and labor relations expert. Then there was Dwight Bakke, of Yale, and Fred Harbison, of Princeton. Cornell always upset the Governor, so he did not put someone from Cornell on that panel.

At any rate, he said, "Let's take a new look." They did and they produced the famous Taylor Committee Report in about three months time. Incidentally, I think that's unheard of, also.

And I have never seen a report so directly translated into law. Dick Winfield was the Assistant Counsel in the Governor's Office who was assigned the job of putting this report into law. There were only a couple of things about it that were changed on the way through. The mini-PERB concept was not there, and the de-certification of employees in the event of a strike was not there. The Bar Association reasoned that if you have a strike, with whom do you deal if you decertify the union? With whom do you deal to get them back from the strike? A few things like that were changed. At any rate, the Taylor Law did become the law of our State. That was the atmosphere under which I became Chairman of the Board.

I served as Chairman of the Board for ten years under three governors. Two years before the end of my term, I resigned to take on what amounted to a national consultancy with the Carnegie Corporation for states that were involved in or had passed some kind of public employment labor relations law. And out of that experience, I'd just like to indicate what I think was the Rockefeller vision and legacy.

First of all, I'd like to note that I think the Governor was always one to recognize that we live in a world of change. I think that was evident because we had gone on for several hundred years since our founding saying that collective bargaining did not belong in the public sector. He was always willing to look at changing circumstances — to keep an open mind. He had vision and perspective. We talked a lot about his pragmatism and the "art of the possible." He established a tone of fairness to all the parties: to management, to labor, to government. Governor Wilson has talked about "balance." Nelson had the uncanny ability to be able to look at a problem from all perspectives, to look at all the people involved, at all the different points of view, and to come up with something which he thought was inherently fair to all concerned.

In this spirit the Taylor Law was developed. Over the intervening 15 years this has changed very little. In essence, the Taylor Law concluded that collective bargaining does belong in the public sector, but it has to be different than that of the private sector. It did not accept the right to strike and a great many people — scholars even of that time — still feel that you really can't have any meaningful collective bargaining unless you have the right to strike. That was challenged in the Taylor Law, and I would say that now, after twenty years of experimentation have taken place in this country, it has been proven conclusively that there can be meaningful participation by employees without simply relying on slugging it out on the picket line. What we are doing across the nation is trying all kinds of experiments, and the Taylor Law was certainly one of the first of these. We are experimenting with all kinds of dispute settlement techniques that can be substituted for the right to strike, and this is having a tremendous impact also on the private sector.

When I was a student at Cornell, for example, arbitration was a singular concept. The idea was similar to a court; if you have a dispute, you go before a judge. The judge or jury makes a final decision. Grievance arbitration had been largely developed by George Taylor. Essentially, if employees had grievances, a grievance procedure was developed where the last step would be grievance arbitration. That was it. At least 25 or 30 different kinds of arbitration are now being utilized with all kinds of combinations. The so-called Med-Arb combination (mediation and arbitration), last-offer arbitration, three-choice arbitration, and arbitration by all kinds of tripartite panels are examples. There's every kind of format you can imagine.

I remember, for example, in one of the legislative committees I went before, I recommended that New York State adopt what I called "a three-choice system" of arbitration for teachers. If everything had been done that could possibly be done, after fact-finding and hearings and all the rest, if they still couldn't settle the dispute, then we would go to tri-partite, three-choice arbitration where the arbitration panel would have the right to choose between the employer's last best offer, the employees', and the fact-finder's recommendation. Our Legislature did not adopt that. However, it's interesting that the State of Iowa read that testimony and adopted it, not only for teachers, but for all public employees in the State of Iowa. Iowa has had ten or twelve years of experience with that system. I've been in Iowa a number of times working with them, and I have been amazed to hear employers stand and applaud the law. I never thought I'd hear employers applaud arbitration.

In short, what has happened is that this experimentation which Nelson Rockefeller and his cohorts were willing to engage in has spread throughout the Nation. As I earlier indicated, I have had the chance now to work with many governments resulting from the Carnegie project in which I was involved. I've had the chance to travel from Alaska to Florida and from Maine to California. Many states have copied the Taylor Law almost intact, or sections of it. Florida, the state I am now living in, copied it almost intact. The Constitution there did not draw a line between public employees and private employees, and the court said to the Legislature: You either pass a law or we'll pass one for you. What they did was to copy the Taylor Law.

Thus, Nelson Rockefeller's major assets were his vision and perspective. One might ask the question: when the Taylor Law was hated as much as it was originally — particularly by unions —how in the world did Nelson Rockefeller manage to get the endorsement of labor leaders, especially when he was running against people like Arthur Goldberg, who had originally been counsel to the steel workers? Well, as I look at it, it came out of one of those basic qualities of his — he was willing to look at an issue squarely. He kept that open door; he was willing to talk with everyone. They knew that, even though Nelson didn't agree with all they wanted, he at least could approach controversial issues with an open mind.

The final thing I would point out, in addition to his struggle for fairness, equity, and balance, was his basic belief in negotiations as a system of dealing with controversy. He was a master, in my view, of managing confrontation. He struggled to substitute negotiation for confrontation. He loved to go into a problem situation where there was massive confrontation, get the best minds together, and solve any problem by negotiation. The John

Delury situation was a case in point. I believe that, if Nelson were here, he would still say (when he got John Delury out of jail and negotiated the sanitation settlement), that the resulting reactions were a major reason why he was not able to get the presidential nomination.

He was able to deal with confrontation as a manager. That was a massive asset. I think that in our business we would call him a master mediator. He was able to manage the situation where everyone was mad, where everybody was emotionally upset and disturbed - calling each other names, where emotion had knocked reason out of the window. He was able to relate to that situation, capture reason and bring it back into the situation, and develop an agreement. This is also having a big impact, I think, on the private sector, because I believe that those perspectives are now paving the way for the biggest innovation in United States labor relations since our founding. The thrust is to change our industrial relations system from one of massive confrontation as in the strikes and riots of the 1800's, to a much more cooperative labor/management atmosphere.

If Chrysler goes out of business, labor is hurt as well as management. Douglas Fraser now sits on the Board of Directors of Chrysler, and there is beginning to be a whole different atmosphere — a reduction of confrontation — and a whole different structure in the labor relations picture. I think that is the kind of attitude which Nelson's vision has brought about, and I think as we look down the road, maybe scores or maybe even a hundred years hence, we'll appreciate the kind of vision and perspective he brought to the American industrial relations scene.

I have attended literally hundreds of ceremonies and ceremonial occasions. The one, of course, that stands out in my mind was the Rockefeller memorial service in New York City's Riverside Church. It had to be unusual, when Lionel Hampton and his ensemble were on the platform and the recessional was "Sweet Georgia Brown." The minister said that this was entirely appropriate and I think it was. But the thing that stuck in my mind was when one of the Rockefeller children closed his remarks by saying this: "The world is a little better place because Nelson stopped by." And I think that you will find that the state of industrial relations is better in America — not only in New York State — since Nelson Rockefeller was Governor.

LOUIS LEVINE: Thank you very much, Bob. Now we're going to hear from Mel Osterman about his remembrances dealing with his fond tour of duty, from 1969 to 1974, as the Director of the State Office of Employee Relations (OER).

MELVIN OSTERMAN: A point that occurred to me as Bob was talking (and, indeed, from other speakers as well this morning) was the extent of loyalty that Nelson Rockefeller engendered from his staff. There was a session this morning on the "Governor as Manager," and there was some suggestion that there was a problem defining terms. Just what was a "manager"? Nelson Rockefeller was certainly the most effective manager that I ever met or ever heard of. He could get more out of his staff than almost anybody I know. Somebody said this morning that he made you feel exceptional, that you and he were the only two people in the world, and that was true.

Part of the process of collective negotiations requires long hours. It is a confrontational process; you go to two or three in the morning. There is some mystique that a settlement at four o'clock in the morning is better than one at three-thirty in the afternoon. You put in some long hours while you were bargaining, and every once in a while Nelson Rockefeller would pick up the phone and call my wife and say, "I just wanted you to know that the people of the State appreciate what Mel is doing for them. We are all impressed by his dedication." Well, dammit, you knew his secretary wrote that and handed him a note, but you gave him an awful lot of points, and you were really willing to knock yourself out for somebody who would do something like that.

It is not necessarily flattering to me to suggest that I am venerable. At the same time, I must concede that I have certain of the hallmarks of antiquity. I served as an Assistant Counsel to Governor Rockefeller long before there was a Taylor Law. I served as a Counsel to the Taylor Committee and represented the State of New York in the proceedings before the Public Employment Relations Board which led to the establishment of the present State negotiating structure. As a Special Assistant to the Governor, I represented the State in all of its early negotiations with the unions representing its employees. From 1972 to 1975, I served as the State's Director of Employee Relations. Since that time, although engaged in the private practice of law, the great bulk of my practice has been involved in the representation of local governments — primarily school districts and villages — in collective negotiations under the Taylor Law. That experience has given me some credentials with which to speak of the impact of the Taylor Law upon public sector management.

It is fashionable to recall the opposition of organized labor, particularly in the City of New York, to the very enactment of the Taylor Law. It is a general rule that representatives of public sector unions are more colorful than representatives of management. One recalls, perhaps with fondness, Victor Gottbaum's comment that the Taylor Law was the "bastard offspring of diseased bi-partisanship." You may recall that the Taylor Law was characterized at the time of its enactment by public sector unions as the "RAT bill" ("Rockefeller-Travia Slave Labor"). I can now smile when I remember that I, as a representative of the State, had "all the charm of a southern textile mill owner."

One should not conclude, from the vivid reactions of our State's labor leaders, that public sector management was any more enthusiastic about Governor Rockefeller's commitment to collective negotiations as a method for determining the terms and condition of employment of public employees. Indeed, it probably does not over-state the vigor of their opposition to suggest that many of our State's elected officials viewed collective negotiations as only a short step away from true communism. Words like "invasion of sovereignty" or "usurpation of power" cropped up regularly in at least the private conversations of these officials.

Such a reaction, while perhaps couched in overly florid terms, is understandable. The job of an elected public official never is an easy one. He or she is forced to reconcile a host of competing priorities in what, hopefully, is the public interest. Every public official constantly is required to balance the demands of taxpayers for lower taxes and, simultaneously, for improved services. There never is enough money to fund all of the things government needs to do or might do. It is unlikely that there were many public officials who deliberately sought to depress the wages of public employees as a method of making tax revenues available for more important priorities. Yet, even though inadvertent, it is clear that by the mid-1960's, this had been the consequence of this balancing process.

The Governor's support for what became the Taylor Law made a fundamental change in the methodology by which these competing priorities were to be reconciled. No longer were the wages to be paid to public employees determined by the unilateral — even if benign — determination of the employer. Public employees were given the right to participate — as equals — in the determination of the terms and conditions of their employment. While the Taylor Law denied those employees the right to strike, it required public employers to sit down with the representatives of their employees, to justify their allocation decisions, and to reach agreement as to what wages and benefits should be. This was a profound change in the way government had conducted its business and a real shock to many public officials who, for the first time, became accountable to their employees for a portion of their decision-making process.

We now have had 15 years of experience under the Taylor

Law. I think it is fair to say that the most dire predictions of the advocates on both sides of the negotiating table have not come to pass. The Law has worked well. While organized labor still articulates the denial of the right to strike as a denial of manhood, we need only look at the membership rolls of our State's public sector unions to conclude that, from their standpoint, the Law has been a dramatic success. More than 80 percent of public employees of New York State belong to or are represented by public sector unions. Compare this to the 25 percent of their counterparts in the private sector. The wages of public sector employees have shown dramatic increases since the early days of the Taylor Law.

The benefits to public sector management have been no less great. I would address this point, not as a labor lawyer — one who earns his living from the process — but from the viewpoint of my experience as a public administrator and as a teacher of the process.

It may be difficult to characterize the significant increases in public sector salaries, with a concomitant substantial increase in the expenditure of tax revenues, as an advantage to management. Yet, for years, the low salaries paid to public sector employees served as a significant deterrent to attracting the kind of employees whom we would like to think enter public services. When government is paying 25 percent less than the private sector employer across the street, it will be difficult for government to attract the brightest and the best employees. We rely, for example, upon our public schools for the instruction and training of our future leaders. When college students are making career choices, are they likely to be attracted to public education as a profession if a school teacher is required to start work at $4,000 a year at the same time private industry is paying a secretary $6,000 a year or a plumber $8,000? The ordering of priorities, which resulted in public sector salaries becoming dramatically more competitive, has had significant impact on the quality of the public service.

Even beyond this, there has been a dramatic change in the attitude of public employers toward their employees. One cannot expect an employee suffering from benign neglect to necessarily appreciate the good-faith of his neglector. A result bi-laterally achieved is inherently more satisfactory than one imposed, however humanely, by an employer. The quality of the bargain inherently has an impact upon the morale and commitment of public sector employees.

These are advantages, however subtle, of which every public sector employer has been the beneficiary. There, however, are even more practical benefits to the process of public administration. Consider my experience with the State of New York as an example. Even before the Taylor Law, there was a process of informal negotiations pursuant to which representatives of the Civil Service Employees Association, representing the great bulk of its employees, would make an annual approach to the Director of the Budget for what they regarded as appropriate salaries for State employees. On another front, representatives of CSEA actively lobbied before the State Legislature in an effort to achieve legislative improvements in the terms and conditions of State employment. Tier I of our State's Retirement System, which was legislated long before there were collective negotiations, is a testament to the effectiveness of this process.

But salaries and even fringe benefits are only one part of the personnel practices of any public employer. With respect to other areas — attendance and leave policies or general personnel practices, for example — the State of New York was in a shambles prior to the enactment of the Taylor Law.

For some time, the Department of Civil Service had promulgated an Attendance Rules Manual which purported to set forth many of the personnel practices by which State managers were expected to regulate working conditions of State employees. Other rules were promulgated by the Division of the Budget and the Department of Audit and Control. Yet, in real life, there was little effective control over the administration of those policies. State agency heads had created an informal category, often described as "administrative leave," by which agency heads arrogated unto themselves the right to grant paid and unpaid leave for such purposes as they deemed appropriate. While thousands of hours were spent on union activities by various officials of CSEA and other unions, there was no effective control over the number or nature of those activities. There was little basis for comparing personnel practices in one agency with those in another. In many ways, each of the State agencies operated as an independent feudal fiefdom, more often than not making up its own ground rules as it went along. Indeed, in our first negotiations with CSEA under the Taylor Law, we had no really hard data on even the number of employees the State employed!

Enactment of the Taylor Law and the onset of collective negotiations made significant changes in these practices. A State agency was created, the Office of Employee Relations, with a broad range of responsibilities for all aspects of the employment relationship between the State as an employer and its employees. The Director of Employee Relations was made part of Governor Rockefeller's immediate staff, bringing together all of the personnel of the Executive Chamber to deal with the State's employment relationships.

Collective negotiations vastly improved the State's record-keeping practices. It was no longer satisfactory to argue at the negotiating table that we did not know how many State employees there were or what their terms and conditions of employment might be. Certainly, it was embarrassing in the early negotiating sessions for CSEA to point out to the State's negotiators that a particular personnel practice existed in one or more State agencies. And, they did so with embarrassing regularity.

To deal with these embarrassments, the Governor's Negotiating Committee, and subsequently the Director of Employee Relations, found it necessary to take a much greater role in centralizing responsibility for the State's personnel practices. The mere fact that we were negotiating what the State's personnel practices *should be*, required the State administration to start from a premise of what those practices *were*. Beyond this, the mere fact that those practices were negotiated and reduced to writing established parameters which gave the practices an enforceability which did not exist before.

In many cases, practices CSEA claimed to exist, which were regarded as abusive or improper by the State administration, were eliminated from the written agreement. The concept, for example, of administrative leave vanished with the onset of collective negotiations. Limitations were imposed upon previously unlimited category leave. Guidelines were established for many fringe benefits which previously had been administered only by whim and caprice. Deviations in practices among State agencies were eliminated. We now had achieved, with the conclusion of collective negotiations, a single document — a collective agreement — which set forth exactly how much sick leave and personal leave were to be provided to State employees, the mechanisms by which overtime was to be computed, and the amounts the State would pay to employees for travel reimbursement. In short, the bi-lateral process of collective negotiations forced the State — in the vernacular — to "get its act together."

It is possible to argue that many of these improvements in the State's personnel practices resulted merely from the passage of time. Experience with another unit of State government, the State judiciary, suggests that such an analysis is incorrect. On April 1, 1977, as the result of the passage of Chapter 966 of the Laws of 1976, the State became the employer of each of the ten thousand non-judicial employees of the Unified Court System. Although the Office of Court Administration had existed for many years before, it found, quite suddenly, that it had the responsibility, not for twenty-five hundred employees, but for ten thousand. I was asked in 1978 to represent the Office of Court Administration in negotiations with two thousand of those employees employed in the City of New York.

I entered upon that assignment with a sense of *deja vu.* The Taylor Law had been in place for ten years. Although the Executive Branch by this time had made significant progress in improving its personnel practices, these improvements had not been shared by the State judiciary. I found myself, as I had ten years before in the Executive Branch, in a situation where the State did not know the number of its employees, what they were paid, or what their terms and conditions of employment were. Unrecorded and often improper personnel practices abounded in each of the four hundred negotiating units in which court employees were represented. It took several rounds of negotiations with the employee organizations representing these employees before a sense of order was restored to this significant segment of State employment.

The improvement in personnel practices experienced by the State has been shared by almost every other public employer in this State, however small the employer. Collective negotiations under the Taylor Law inherently constitute an adversary process. To participate effectively in the process requires both sides to assess not only where they *should be* but where they are. While some may argue that individual benefits of public employees are excessive or abusive, for the first time we know what they are, at least, and have a mechanism for changing them in the future. This has made a fundamental change in the processes of public administration. It is a change which has redounded to the benefit not only of public administrators but to the public they serve.

Collective negotiations have offered public employers the opportunity to undertake a variety of experiments, which hold out the possibility of dramatic change in public administration. During the first years of the Taylor Law, the State, for the first time, imposed a variety of controls on its own personnel practices. During my tenure as Director of Employee Relations, we negotiated and set into place a negotiated disciplinary procedure which gave State managers an effective tool to control aberrant and improper employee behavior. In one year, the number of disciplinary proceedings against State employees increased from 75 to 2,000. The State has been able to implement a program of progressive discipline by which improper conduct is corrected at an early stage and a State employee, who otherwise might become a serious problem, is returned as a productive member of the work force. In 1974, we entered into an experiment in productivity bargaining by which the State and its employees would work together to improve the efficiency of State service, and the employees would share some of the benefits of those improvements. In later years, the State experimented with a system of intensified evaluation of its employees and the possibility of rewarding exemplary performance with cash incentives. While not all of those experiments were successful, without collective negotiation, it is doubtful that they even would have been attempted.

The purpose of today's program is to review Nelson Rockefeller's contributions to this process. His role was critical to its success. It is a fundamental rule of life for politicians that, when a problem arises, the first solution is to throw a committee at it and hope that it will go away, at least for a period of time. That is not what Governor Rockefeller did with respect to the growing pressure of public employees for a greater role in the determination of their terms and conditions of employment. The Taylor Committee was created and its work completed in little more than three months. Its report, even fifteen years later, remains one of the hallmark documents in the field of public administration. Legislation implementing the report's recommendations was introduced almost simultaneously with the issuance of the report. Governor Rockefeller did not rest merely with the recommendations of this committee. He worked long and hard in the succeeding year to overcome the objections to the new law. Without Governor Rockefeller's relationship with Assembly Speaker Anthony Travia, a relationship which both parties worked very hard at, the law simply never would have been enacted.

The Governor's role did not end with the enactment of the law. His commitment extended to making the law work. He encouraged his staff to turn their attention to problems of employee relations and to put into place management teams which would permit the State to fulfill its obligations under the new law. The Governor supported the efforts of Abe Lavine, the State's first Director of Employee Relations, to create a new class of State employees, the Employee Relations Officers, to be installed in each State agency, and to give them a special employee relations capacity. He supported the efforts of the Director to staff the Office of Employee Relations with the best possible professional employees, regardless of political affiliation.

When I was Director, as Abe Lavine had been before me, I had essentially unlimited access to the Governor. If I needed to see him, he would see me, and he would see me promptly. One of the hardest parts of the job (and I suspect this was not true just for me but it was probably true for all the commissioners), the toughest part of the job, was knowing when you had to ask. That is, what you could do on your own and what you had to have his authority to do. But if you needed to see him, he was available. It might not be the longest conversation in the world, but he treated his staff with a significant amount of respect. I guess there were some of us who got too testy and got slapped down for it. But if you needed to see him, if you had a decent track record and didn't abuse that privilege, you got to see him; he gave you the support that you needed.

The Governor was committed to appointing the best possible people to the Public Employee Relations Board, the State agency charged with the administration of the law — members who had practical familiarity with the operations of government. He selected them for their experience and expertise, not to repay political obligations. The Governor supported the efforts of Robert Helsby to bring together his truly dedicated and competent staff. Perhaps even more importantly, the Governor determined that members of his staff should go out of their way to respect the independence of the new agency. That was not necessarily a foregone conclusion. PERB was established not only to oversee the administration of the law; it was empowered to judge and make effective decisions concerning the conduct of the State as an employer in collective negotiations. Many of PERB's decisions did not go in the direction that the State administration would have preferred. At an early stage, PERB enjoined the State from proceeding in collective negotiations with the Civil Service Employees Association. It established a pattern of bargaining units significantly different from that which the State had recommended. On a number of occasions, it found that the State had violated its obligations under the law.

It would have been easy to impose the majesty of the State upon PERB in an effort to insure that its decisions were more supportive of positions taken by the State. We were enjoined by the Governor from doing so. We were told that the agency would not succeed, nor would the law it supervised have a chance of success, if PERB was, or was perceived as a tool of the Executive Branch.

During my tenure as Director, I had essentially unlimited access to the Governor for guidance as to the positions we were taking in collective negotiations. In short, the Governor did not merely give lip service to the law he had brought into being. He cared deeply about its success. He was willing to allocate the resources and his own time and effort to make the process work.

Whatever you may think of Nelson Rockefeller's political views, the Taylor Law today is a testament to the intelligence and commitment of a dedicated public servant. I had the opportunity for a number of years to share a small part of Nelson Rockefeller's service to the people of the State of New York. It is a privilege that I will always treasure.

LOUIS LEVINE: Thank you. Our next presenter/reactor is Professor Joseph Zimmerman, professor of government, political scientist, and former Research Director of the Committee on Transportation.

JOSEPH ZIMMERMAN: I approached the Rockefeller administration from a different perspective than our other speakers. Since the spring of 1965, my public employment at the Graduate School of Public Affairs has been with the Legislature, either as a staff director or research director for joint committees or committees in one house. So I viewed the whole process to some extent from a legislative perspective. I approached the Rockefeller legacy from two aspects that have not yet been brought up.

I tried to take a comprehensive view of the Governor's role in labor-related matters and, among other things, I point to his use of the executive veto to disallow a number of bills. It has been stated that 1965 was the best year in terms of the Governor's relationships with the Legislature, but, on the other hand, 1965 was the year in which he set the all-time record of any Governor, in any state, in terms of the percentage of bills as well as the absolute number of bills reaching his desk which were vetoed. There are reasons for that. That veto record by itself does not necessarily suggest that the Governor had bad relations with the Legislature.

VETOES OF LABOR-RELATED BILLS

Governor Rockefeller holds the record for the largest absolute and relative numbers of vetoes of bills passed by the Legislature. He disapproved 34.6 percent (567) of the 1,641 bills reaching his desk in 1965.[1] Labor-related bills invalidated by the Governor fall into three principal categories: pension and retirement bills, bills which infringe on local discretionary authority, and measures sponsored by private interest groups. Many of the pension and retirement bills also involve infringement of local discretionary authority. These bills commonly apply only to New York City.

Pension and Retirement Measures

Illustrative of actions taken by the Governor during his first year in office was his veto of a bill increasing retirement benefits for uniformed members of city fire departments who continued in service beyond the minimum period of service elected by them for retirement.[2] The bill was tailored to apply principally to New York City firemen and was disapproved because it was actuarially unsound and contained other defects. A second bill disallowed in 1959 would have eliminated the requirement of mandatory membership in the Retirement System for those on "Social Security" and, in addition, would have allowed a member to withdraw his accumulated contributions every 15 days.[3]

In 1960, Rockefeller disallowed a bill amending the New York City Administrative Code to permit members of the New York City Teachers' Retirement System to claim service for time spent in study under the Federal "G.I. Bill of Rights" while the members were on leave of absence without pay.[4] In 1960, Governor Rockefeller also agreed with Mayor Robert F. Wagner of New York City that a bill should be vetoed, because it was discriminatory in not covering all city employees and would result in a substantial increase in city expenditures.[5]

Governor Rockefeller, in 1962, invalidated seven mandated pension bills — affecting New York City's teachers, policemen, and firemen — because of the cost mandated upon the city.[6] On the other hand, the Governor approved the Mitchell Bill mandating "long overdue additional benefits for retired New York City school teachers," because there was no evidence that the Mayor intended to act to solve the problem.[7]

The following year, the Governor rejected a bill, opposed by Mayor Wagner, that would have mandated a supplemental retirement allowance for each member of the New York City Teachers' Retirement System who retired between September 2, 1956 and February 15, 1958.[8] This bill obviously was designed to cover only "special" retired teachers. In the same year, Rockefeller also vetoed a bill mandating a retirement plan at guaranteed half-pay after 25 years service in the State Employees' Retirement System for sheriffs and their subalterns.[9]

Governor Rockefeller also vetoed four bills that would have provided that retirement benefits for police, and firemen in one instance, under various pension plans, be based on compensation earned during one year of service rather than the present average of three years' salary.[10]

Local Discretionary Authority

Interest groups unable to achieve their goals on the local government level often turn to the State Legislature with a request that the Legislature mandate local governments to initiate an action favorable to the interest groups.[11] If enacted into laws, these mandates can restrict severely the discretionary authority of local governments and create serious financial problems for substate units.

In 1959, Governor Rockefeller vetoed a bill permitting police officers to live outside their employing municipalities because the bill would not allow municipalities to establish their own residency rules to meet their particular needs and would discriminate in favor of policemen as against other municipal employees.[12]

Private Interest Groups

One of the first major issues attacked by Governor Rockefeller in the labor relations area was union racketeering, and the Governor was successful in persuading the Legislature to approve his program bill to deal with racketeering in labor unions.[13]

Relative to the technical difficulties surrounding the problem of the application of the labor law to farmers, the Governor, in 1959, vetoed a bill authorizing the Industrial Commissioner to revoke, suspend, or refuse to renew the registration of a farm labor contractor or a crew leader who breached contracts with farmers, when it had been established judicially that such a person had given false information about the terms and availability of migrant laborers.[14] The Governor was convinced the bill was biased against the crew leader and the bill would be unworkable.

Another vexatious problem cognate to farm labor contractors was illustrated by a bill amending the Civil Practice Act relating to labor disputes involving transportation of farm products. Farmers and farm groups had been plagued with the threat of various forms of strikes and work stoppages, seriously affecting the harvesting and transportation of perishable farm products. This bill attempted to deal with "this unique problem of the farmer" by an amendment to the Civil Practice Act, commonly known as the "Little Norris-LaGuardia Act," and an anti-union injunction law. Rockefeller listed five ways by which the bill failed to afford protection to the farmers. He also adduced four items distinctly unfavorable to labor, in that the bill would permit a court to issue an injunction in labor disputes involving transportation of perishables and dairy products without giving the union an opportunity to be heard before an order was issued.

Rockefeller was constrained to disallow the bill.[15]

A final illustration of the Governor's analytical powers is revealed by his veto of a pair of bills sponsored by barbers and their professional cousins in hairdressing and cosmetology. Under provisions of the first bill, registration of the barbering industry would have been shifted from the Office of the Secretary of State to a newly created, seven member Board of Barber Examiners, six of whom must have been licensed barbers for at least ten years prior to their appointment. The Governor recited Governor Thomas E. Dewey's 1946 approval message of a bill designed to protect the public from incompetent practitioners and the right to engage in the trade. The Governor ruled that public regulation was preferred to private regulation of the industry and indicated he disallowed the bill because it: removed the apprenticeship route to becoming a barber; blanketed into the trade, without an examination, those who had been practicing without a license prior to July 1, 1961; deleted from existing law the reciprocal licensing features granted to barbers from other states; and required part-time inspectors to be appointed from among practicing barbers licensed for five years, thereby subjecting the inspector to a clear conflict of interest.

The second bill would have amended the General Business Law so as to make it practically impossible for a licensed hairdresser to treat patrons in their homes. Such a requirement seemed quite unreasonable to Rockefeller. While the bill afforded licensing authorities the opportunity of closer supervision and inspection, the bill ignored qualified licensees who could not, for a variety of reasons, work regular hours. Furthermore, the Governor pointed out that this bill effectively could transfer the regulation of the hairdressing and cosmetology industry from the present public authorities to the owners of licensed beauty parlors.[16]

TAYLOR LAW LEGACY

Soon after assuming office, Governor Rockefeller became acutely aware of the shortcomings of the Condon-Wadlin Act, and in 1963 he signed a bill providing milder sanctions for violations of the Act. In his 1965 State of the State Message, the Governor recommended that the milder temporary sanctions, approved in 1963, be made permanent. The AFL-CIO was opposed to the Governor's proposal and was successful in having the Condon-Wadlin Act repealed. The unions also persuaded the Legislature to approve a watered-down version of a labor law which Rockefeller rejected as unworkable.[17]

During the 1966 session, the solons did not find time, or perhaps they lacked the inclination, to deal with the urgent matter of revising the Condon-Wadlin Act, except to enact a stop-gap bill to head off a new transit strike in New York City. Governor Rockefeller, however, appointed a special panel of national leaders in the field of labor relations to make recommendations for legislation for the protection of the public from illegal strikes. The final report of the special panel, chaired by Professor George W. Taylor of the University of Pennsylvania, was made public on April 7, 1966.[18]

The principal proposal contained in the Governor's 1967 State of the State Message was enactment of a new public employees' act embodying the recommendations of the Taylor Committee. The legislature responded affirmatively and enacted the Taylor Law.[19]

An illustration of Governor Rockefeller's firm adherence to the Taylor Law was his disapproval of a bill providing each employee of Manhattan State Hospital, on Ward's Island in New York City, toll-free use of the Triborough Bridge when traveling to or from work in their private automobiles, because the bill would change the terms and conditions of employment for one group of State employees outside of the agreement negotiated by the Governor's Negotiating Committee and the Civil Service Employees Association.[20]

The prohibition of strikes contained in the Taylor Law has not been totally effective, as there have been an average of 20 strikes a year, including an occasional major strike by teachers and sanitation employees in New York City. Nevertheless, 99 percent of the contracts are negotiated successfully each year without a strike.

One can conclude, without fear of contradiction, that the Taylor Law has increased the political power of public service unions in general. In particular, the political clout of public employee unions was increased by a 1977 law authorizing a union representing State employees to request the withholding of an agency shop fee from the paychecks of non-union members in the bargaining unit.[21] The law contains a provision requiring a union to return, upon the demand of an employee, a part of the agency shop fee representing "the employee's pro rata share of expenditures by the organization in aid of activities only incidentally related to terms and conditions of employment." Unions have been slow in providing refunds upon requests and often refund only small amounts, necessitating a court challenge by the requesting employee.

The additional millions of dollars generated by the agency

shop fee are utilized for political purposes, with funds being given in large measure to incumbent legislators who voted for the Agency Shop Law and its extension. While macing and political assessments are illegal, the agency shop can be viewed as an indirect and legal form of macing from the standpoint of public employees required to pay the agency shop fee.[22]

SUMMARY AND CONCLUSIONS

Governor Rockefeller found the executive veto to be a most effective weapon in protecting the public against labor-related bills conferring special pension and retirement benefits upon individuals, infringing local discretionary authority, or bestowing inappropriate regulatory powers upon private interest groups. Since his retirement from office in 1973, there has been a decline in the employment of the veto power by the governor, with the sharpest decline occurring during the administration of Governor Hugh L. Carey. Without a detailed analysis of all bills signed into law since Rockefeller resigned from office, one can not determine whether labor-related bills that would have been vetoed by Governor Rockefeller have in fact become law.

While Governor Rockefeller is not responsible for the Agency Shop Law, the Law is a product of the Taylor Law. If the Taylor Law had not been enacted by the Legislature and signed by Governor Rockefeller, it is improbable that an Agency Shop Law, with all its political ramifications, would be on the statute books of the State of New York today.

LOUIS LEVINE: Ladies and gentlemen, the floor is open for questions.

ROBERT HELSBY: Not a question, just a comment. I wanted to tell Mel that Jerry Wurf's characterization of him was relatively mild. The first meeting I had with him, Wurf's first question was, "When did you come out of the woodwork?" After that he got obscene. We learned later, after that first meeting, that there was something going on over at the Mansion, and I had to talk to the Governor and related this sort of casually. We learned later on — after we had an established relationship — that the Governor had gone to Meany, related what had happened that day, and Meany got back to Wurf.

MEL OSTERMAN: Abe, when he met my wife this morning, commented that he had done me a substantial disservice, because he had suggested that I succeed him as Director of Employee Relations. He suggested perhaps that that was the biggest grudge I had against him. He's wrong. He made, really, one of the dumbest decisions that anybody ever made. Back in 1969 — I guess it was — we decided that we would negotiate concurrently, during the pendency of the election, with both CSEA and with AFSCME. We conducted two simultaneous sets of negotiations. They were extraordinary, and we had to keep the pacing of the negotiations equal.

There was a time when the AFSCME people had TV cameras outside of the door of the negotiating room. They would rush to the door with an offer. We kept saying, "We won't make you an offer unless you agree not to go on TV." It was a very ugly scene.

We finally reached agreement with CSEA on Friday night, about two o'clock in the morning. We hadn't finished with AFSCME. We didn't have a session with AFSCME until Monday morning. We enjoined upon CSEA that they had to keep it quiet; they could not talk about it. We worked with some of them over the weekend.

At that point, I was commuting back and forth from New York City. I went home. I came back on Monday, and we were supposed to go finish up with AFSCME that morning. I came into the office and Abe said, "Gee, Mel, I think I had better finish up with CSEA. You go down and talk to AFSCME."

I walk in, and Jerry Wurf is there. We didn't expect Jerry Wurf to be there that day, and Jerry said, "Gee, the rumors are you settled with CSEA." And I said, "Oh no." I knew that Abe was back in the office finishing up with CSEA. I didn't really know what the status of the negotiations were. I continued to dance; I probably lied. Two o'clock, three, three-thirty — the red head edition of the *Knick News* came out, and the headline across the front: "CSEA Settles with the State." I have rarely had as bad an hour in my life!

MILTON MUSICUS: I just want to add to what Bob Helsby mentioned as to how he was selected for his job. I never really found out how the Governor selected people for jobs. I think that if you were ensconced in a fairly secure berth, he would yank you out and assign you somewhere else. That was my experience, when I was designated as Director of the Mental Hygiene Facilities Improvement Corporation. I was handed the legislation, a $500 million appropriation and told to "go ahead and build." I did not know what I was going to be doing.

Soon thereafter, I was amused by Bob's predicament. Bob came to my house one day and said: "Milton, I'm being offered this job. How do I get out of it?" I said, "You better take it whether you like it or not. If the Governor offered you a job, I think you would be criticizing his judgment if you said you didn't want it." Bob accepted the job offer, and I wondered often whether Bob did express his concerns. The Governor's offer of a job was a challenge to forge new programs — which few could reject.

ROBERT HELSBY: But, you see, Milton, that's a good example of how he knew so much more about Helsby than I knew about Helsby. Because in retrospect, if I had not been forced into that, if I hadn't taken it — as I look back on my career — I would have missed so much.

MILTON MUSICUS: Bob, every one of us experienced that. Since when was I a construction man? And yet, I directed, ultimately, a construction program of two billion dollars, and then was selected by the Mayor of New York to direct the City's construction programs. The Governor did indeed change our lives. And, to this day, I don't know how he selected some of us for these positions.

I observed him in his relations with labor leaders. The one I knew best was Peter Brennan, who headed the construction worker unions. I observed the way the Governor dealt with Peter at meetings. What did a Rockefeller have in his background in common with Peter Brennan? Nothing. But he made Peter feel as if he was the greatest guy there ever was. I attended meetings of other chief executives who also awarded tremendous amounts of construction work, contracts that cost billions of dollars. If the purpose of these meetings was to establish rapprochement with leaders such as Peter Brennan, it didn't work. I don't know all the reasons that brought the Governor and union leaders into close working relationships, but I do know that when Rockefeller spoke to Peter they were equals. When I observed the other chief executives, they could not speak with the labor leaders as equals, and they were not able to get the support of the unions.

ROBERT HELSBY: You'll recall that when we started out with the Taylor Law, the Governor designated a committee composed of Ursa Poston, Norman Hurd, and, I think, Bobbie Douglass. That was the committee that was to handle labor relations for the Governor. You can imagine, first of all, just the problem of getting that group together. I'll never forget the day I went to the Governor's office, and this illustrates his willingness to listen.

It was just the two of us, and I said, "Governor, if you'll allow, you cannot conduct labor relations with a committee. With

160,000 or 180,000 employees, whatever it is, you ought to have a vice-president, as General Motors and other large companies have, for labor relations." And he created the Office of Employee Relations.

I think that OER in New York State was the first such agency in any government I know of in the country. Now virtually all of the major states have them; universities have them; governments have them. That's the kind of receptivity he had. If you would make a case, he'd listen.

Then there is the business of autonomy. Of course I was in a very good position. (Somebody used to remind me, "Look, you didn't want the job, so if you lose it, big deal.") We were a fledgling agency. We didn't really know what we were doing.

On the business of the State bargaining unit question — the question of: What kind of unit should there be in the State government? We knew that New York City had simply tried to follow the private sector model, and they very quickly had four hundred bargaining units in New York City. How would you like to be one employer with four hundred units? Well, we knew we didn't want that.

The Legislature gave us certain criteria. We established units that nobody asked for. They challenged that in court, and, of course, we had some 28 unions on our doorstep wanting what they called "a piece of the action."

But Nelson understood what our agency had to be, as probably no one else in the country did. He understood that if the independence of the agency was destroyed, then you destroyed the system. You don't have a referee or umpire of perceived integrity.

And also consider the other aspect of it: that speaking in political terms, this was an advantage to him as Governor. Case: Fire-fighters in New York City came to an agreement, and the *New York Times* and the *News* came barreling in and said to John Lindsay, "What's in the agreement?" And he said, "I won't tell you until it's ratified. You know the problems before ratification, upsetting the ratification vote and so on." The newspapers said, "Hold it, this is the public sector. It's taxpayer money, we have a right to know what's in that agreement." They came to the Governor and said "This is all wrong." What did the Governor do? He dropped it in PERB's lap and said, "We don't know what is appropriate for the public to know and when." And we made a study. The study's on record. We distributed it to all the parties, but, you see, if he hadn't had that kind of autonomous agency, he couldn't have done that. And he understood that.

MILTON MUSICUS: There is a common thread in all work

assignments the Governor made. He gave a tremendous amount of autonomy, and he expected results overnight or last night. If you wish to talk about hours of work, you should have been there the first year, when we started at 7:30 in the morning and got home after midnight! I was brought in to work on the reorganization of State government, but I was told that during the day I had other responsibilities. I was supposed to direct the reorganization study at night!

LOUIS LEVINE: It's interesting to note the comments regarding the trade union movement and the Taylor Law. The ones who most benefited from the Taylor Law — the State, county, and municipal employees — never supported the Governor in any of the three election efforts. They got the most out of him in terms of this law, state-wide, and they never supported him. It's most intriguing to look at that. Some of the others vacillated; some years they supported him, in others they didn't. That group never supported him.

And to this day if you ever talk to Gotbaum, he still becomes violent on the subject. He still talks about the "RAT Law," and he still talks about all of the negative aspects of the Law, even though he knows the benefits he has gotten from this Law. Without it there would not be a "District Council 37," there would not be a CSEA - none of those things would have taken place. He knows what he's gotten, and yet he continues to deny it. So, the benefits sometimes are given to people, but don't always expect that you're going to get paid back for it. In the labor movement, that's a given. The more you do for someone, the less you should expect back in return.

ROBERT HELSBY: Isn't that true in a lot of areas though? I think we have assumed that because we do things for people, they'll be grateful and support us. I think all of us have been victims of that. We've done a lot for certain individuals, and we've gotten a kick in the head for it. If you aren't careful, you become cynical. And you find yourself saying, I'll never do anything for anybody again. You can't do that. You do a job well to the best of your abilities.

I'm not quite sure I understood it when George Meany was as much of a pro-Rockefeller man as he was. Incidentally, I'll never forget the time I got in the middle of a George Meany — Richard Nixon — Nelson Rockefeller — Malcolm Wilson — Norman Hurd fiasco. It was on one subject, one very easy subject, and it involved AFSCME. The question was whether they were going to have an in-person ballot or a mail ballot in the elections in the Mental

Hygiene Unit. Very simply, CSEA felt that if they could have a mail-ballot election, they could win it, and AFSCME felt that *they* could win it with the other procedure.

Mel Osterman was in the middle of that — the whole business. It was a very good example of the kind of high-level pressure on all kinds of people that can arise. Nelson was able to keep all of that in perspective. He was not about to pressure my Board to try to get us to do something that he felt we ought to do. He respected the integrity and the autonomy of the Board, because, if you destroy that, you destroy the whole system. That is the thing that has been copied, and I have been able to work with other states around the nation on that kind of concept.

JOSEPH ZIMMERMAN: Could I ask Alan Miller if he might comment, from the standpoint of the Commissioner of the agency with the most employees during the period, as to what impact it had on him as the manager?

ALAN MILLER: My recollections are many — both as the Commissioner and also as the individual trying to sort it out. It was a very complex law and I think many of us had mixed feelings. The idea of finding some orderly and useful, effective way for the managers of State programs to be able to work with representatives of the employee unions, is something that I was entirely sympathetic to and had been improvising ways of doing, even before the Taylor Law — but it was improvisational and amateurish. Clearly the Taylor Law accelerated the process. We had to become better at it.

The kind of structure that developed at the State level with the Office of Employee Relations was very quickly, almost simultaneously as I remember, paralleled by the development of some competent capacity within our own department to do the same. I think there was an immediate increase in our abilities to do, more professionally, what we had been struggling to do more amateurishly.

Of course, it's hard for me to think of any of it without putting aside the anguish that we all went through as a result of one of the first tests of the Taylor Law. A dispute between two of the employee unions took place over the corpus of our department, which led to perhaps the first, and one of the most massive, public employee strikes in New York State history.

ROBERT HELSBY: That was probably one of the most difficult hours I put in, and this involved AFSCME, because at one o'clock in the morning, Jerry Wurf — who was there — let it be known that if he could get the kind of unit structure he wanted out of PERB, then he would call off the strike scheduled for the next morning at eight o'clock in Mental Hygiene. That was a tough hour, and yet, really, I guess like Harry Truman said about the firing of MacArthur, to me it was very simple. I had no problem with it at all and moved very quickly. If we succumbed to any pressure, whether it be Jerry Wurf or the Governor or anybody else (there are no secrets in labor relations), everybody would know about it before the sun had set and the integrity of our Board was out the window. I knew after all the hearings — 6,000 pages of testimony — that what Jerry Wurf was seeking was essentially the kind of unit structure we were going to decide upon. It would have been very easy for me to have said, "Well, this is what you're going to get." But I couldn't do that, because that would have been seen as a forced decision based on that kind of pressure rather than on its objectivity and merit. That's the Board down the drain.

ALAN MILLER: It was very interesting, dealing with the event itself, finding that it was something that was survivable, and then all of the work of learning what to do afterwards. If the Law and the Board survived that, it seemed to me they were viable.

ROBERT HELSBY: If it had not been for a Governor with that kind of vision — that kind of perception — we couldn't have done the kind of things we did, because we knew we had the backing of somebody who understood.

COMMENT

It's fine for us to talk about the impact of the Taylor Law here at the State level. It's been an interesting discussion. I wish we would pursue a little more about the private sector. If there's any outcome that comes immediately to mind in the Rockefeller administration, that had a state-wide impact from which that State itself almost was divorced, it was the Taylor Act. As you were talking, I thought to go from the extreme of the State to the absurd of the local school board. And I happen to have been president of a school board that particular year. To try to negotiate and to try to make some of these decisions at that level was interesting and less dramatic, but nonetheless set a stage at the local level that probably transcended what was evolving at the State level. If you're focusing on the Rockefeller period — on the impact of it — I think this is an area in which the impact on the localities exceeded the impact on the State itself. Perhaps there is no other major program of which you can say that.

ROBERT HELSBY: I think that's probably right, but I'd still like to ask, "What is the option?" As I mentioned, teachers led the way, not only in New York State, but across the nation, in terms of upheaval — the strikes. They were wanting — they were seeking some kind of meaningful participation in the determination of their conditions of employment.

There are ten states in the country that have no law at all, and I've been in virtually all of them. If you come to the conclusion, that they don't have collective bargaining, you're wrong. In the State of Colorado, when I visited some time ago, there were one hundred and twenty-five school districts and eighty-two contracts. How did they get them? They had no state law. They got them by jungle warfare — not a systematic, orderly procedure. In fact, that was one of Rockefeller's great strengths: he was willing to tackle any kind of a problem going. He was a master of handling confrontation. He'd take on anything and try to put it into some kind of an orderly process.

MELVIN OSTERMAN: One of the things that I'm proudest of, in a strange way, is a statute that doesn't exist anymore. When I was in the Governor's Counsel's office, we had a series of strikes in our non-profit hospitals. We had a law in New York State for a hundred and fifty years, that employees of non-profit hospitals could not strike. Leon Davis was organizing the hospital employees, who were probably the most oppressed class of employees in the State. They were paid dreadful wages.

The Governor saw the problem and was willing to sponsor a law which granted collective bargaining rights. It was the first law in the country which provided for resolution of these disputes by arbitration. It was a dramatic and important law. It's now obsolete because the National Labor Relations Act has pre-empted the field, but this was something that had never been done before. He was going to try it and follow through with it.

FOOTNOTES

[1] For details, see Joseph F. Zimmerman, *The Government and Politics of New York State* (New York: New York University Press, 1981), pp 200-04. For a general analysis of the use of the veto power in New York State from colonial times to 1973, see Frank W. Prescott and Joseph F. Zimmerman, *The Politics of the Veto of Legislation in New York State*, 2 vols. (Washington, D.C.: University Press of America, 1980).

[2] *Public Papers of Nelson A. Rockefeller: Fifty-Third Governor of the State of New York*, pp. 338-339, (1959).

[3] *Ibid.*, pp. 156-157.

[4] *Public Papers*, 1960, pp. 316-317.

[5] *Ibid.*, pp. 196.

[6] *Public Papers*, 1962, pp. 341-342.

[7] *Ibid.*, pp. 492-493.

[8] *Public Papers*, 1963, pp. 296.

[9] *Ibid.*, pp. 291-292.

[10] *Public Papers*, 1969, pp. 550-552.

[11] For an analysis of the problem of mandates in the fifty states, see Joseph F. Zimmerman, *State Mandating of Local Expenditures* (Washington, D.C.: United States Advisory Commission on Intergovernmental Relations, 1978) New York State had the largest number of mandates among the fifty states.

[12] *Public Papers*, 1959, pp. 389-390.

[13] *Ibid.*, pp. 177-178.

[14] *Ibid.*, pp. 280-281.

[15] *Ibid.*, 1959, pp. 360-362.

[16] *Public Papers*, 1961, pp. 294-295 and 406-407.

[17] *Public Papers*, 1965, pp. 277-278.

[18] *Public Papers*, 1966, pp. 767 and 877-929.

[19] *Public Papers*, 1967, pp. 17-26.

[20] *Public Papers*, 1968, pp. 278-279.

[21] *New York Laws of 1977*, Chap. 677-78. The "agency shop" is a requirement that non-members of a union must pay an agency shop fee equal to union dues.

[22] See: *New York Civil Service Law*, Section 107(3) (McKinney 1973), and New York Election Law, Section 17-156 (McKinney 1978).

Chapter VIII

Innovations in Public Finance

FRANK WILLE: It's a great pleasure to be able to introduce Ed Kresky as the theme setter for this particular panel session in public finance. Ed and I first knew each other, when he was a Program Associate in the Secretary's office, and I was in the office of the Governor's Counsel. I only got involved with some of the details of legislation, and some of the ideas connected with the State University Construction Fund and Mental Hygiene Facilities Improvement Fund, the South Mall, and things like that, but Ed saw the bigger picture. Since I only had a little piece of this mosaic, I am very interested in hearing the things I didn't know when I was in Counsel's office. At the moment, Ed Kresky is a partner in the firm of Wertheim and Company, and he has had a very active role in a number of public activities since he left State government. I don't know if he still serves on the Metropolitan Transit Authority (MTA) or Municipal Assistance Corporation (MAC), but he's had a very active career in public finance as well as other things since we've been in Albany. So I introduce Ed Kresky, and we'll hear all there was to know at the time about public finance.

EDWARD KRESKY: No, I'm not with the MTA, but it isn't much better than that. I don't know where the great deficits are, but I hasten to add to those sitting on the right that the next half hour will produce just enough hot air so that the chill in the room will disappear. This is some topic — "Innovations in Public Finance"! When I got the programs for this meeting and reunion, I understood why "Innovations in Public Finance" was on the program, but Mary and I were really astounded by one point in the program, which we heard yesterday. It was on "Nelson Rockefeller as Manager." We thought about "Nelson Rockefeller as Manager" and observed: What are we doing here in Albany to try to learn about that? We thought he was an able executive and political leader, but a manager? — no.

But as I see it, the trip to Albany and the program Norm devised was very sound. We learned an awful lot yesterday, and I learned it from my former professor and dean and my mentor for many years in the Rockefeller Administration, Bill Ronan, and from my friend, Warren Anderson. They were wise enough to look in the dictionary. For those of you who missed it, I think Warren found it in the *Random House Dictionary*. One of the descriptions of the word "manager" is "a manipulator of resources to meet expenditures." That proved to me conclusively that Nelson Rockefeller was not only a manager — he was probably a managerial genius!

When looking at the theme of this particular session, I feel that, putting aside Attica, no area of Nelson Rockefeller's fifteen-year career as Governor is more controversial and remains more controversial than the so-called "innovations in public finance." And it is with some temerity that I get up here to talk about it, particularly as the discussants are not exactly novices in the area of public affairs and finance.

You know, there's somebody missing here today. If we would all close our eyes and think about this town — there truly is somebody missing that belongs here as a discussant. Yes, if I close my eyes and think hard I can see the soft-spoken, well-mannered ghost of Arthur Levitt here this morning — to commune with us on a subject he held very dear to his heart.

Arthur retired as State Comptroller in 1979 (I think he originally ran on the ticket with Governor Cleveland, but I'm not sure. It might have been later), and he was for many years director of the Lincoln Savings Bank and maintained an office at the Bank. That office was one floor below Wertheim's offices in the Pan Am Building. As I was a very good friend of Arthur Levitt, his son, I said, "Why don't we have the old man up for lunch?" Which we did.

It was a very, very nice lunch. In fact, this lunch took place not more than a few months before Arthur's death. He seemed in good shape. My presence at lunch started conversations about Nelson Rockefeller as Governor, and he was very complimentary. He said, "He was a wonderful Governor and a wonderful man." We talked about all those things that we talked about yesterday —his drive, his charisma, his desire to do things, and so forth. And throughout I was watching him carefully, because I knew what was coming next.

Arthur went on about Nelson, and he then turned and said, "But you know, there's one area that I didn't agree with Nelson on." I said, "Is that so?" (I thought disarming would be the correct way to go.) No way — he started and he moved in his chair and this normally gentle person, at least to me he was always a gentle soul, started to flush in the face. Putting his knife and fork down on his plate, he reached into his pocket and he pulled out that 3 x 5 card on which he had listed the amount of moral obligation debt the State owed ... and the damn card was up-to-date! The last time I saw him do this he was still in office and the numbers now were slightly more. I said, again in a faulty attempt to disarm him, "It is remarkable that these numbers are up-to-date..." And he knew exactly what the moral obligation debt was.

He started lambasting about the moral obligation debt, and then I came to this terrible bend in the road. "Do I use my ace card on this 77- or 78- year old gentlemen ... that he approved each and every one of these financings?" "But then, ... maybe that's sort of ridiculous," and I dropped the idea.

By then, Arthur turned to the final subject of luncheon: What a terrible tragedy for the United States that Nelson Rockefeller never became President. (Because of the printing presses in Washington, there would have been no need for moral obligation debt!) He thought that Nelson would have been a wonderful President, a view shared by most of us here today.

I guess that was the last time I saw Arthur Levitt. Mary and I were in Europe months later and read of his death. But he's not with us, and hopefully some of our discussants may take up some of the Arthur Levitt challenges to Nelson Rockefeller's innovations in public finance. To a degree, I intended to do so myself.

Yesterday, Malcolm Wilson, in what can only be described as "pure Wilson," gave a wonderful reminiscence of Nelson Rocke-feller as Governor and very importantly, the 1958 campaign wherein a few old veterans like Governor Wilson, Bill Ronan, Dick Wiebe and June Martin were active participants. It was a very interesting campaign. Nelson Rockefeller was running on the Republican ticket against a very fine Governor, Averell Harriman, but they really did a job on Harriman. Happily, I had very little to do with that campaign. I was working for the Constitutional Revision Commission discovering how much of Article 8 of the Constitution could fit on the head of a pin, and then how much we could remove from the Constitution. But they did quite a job on Harriman. They talked about his reckless finances. They talked of an $850 million deficit, if I remember correctly.

And in the early months of the Rockefeller administration, the Governor gave his first Budget Message. I was not in Albany for that first Budget Message, but I gather it was actually read to the Legislature, or portions of it were read to the Legislature. It was a remarkable document. I quote from it — "The State of New York today is faced with its most serious problem in more than a generation." And then Governor Rockefeller stated his fiscal objectives: 1) there would be a minimum of bond financing, and 2) there would be a re-establishment of sound fiscal policies based on the principle of "pay-as-you-go."

Having set out his thoughts in his first Message, and, in fairness, most people believed each word that Norm Hurd wrote (or his associates wrote) in that very first Budget Message, Nelson was determined to avoid excessive borrowing, and he was determined to "pay-as-you-go," which of course was a very normal objective after the reckless finances of the Harriman years.

I'd like to digress for a moment to the Harriman years, because yesterday Jack Germond was talking about Governor Rockefeller being very green when he arrived in Albany in January of 1959, along with the Rockettes and George Balanchine. The latter two left soon after the inauguration and Nelson stayed on for 15 years. But there is a story about Governor Harriman in his first year of office and it shows how green he was. Harriman was a little hard of hearing. As a matter of fact, he was quite hard of hearing, and his Budget Director, Paul Appleby (also of the Governor's own generation) was a bit hard of hearing as well. A friend of mine, who was a high official in the budget office, was asked by Harriman, as all governors do ask when they come to office for their first term, to try to help get a tax increase so he could do something for the four following years. My friend had to do a chart, which was traditional in the budget office, of what the impact of various proposed tax increases would be on the taxpayers in the State. He presented it one night at the Mansion, and Dr. Appleby and the Governor were looking at the chart, and they didn't hear each other too well. One would talk about one thing and the other would answer, talking about another matter.

Governor Harriman used to wear Ben Franklin glasses, and he was a handsome gentleman. He was looking over these spread sheets of the tax proposals and he kept calling the tax-payers "stockholders". So he was a little green in 1955, and Governor Rockefeller was a little green in 1959, despite both of them having many, many years of intensive and highly important public service before being elected as governor.

Well, Rockefeller, having outlined his fiscal parameters for his first term in office, had to do certain things. So they increased taxes and put up some constitutional amendments for referenda votes in order to borrow. At the same time, as Bill Ronan recounted yesterday, task forces were organized. Now Bill said 42 task forces; I thought it was 48, not 42; I'm not quite sure. Quite an army of task forces were organized by Governor Rockefeller for the redoing of the economy of the State of New York — redoing the structure of government and the functions of government. Although there were many, two, I think, were particularly pertinent to our discussion today. One was a task force (they all had wonderful titles) to insure the supply of middle-income housing, and it was headed by Otto Nelson, who was a senior officer of the New York Life Insurance Company.

Otto Nelson came in with a report on middle-income housing, and, at that time, the State was doing very little in that field. Low-income housing through Federal and State programs existed, but there seemed to be a great void in producing middle-income housing in major areas of the State.

There was another task force — the task force to review higher educational needs and facilities. That was a three-man task force, perhaps the most distinguished of the forty-eight or forty-two task forces, and it was chaired by Henry Heald. He came in with one of the most significant reports filed in the Rockefeller years, and it was a report which brought forth an enormous expansion of public higher education facilities in the State of New York.

Both reports were pretty well in hand by the end of 1959 and, at that time, the Governor looked at these reports which called for some significant changes in direction. The Heald Report called for enormous demands to be placed upon the State to provide more in the way of higher educational opportunities and the Otto Nelson report did the same in the area of housing. Out of those studies came the creation of the New York State Housing Finance Agency in 1960 and the appearance of a pipe-smoking lawyer from Wall Street.

I look at my friend Dick Weibe in the audience. Dick played a great part in some of the early thinking on these efforts. He was never very shy in his work patterns, and he dealt with John Mitchell quite a bit. A number of years later Dick, Bill Ronan, and I were having lunch with John Mitchell (at the time of the birth of the MTA), and Dick went to take a telephone call. John Mitchell took his pipe out of his mouth and he asked, "What law school did Dick go to?" Well, I guess it was the Ronan Institute of Law. That was the closest Dick ever got to law school.

We'll discuss the moral obligation debt, in the context of our morning's program. It was an important change in financing procedures. The thinking behind it was widely used in this State and elsewhere around the United States. Yet in the context of Nelson Rockefeller as Governor of New York, the moral obligation

"LEAVES NOTHING TO THE IMAGINATION!"

Political cartoonist Hy Rosen's 1967 comment on Governor Rockefeller's reaction to New York City Mayor John Lindsay's request for increased State aid. The original of the cartoon, which appeared in the Albany Times-Union, was signed and presented to the Governor by Mr. Rosen.

debt concept was merely an instrument. The Governor was not a technician. He was interested in building middle-income housing. He was interested in sparking the growth of the State University and, later on, expanding the mental hygiene facilities; building the community colleges; municipal hospitals; and then, in a very, very grand piece of legislation, a whole new concept of overall urban development through an Urban Development Corporation.

199

Rockefeller's interest was not in the technique of moral obligation debt and in its methodology. We heard, at great length and with a good deal of humor and insight yesterday, that the Governor was a person who did things or built things and wanted to reach what he perceived to be his public policy goals. And he was hampered in reaching some of these goals by his first Budget Message. His desire to use moral obligation bond issues grew over the years, and I think he really believed they were just a whole pack of user fees. One way or another, whether it was paid by a municipality or by a college student or it came out of a rental fee, he viewed the payment as a user charge.

I think the moral obligation debt concept is very important, but the fact is, that it was methodology designed to achieve his public policy goals in a whole bunch of areas. Today it's grown immensely. I don't know whether I'm happy or sad to say that I have been a participant in its greatest growth, and I have with me my good friend Dick Netzer who serves with me on the board of MAC. It is interesting that, of $12.5 billion of moral obligation debt, MAC has a modest $7.9 billion. The moral obligation debt concept was designed to meet the needs — the physical development needs in the State as the Governor perceived them. But, when the City of New York was going belly-up in June of 1975 and there was no way of figuring out what to do, up trucks the moral obligation debt again. The Carey administration was very determined that there would be no further expansion of moral obligation debt. And it would live through some very difficult experiences it felt it had inherited from the Rockefeller years. But there was a desire to get the commercial banks to buy MAC paper, and they couldn't buy MAC paper without the moral obligation back-up.

Even Arthur Levitt once bought $25 million worth of MAC bonds for the Pension Funds. It took phone calls from the Governor and Senator Anderson, from Speaker Steingut, and from about 20 bankers. He bought $25 million — holding his nose all the way. He resold them a year and a half later at a large profit. Levitt thought it was a terrible investment when he bought the MAC bonds, yet he made quite a bit on them.

So, I'm not trying to slough off moral obligation debt. It's been used in strange ways, used in ways never contemplated — particularly, in the MAC experience, where MAC doesn't build anything, but acts as a banker for the City of New York.

There were a number of other areas that I'd like to touch upon where there was some innovative financing which was much sounder and received wider public approval. The Governor was convinced that the automobile should also pay for the improvement of mass transit. A great tussle and foot race occurred, between John Lindsay and Nelson Rockefeller, over who was to get the Triboro Bridge and Tunnel Authority excess revenues, which were held by an old gentleman by the name of Robert Moses. John Lindsay came up with this idea of getting some of this Triboro money and getting it into the New York City subway system. And in 1965, in his first year in office, he came to Albany with that idea. Well, the idea was obviously too good an idea to be wasted on John Lindsay, and his bill got no place. But "our Bill", Bill Ronan, got into this act and the MTA was created.

One of the reasons for the creation of the MTA was to get our hands on this Triboro Bridge and Tunnel money. There was a little problem. There was a Trustee for the bonds of the Triboro Bridge and Tunnel Authority, and the Trustee was a bank. I can't quite place it — I think it was called the Chase Manhattan Bank, and it had a Chairman with a last name very similar to that of the man who was Governor, which happened to be a strange thing. Not that strange. After all, when Governor Lehman was in office, his brother Irving Lehman was the Chief Judge of the Court of Appeals. So we'd had brother acts in this State before.

Well, it was getting to be February 1968, and this law was supposed to come into being, and the Commissioners of the MTA would become the Triboro Bridge and Tunnel Authority Commissioners. Robert Moses said there was no excess money and you could look at the books at Triboro, and you could not find more than $5 million of excess. But the law said that the MTA Commissioners would become the Triboro Commissioners and the Chase Bank sued. They had to, as Trustee. The Trustee said that the new Commissioners of Triboro, the very same railroad and subway Commissioners, would not be able to fairly deal with rubber and rail simultaneously. Well, they had no desire to deal with rubber and rail — they wanted Triboro's money! And they went to court.

Well, this was a very, very difficult thing for Governor Rockefeller's brother — to sue the State. His brother was a very cagey guy; he left for Russia on a business trip. So he was out of the country and the suit began. The Governor was in sort of a slow period in Albany, so he decided he would take some of his vast legal knowledge and apply it to this problem. And there were very, very distinguished lawyers involved. For example, Governor Dewey and his partners were representing the Chase Bank and Sam Rosenman was representing Bob Moses. It was in the courts, and it was embarrassing.

Well, the Governor did what he always did: he called everybody to the 3rd floor of 55th Street for a little meeting.

Everybody was there but the judge: the Governor's Counsel, Mr. Lefkowitz, Governor Dewey, Sam Rosenman. One would think one was going to have a seminar on New York State government and its history, going back to Rosenman's being Counsel for Governor Roosevelt.

They all sat around the square table. Of course the center of the table was where Governor Rockefeiler sat. And they all somehow or another came to an agreement, and the next thing you know we agreed to offer the bond holders a quarter percent more interest and the suit was to be disbanded and the bond resolution amended. So the Governor also played judicial roles in office, particularly, if it was to meet a certain program need.

It's astounding but in the years from 1972 to 1982 the Triboro Bridge and Tunnel Authority put $1.2 billion into the coffers of the MTA and its subway and commuter rail systems. That's operating money, not bond money to buy equipment, but money to keep fares down. We'd have a $3 fare without Triboro. So it was innovative, and you needed a shoe horn here or there. Getting the consent of bond holders took a little while, but everything was achieved and rubber was paying for rail.

The temerity of Governor Rockefeller was something impressive. I was brought up on public administration, and there were these demi-gods — Robert Moses and a guy named Austin Tobin. He was tough. Austin, when you looked at him, and he was sitting in 55th Street, sounded like he came from Trenton. When he was down in Trenton, he sounded like he came from Albany. Austin and the Port Authority had a very good thing going. Just the fourteen lanes of the George Washington Bridge were enough. My God, you could pave the Adirondacks with that kind of money.

Well, we had one hook into Austin in 1959, and it ended up as a general obligation bond. You may recall the State-guaranteed commuter car bonds. There was one Pyrrhic victory in 1962, when we got rubber to pay for rail with the rehabilitation of the Hudson and Manhattan Railroad H&M) by the Port Authority, but it wasn't the greatest success. As I look back on it, I was had by Austin and his lawyers, and years later we became very good and close friends. He was a remarkable man. We got a law written on the H & M and the World Trade Center, and Austin beat us again in the bond resolutions. At that he was a master.

As a result, until the Carey administration got some buses from the Port Authority, they just did the H & M, and they made a good railroad out of it. But they're very clever: the fare is still 30 cents — the same fare as 1962. If the H & M deficit goes up they can spend so much less for other transit purposes. They tell us in New York — "Well, you know, there's pressure in Trenton." The fact is that it was a stalemate between Nelson Rockefeller and the Port Authority. The Governor got control of every agency affiliated with the State of New York and its subdivisions except the Port Authority.

There were a lot of other innovations that Governor Rockefeller used. There was the old so-called "first instance appropriation." Boy, he turned that into a fine art! It was a relatively little-used thing. There were some old first instance appropriations — some for the Power Authority — on the books for 35 years before being repaid. Every time there would be a new Budget Director, there would be a new or revised agreement entered into between the State and the public authority.

But Governor Rockefeller was really a master at that. We had a study commission chaired by Bill Ronan on whether the State should buy the Long Island Railroad. I was the entire staff for this study. (Somehow, none of the conclusions were foregone as we began.) Then Bill Ronan and Bill Shea negotiated a purchase price for the railroad of $65 million. The question never even passed through my innocent mind: "Where do you get the money for this?" Of course, it was a first instance appropriation, and we bought the railroad.

The Governor also began to try to get general obligation bond issues approved by the Legislature and the voters. In 1967, a massive $2.5 million bond issue for transportation was approved. Another one a few years later (which featured a great action photo of Nelson Rockefeller, Mayor Lindsay, and Bill Ronan in a subway car), went down to defeat. The Pure Waters Bond Issue passed, others failed at passage — most importantly, those that could have provided lower-income housing.

Lease-purchasing was another wonderful area of the Governor's financial activities. He worked out one of his great lease-purchases of all time, when Albany County provided the security for a new State Capital in New York.

In concluding, I would hope my fellow panelists have more to add than I can in trying to go over this bunch of innovations. Was it too much, too soon? Bob Connery, in his book on Governor Rockefeller's career, felt it was. But that was the nature of the Governor. He was not interested in what could be done ten years from now. He was not interested in doing things years later. He was, as Malcolm Wilson said, a man who would unabashedly send ten to fifteen major proposals to the Legislature. He would push them forward with an enormous amount of energy. Some of it may have been a little too rapid. There has been that criticism. I will leave that to those more qualified and more distinguished in this area to discuss.

I guess there's one special question that I'm interested in and that is: Did these innovative financings contribute to the fiscal crisis of the City of New York in 1975 and '76? There I say no, because if you think there was innovative financing by Nelson Rockefeller, you should research what went on in the City of New York! I mean, they were geniuses at it. Actually, I'm sure Random House, when it used the phrase "manipulation of resources to meet expenditures," had in mind former Deputy Mayor Jim Cavanaugh.

Rockefeller's innovative financings were done up front. He told you what it was going to be. He told you he was using moral obligation debt. He would say, "I want rubber to pay for rail." But not in New York City. Little was done up front; much was done under the rug. Although the large amount of moral obligation, lease-purchasing, and other forms of debt that the Rockefeller years produced didn't help in the New York City fiscal crisis, I contend that it was not a contributor to the crisis. In fact, it was the reverse, for the New York City fiscal crisis created a fiscal crisis here in Albany, for some State public authorities, that probably wouldn't have otherwise occurred.

Another question I guess I should ask as a banker is: Were these innovative financing techniques responsible for the long march of the State of New York from 'AAA' to 'A'? Not really. The maturity of the State's economy, the need for re-industrialization, and high urban unemployment were not caused by innovative financing, but these economic factors contributed to the downgrading of the State's credit.

In the end, was it all worthwhile in retrospect? Yes, I think it was. I look at our neighboring states of New Jersey and Connecticut with their 'triple A' ratings, but in many respects they're not top-rated states. I look at the State University system of Connecticut: some of it is sad, operating in old garages, and one can see the shambles of wear and tear in schools that have just not been maintained. Look at the State of New Jersey and see how the youngsters are deprived of full educational opportunities, because of the lack of vision in New Jersey to do more for their public services.

We don't have a 'triple A' rating, but what we do have is the heritage of Nelson Rockefeller, an incredible set of facilities and services that were meant to meet genuine public needs and have done so in a remarkable fashion. It doesn't come cheap — God knows — with all the taxes. But you don't get something for nothing. And I've seen all too many states in this country where nothing is being given and they have a 'triple A' rating. I'd rather have what Nelson Rockefeller left behind: the great State University and City University systems; the enlightened programs in mental health, community affairs, the arts, and so forth. The subways and the commuter railroads now do run and are improved. The fact is they're not the world's greatest railroad system like we were promised in 60 days — but, then, Nelson didn't say which year!

Which reminds me of a little story, and I'll close on this note. Before the end of that sixty-day period during which we were going to make the Long Island the world's greatest — the world's finest — railroad (the service at the time was terrible), the *Daily News* ran a little box which read as follows: Dateline: Albany, June 23, 2002. Governor Nelson A. Rockefeller, Jr. today announced that in fact, the Long Island Railroad is the world's finest railroad. The Governor was quoted as saying, "I wish Dad were alive to see this."

FRANK WILLE: I'm a little bit sorry that Ed Kresky started out with that quote from the 1959 budget message, because those of us who were recruited into the service of Nelson Rockefeller back in those days looked at those words too and thought: By golly, there's a courageous man who knows how thoughtful people react as observers of the public scene — I'd like to go work for that man. There are any number of us who said that. I spent the next four years in Counsel's office working on those embellishments of revenue bond financing and moral obligation bonds, about which Ed spoke, but I never lost my respect for the Governor's courage when it came to matters of public finance. I think that one of the principal areas in which it took a great deal of courage to try to do what the Governor did, was in the Urban Development Corporation (UDC). One of our panelists is Ed Logue, the former Chief Executive Officer of the Urban Development Corporation. I'm going to call on Ed to discuss Ed Kresky's remarks in the context of urban development and renewal in the State, and in New Haven and Boston, as well.

EDWARD LOGUE: This retrospective is about some of the beginnings of UDC: tales that I do not believe have ever been told before, at least not in one place. It's personal, but that is part of why we are all here. To me, innovations in public finance are not something you write complicated monographs about. You find out who the actors were — who were the people involved. Now, believe it or not, I'll tell you something you don't know: I knew John Mitchell before Nelson Rockefeller. In New Haven in 1955, Mayor Dick Lee had just put me in charge of creating the development program. We were a 'triple A' city for the same reason Ed just described, nobody had borrowed any money for years. Our investment banker was the First National Bank of Boston, and our bond counsel was Storey, Thorndike, Palmer and Dodge. This was not the Boston of today; this was the Boston of thirty years ago. Dick Lee and I had some creative ideas about what we were going to do with bond proceeds, and the First National Bank and their lawyers said, "No."

I called up some of my new friends around the country, who were experts in creative urban renewal, because this was a beginning of a new career for me. And I asked, "Who's the best lawyer in this business of municipal bonds?" And of course they all told me, "John Mitchell." I called John Mitchell in New York, and I explained who I was and what I wanted and I said, "Are these people in Boston telling me the right answer?" He said, "No, of course not. Get yourself another lawyer." I got a good Connecticut lawyer and a good Connecticut bank, and New Haven went on from there. So I've always been grateful to John Mitchell for that advice ... for which he never sent me a bill!

After a while I moved along to Boston. We organized the Boston Redevelopment Authority (BRA), which very few of you really know anything about. I won't tell you a lot about it, but I'll just tell you that we merged the Boston Redevelopment Authority and the Boston City Planning Board. We put in one place the power of eminent domain, the power to give tax abatements, the power to override all codes — and had no civil service for any new employees. The BRA was going full blast, but that was only urban renewal projects. There was a lot of public building to be done to fill out the urban renewal projects. That was to be done in the old way, and that was driving me nuts.

I read an article in *Fortune Magazine* about something called the State University Construction Fund. And I called the author, Walter McQuade, who is a friend of mine, and I said, "Walter, is this guy Adinolfi as good as you say he is?" He said, "He's better." So I began an effort in seduction, which turned out the other way. I got Tony to come to Boston as a consultant and together we wrote something called the Public Facilities Law, which does little things like this: The Public Facilities Commission, again without any civil service (but with the power of eminent domain), consults with the Fire Chief, the Police Chief, and all the other chiefs, and then can go ahead and build what it wants where it wants. Even with schools, we were able to get a law through that provided that the Public Facilities Commission was required to consult with the Superintendent, not with the infamous Boston School Committee. If the Superintendent didn't like what was being proposed, he had thirty days to propose an alternative. And if that wasn't acceptable, the State Commissioner of Education had the opportunity to choose between the two proposals only. The building program got going but Collins [Mayor of Boston] decided not to run for re-election. The day he told me that (the story about Adam and Eve and the apple), he said, "Did you ever think about running?" Of course I had, a little. I did it, and it didn't work.

Then I became a professor and a consultant. What I didn't know, was that Adinolfi then lived next door to ... guess who? Al Marshall! Rockefeller called me one day in mid-January of 1968, and Janet Murphy said, "The Governor is on the phone." I said, "What Governor?" And he gets me, and he just pours it on. Remember the way? I suspect each of us has never been more flattered by anybody, including our spouses, in our whole lives. So he tells me I'm the greatest thing since whatever. He said, "Can you come to New York?" I said, "Sure, when?" He said, "Tomorrow."

So I went down there, and I met three characters named Douglass, Lefkowitz, and Urstadt up in the fourth floor conference room at 22 West 55th. They said, "Here's the bill." What they didn't know about me was that I had written and studied an awful lot of legislation in my time. I'd been taught how to do this in law school — and by John Bailey, the longtime Democratic State Chairman in Connecticut. I don't claim any other talent, but I know how to draft. That day, I discovered there's a trick in New York, one I suspect was invented by Robert Moses.

If you read certain kinds of New York legislation carefully, it all appears to be heading in one direction. It is all very re-assuring if you miss that key clause, which then takes you in the other direction.

I read the bill and said, "This is a great piece of legislation, but it won't work." They didn't really want to hear why. So they said it was time to get the Governor.

The Governor came up. He repeated the flattery. I decided, then and there, that I was going to give back to him what he was giving me. I said, "Thank you, Governor. I've wanted to meet you for a long time, because of all the public officials I've ever known, or known about, who were creative and had innovative ideas, you're just about the only one who creates structures to make those things happen." Half of us in this room were involved in New York State structures that didn't exist in 1958.

Then I did something not very nice. I said. "This is the greatest development bill that I've ever seen. You can build new towns with this, you can put housing all over the State, you can do industrial development, you can do anything. But it won't work." He said, "Why won't it work?" I said, "Let me give you an example."

207

"I assume you want to do a lot of things in New York City." He said, "I sure do." I said, "John Lindsay will have to approve them." He said, "What the hell do you mean?" I said, "Well, under this bill UDC will have to get a building permit from the Building Commissioner of the City of New York." If you know anything about building commissioners, they can give you a permit or deny you a permit, depending on how they feel that morning or what they're told to do. I said, "You want to do innovative things with this legislation." He said, "That's right." I said, "If you're going to do innovative things, you've got to pass Lindsay's zoning and planning operation. You've got to do it his way." He looked at me and said, "You're right."

That was perhaps unfair of me. If I'd said Frank Sedita, then mayor of Buffalo, I wouldn't have dissuaded him, because he figured he could handle the Frank Seditas. He could handle any one of them. But the one guy he knew he couldn't handle was Lindsay — so I used Lindsay as the example.

Then he said, "Come on downstairs." There he said, "I think I can get this bill passed."

Well, he did, he didn't, and then he did. I began a long and pleasant association with the Governor and many people in this room and, particularly, with Norm Hurd and Al Marshall and Dick Dunham. I never worried about the lawyers too much because I am one of them myself.

But having used John Lindsay to get the override, I then met a fellow by the name of George D. Woods, the Governor's choice to be first chairman of UDC. I was the first President and C.E.O. Sitting in 55th Street, in June of 1968, the Governor said, "Well, here are the three of us. Ed, you're supposed to know something about cities. George, you're supposed to know something about finance. And I'm supposed to know something about politics. Let's see what we can do."

Now to UDC innovations in public finance. I bet if I took one of those instant polls you can take in Columbus, and I asked you this question: Who had the brilliant idea that the UDC should have general obligation/general purpose bonds? Most of you would say: Ed Logue. You'd be wrong. This was George Woods' idea. Where did he get the idea? That's the way the World Bank did it! He said, "You're going to have good ones and bad ones, and you will want to do all kinds of things, and you should want to package them." And there we were. George Woods, former Chairman of the World Bank, former Chairman of the First Boston Corporation, one of the canniest investment bankers in the world — said that's the way it should go. Who am I? Just an urban developer from Boston. So I said, "That sounds good to me." We started down that road. I thought it was a good idea, and I came to like it and identify with it. Years later George became a little forgetful about the origin of that policy.

You will all remember, that the idea in 1968 was that the UDC was to do housing and industrial development, and economic development, and all that stuff. Most of you probably do not remember that something else happened in 1968. The Congress of the United States passed a little tax law that said, in effect, "Industrial bonds are not a good idea." So the basic financing system, which was supposed to be a very balanced program, disappeared about three months after the law was adopted.

We had an awful time getting the Treasury to tell us what we could do. David Kennedy was Secretary of the Treasury at that time. We had a meeting at 812 Fifth Avenue, and the Governor took Kennedy off in the corner and he said, "We've got to get an answer; we've got to get a ruling. You have to give us a numerical quantity." Finally, Kennedy gave us a ruling that said: 90-10. That meant that if we had an issue and 90 percent of the dollars went for housing, we could use 10 percent of the dollars for anything we wanted. Again, a forgotten matter.

Another gentleman I met was Colonel Levitt. George Woods and I went to see him. George had said to me, "We've got to ask for as much as we can, because it's going to take a while to get this stuff finished, and we don't want to bother anybody while you're half built." So, George said, "Arthur, we want $350 million for the bonds." And Arthur said, "No." And I showed him the first round of projects. And he said, "OK, you can have $250 million." I got $250 million worth of construction under contract — not completed — under contract. And I went back to Colonel Levitt and I said, "It is time for us to get some more. I do not want to be in the position of doing more building unless I have the money in hand." He said, "Don't be silly. You come to me when you need the money, that is when you've got bills to pay." That was Arthur Levitt. This conservative paragon, this pillar of caution. Arthur Levitt said, "No, you've got to do it this way." OK. He made us take the risk, and, of course, he did not accept any responsibility then or later. As has been said — we wanted to build, so we did as he advised.

We kept the peace in the Legislature. I'll never forget the first time I met Malcolm. He said, "Well, Ed, I know you're a Democrat, but at least you're not a West-Side-Reform-Democrat." And the more I came to know that bunch, the less chance there was that I'd ever become one.

As Dick Rosenbaum and Chuck Lanigan could tell you, we weren't very helpful to the Republican State Committee when it came to appointments, or architectural commissions. But we did have a simple system for keeping the peace. We had one system for one part of the State, another system for the other part. Once a year, about February, the Governor would call me and he'd say, "I have Joe Margiotta with me, and we just want to renew our understanding." And I would say, "Put him on the phone." I would say, "Joe, you got it. Nothing will be done in Nassau County unless you okay it." Nothing was done in Nassau County. What the heil. They didn't need too much out there. That meant that we had no trouble in the Assembly. Democrats, I never had to worry about.

But then what about the Senate, the conservative Senate? Well, there we had a leader in those days named Earl Brydges, and we had a crazy mayor, E. Dent Lackey from Niagara Falls. Earl was from Niagara Falls. The rule was exactly the opposite. The call would come from Earl, "We need an auditorium, a convention center." "OK, Earl." "We need two hundred units of housing." "OK, Earl." We built the 200, and I would say, "Isn't that wonderful?" And then Earl say, "We got to have two hundred more." The answer was — Joe Margiotta gets nothing, that's what he wants; Earl Brydges gets anything he wants. And that kept the peace at both ends of the State and in both houses of the Legislature.

I was never sure that anybody really told me the truth about what Al Marshall said to the legislators to get the UDC bill passed. For example, I looked at it as something that would allow us to build housing in the Nine Towns Program in Westchester County. Among other reasons, we needed to demonstrate that a metropolitan approach was to be followed in order to be allowed to build in the New York City ghettos, something it was clear we were expected to do. We worked away on this project. I always liked to be prepared and very visual when we came to the Governor — and there we were to brief him on our suburban housing program. We were all set to go, and I described the whole thing and he said, "Are you telling me you're going to do it anyway?" I said, "No, we haven't bought any land. We've just got it under option. If you want to stop it, you can stop it." He said "Go ahead."

In retrospect, there was one thing wrong with this meeting. At nearly every meeting I ever had with Nelson Rockefeller, Malcolm Wilson was in the room. Malcolm was not with us that day. Whether the outcome would have been the same, I don't know. My experience with Malcolm was that he always told the Governor exactly what he thought, and whatever decision was made he was loyal to it.

But we all remember Nelson the enthusiast, and how he got going on this — "What a wonderful idea; it isn't going to hurt anybody too much." He said, "You know, up there in Pocantico, we have a little piece of about 20 acres, over in the corner, separated from the rest of the property. Why don't we see about that?" I thought: Oh my God, Nelson Rockefeller and the Rockefeller family were going to put ten to fifteen acres into this thing. That will take care of that. I left elated.

About three o'clock that afternoon I got a call from John Lockwood, the family's lawyer. He said, "Forget it. It's not Nelson's property; it's the whole family's." That ended the Pocantico portion.

The minor financial innovation in the Nine Towns Program was when the Governor graciously arranged my surrender. We talked about amending the law in 1973 to remove the housing override in the suburbs. I said, "Governor, this land [that we had by now bought] will not sell for what we have paid for it, under these circumstances, so I need an appropriation." Dick Dunham managed to do that, and we received a $3 million appropriation to recoup our entire investment in the Nine Towns Program.

Although the Governor and Ed Michaelian (the Westchester County Executive) supported it, no other elected official did. There was an uproar and finally it was clear we were going to have to surrender. We scored much better in Monroe County and three thousand suburban homes were built. There were others outside Syracuse and Buffalo.

Earlier in 1973, a terrible thing had happened to UDC with our Arthur Levitt-mandated system of financing, and our build, build, build approach to our responsibilities. Mr. Nixon got re-elected President of the United States in 1972 by a rather enormous majority. He decided to celebrate that victory on the 6th of January 1973, by suspending half the laws that dealt with housing and urban renewal in the U.S. That caught us in a very abrupt and painful way. We had always been very forthcoming in our disclosure statements, thank God. When we had to put out the next one after the impoundment, we put it out with the moratorium unresolved. It worried a lot of people in the financial community. I have, more or less, come to the conclusion that a lot of people in investment banking do not do their homework.

Well, we worked hard and rebuilt our credit — we thought. We got a new financial team — first class. Everybody in the market place seemed pleased. Then something else happened. And it had some consequences that have never been adequately understood.

With our financial house in what seemed to me (and George Woods) pretty good order, I started visiting around in June of 1974. The two places I remember in particular were the CitiBank and

Bankers Trust. We visited with one of the top three guys in each bank — in one case, the top guy.

Although they were perfectly friendly to me personally, I was confronted with an avalanche of hostility. As soon as I got out of these meetings, I called Dick Dunham and said, "Something is very wrong." You know what it was? I don't know what people ask people to promise before they resign office. All I know is that in 1974 the Port Authority Covenants were changed, at Malcolm Wilson's initiative.

Wall Street was outraged. And they said these things to me: Nelson we knew. We don't know Malcolm Wilson. The State has violated its word to the investment community. It has changed the law. And we're going to find some way of teaching the State a lesson and testing this moral obligation. Now, I'm thinking to myself: I have a feeling which agency is going to be the guinea pig —UDC. Dick Dunham and I worked the whole summer. I must say, Malcolm was a trooper. It was a hell of a time. They were determined to test the moral obligation clause. And they did. There's more to that story that I can tell, but there is not time today.

One final comment. In the Spring of 1975, I found myself in Johnny Oakes' place at a dinner party. (I'll never forget Rockefeller saying to me, "You know that Johnny Oakes at *The Times*? I said to him one day, 'Johnny, why do I always have these problems with you?' And Johnny said, 'Well, if you'd just do as I ask you to do, you wouldn't have any problems.' I replied, 'I'm the one who was elected Governor. You're not." Johnny never understood that, or so the Governor used to tell!) But anyway, that evening, Jim Perkins, the former President of Cornell, was there, and he asked one question that, I would suggest, is worth pondering. He said, "Ed, just one question. Would all this have happened if Nelson was still Governor?" And I said, "Of course not."

One final note. I don't always agree with Henry Kissinger on everything, but I did agree with one thing. Right in the middle of his eulogy he said, "Oh, what a President he would have made!"

FRANK WILLE: Thank you, Ed, for those insights. As the next panelist to discuss the ways in which the innovations in public finance impacted on his jurisdiction and domain, while he was in State service, I call on Chancellor McGovern of the University of the State of New York.

JOSEPH MC GOVERN: I'm very happy to be here. It brings back a lot of memories. One of the memories goes back to the day in the middle 1960's when Norm Hurd said to me over in the county courthouse, "Joe, how many hats do you wear around here?" The occasion for the remark was that, as a member of the Board of Regents of the University of the State of New York, I had met the previous evening with Governor Rockefeller and with Norm to discuss educational matters, and the next morning he found me wearing a different hat and involved in the sale of the first issue of Albany County South Mall bonds. I explained to Norm that one of my functions in Albany was as a Regent, and, since I received no pay for my services, I really wore no hat there because I couldn't afford one. But I had been Bond Counsel to the City and the County of Albany for over 20 years prior to that time, for which I was paid reasonable fees, and that enabled me to have one hat.

There is a story behind the South Mall, and I think that's really the purpose Norm invited me for. It's an interesting story, and I think it illustrates many of Nelson Rockefeller's qualities. The story goes that, shortly after Nelson came to Albany, he looked out the window of his second floor office, and he saw a piece of the City of Albany with dilapidated housing — much of it going back to the time of the Patroons — and he thought that it should be eliminated and replaced by State office buildings. Of course the Albany Democrats didn't see it that way, because that housing may have looked dilapidated, but it housed a lot of Democratic voters, and that was a good reason for leaving it the way it was.

Well, Nelson got an appropriation from the State Legislature of $20 million or so to condemn ninety-eight acres in the heart of Albany. And the State proceeded accordingly to take title, demolish buildings, and relocate the people. It's been said here, earlier, that Nelson was never one for technicalities and as Ed Kresky said, "Sometimes he never stopped to think where we were going to get the money." He didn't think of that here, because this was 1963, and this was the time when there was a promise of no more State bonding. Nor was there to be any increase in taxes. There was a big hullabaloo about the fact that Nelson was going to increase fees — that they were not to be considered taxes. Governor Cuomo, the other day, referred to "revenue producing mechanisms" — a little variation on "revenue enhancement". But it never occurred to Nelson Rockefeller (at least it seems to me that it never occurred to him), that to finance the State office buildings on this 98 acre plot by a State bond issue would require a vote of the people. And it didn't occur to him, that the people in Montauk or Ticonderoga or Oswego or Otsego wouldn't have much interest in shelling out additional tax money to pay for what was then very unkindly being referred to as the "Rockefeller Center of Albany" or "the Taj Mahal" that was being built in Albany.

The Democrats in Albany started a law suit to try to stop this entire enterprise, but (as I guess they knew they would) they lost. The perennial Mayor of Albany, Erastus Corning, for whom I had acted as Bond Counsel for 20 years, called me on the phone and said, "Joe, Nelson is stuck. We've got a desert in the middle of our fair city and he can't build the office buildings. Can we do it for him?" "Well," I said, "there is a way it can be done, but some legislation will be needed." The way to do it would be, as Ed Kresky in one of his notes in preparing for this meeting referred to it, lease-purchasing on a grand scale. And I outlined the plan which subsequently came to fruition, namely, that the land should be transferred to the City or County of Albany, that the County should issue its bonds and build the buildings, lease them to the State, and the State enter into an agreement by which an annual rental would be paid equal to the debt service. And when the bonds were paid, everything would go back to the State — that was the carrot at the end of the road.

Well, Erastus said, "I was thinking along the same lines." (Erastus Corning was a very astute person in public finance.) "I've been thinking along those lines, and I'm going over and talk to Nelson." That afternoon he called me, and good fisherman that he was, Erastus Corning said, "I gave our ideas to Nelson and he bought them hook, line, and sinker." I remember that expression so well.

Immediately, legislation was drafted by the Governor's Counsel's office, and within a day or two I had a draft down in my office at 4 Wall Street, and we took it from there. I must be very careful as to what I say about what happened from then on, because there followed a long period of negotiating a rather complicated finance agreement between the State and the City and County, and the person who handled those negotiations for the State is sitting right here — Bob Stone — who was then Deputy Commissioner of the Office of General Services working with General Schuyler. Bob and I spent many a day and evening going carefully over every word of the deal.

It gave me great satisfaction and pleasure — it's a small world — when Bob later became Deputy Commissioner of Education for legal affairs and was my counsel, when I was Chancellor of the Board of Regents.

I just don't want to pass by my experience in education in this State without making one observation. Over the years, Governor Rockefeller was a very good friend of education. I think that the State University, the City University, and the independent colleges owe an awful lot to him, because here he was innovative, as he was in other areas. It was in education that I got to know Nelson Rockefeller more intimately than in the area of municipal finance. I have great respect for his dedication to education and his even-handed support of the diversity in education which has prevailed in New York over the years.

Well, the deal was negotiated. There have been references to Arthur Levitt. Arthur Levitt, as he did with other revenue bond issues, approved — this time with a memorandum. But this was not strictly a revenue bond issue. I don't think there had ever been anything like this done in this State. The bonds that the County of Albany would issue to finance the South Mall would be general obligations of the County. Immediately, the question arose as to how the County of Albany, within its debt limit, could finance a project which in its early stages was spoken of as costing $360 million, and which, by the time the finance agreement was signed, was to cost $480 million. Within the last couple of months, the last bonds were sold, bringing the total to $980 million. How could the County handle that? Well, there always had been a provision of law, that, if a project was self-liquidating, the State Comptroller could eliminate from the calculation of debt limit as much of the indebtedness as was supported by revenues received in the previous year. So, by that procedure, each year as the bond issues were sold, the prior bond issues were eliminated from the County of Albany debt calculation.

So here we had a general obligation bond issued by municipalities. That was very different from obligations issued by authorities, which had to depend solely upon revenues or upon the moral obligation of the State. You had a direct obligation of the County of Albany, but it also was supported by a type of moral obligation of the State. One of the limitations, in this financing agreement, was the constitutional provision that the State cannot bind itself beyond one year — the so-called "executory clause" of the State Constitution. I remember very well that when the first issue of bonds was being presented to the investment bankers, I was asked to appear before a number of syndicate members who were thinking of bidding for the bonds. And I said, quite frankly, "There is a legal limitation on the State's lease obligations which are the principal support of these bonds, and what the investor will have to do is set off against that legal limitation the possibility that the State will not pay the rent."

In the practical order, the chances of the State not paying the rent (which would provide debt service for the bonds) were minimal. First of all, the State needed more office space. It was paying rent to private landlords around the City of Albany. As years passed and the bonds were paid off through the rentals, the

State could look forward to the carrot at the end, when all the property would revert to the State. So the incentive to the State to continue, by annual appropriations, to pay the rent that would pay the bonds was really the heart of the security. And it was both a moral obligation and a practical obligation on the part of the State (having entered into this financial arrangement) to continue to make those appropriations.

I remember also, Norm Hurd may remember it too, the day we were to receive the bids for the first issue of the South Mall bonds. That was in late 1965. Norm came over, and he was terribly concerned that the interest rate was outrageously high at 3.85 percent! As a matter of fact, he asked us to hold up making the award, until some consideration could be given to the acceptability of the interest cost. The next few issues were sold at interest costs in the area of 3.7 percent to 3.9 percent. What a contrast with the last issue, recently sold at an interest cost of 9 percent!

To answer some of the questions that have been asked, I believe that the South Mall project, as years pass, will be regarded as one of the glories of the Rockefeller administration. Did it contribute to the financial predicament of the State? I don't think so. If it were to be done today, or even half done, I think it would cost just as much. And the financing cost would be really outrageous. I think if there was a mistake made in building the South Mall (and it did cost an awful lot), it was in Nelson Rockefeller's dynamic drive to get things done and get them done fast — full steam ahead. At the same time they were building the South Mall, they were also building the State University at Albany campus, which cost at least $75 million. They were also constructing that network of roads around and through the City of Albany. So those three things were going on all at the same time. And the contractors practically could name their own figures. Another thing that happened was that there were so many contracts awarded for the construction of the South Mall, that the contractors were in each other's way. As I am told, there were substantial awards of damages to them, because they were interfered with in the completion of their work. I think, if any mistake was made, it was that Nelson wanted too much, too quick.

I'll close with just a brief reference to Arthur Levitt. The Comptroller was a Trustee of the Teachers' Retirement System and the Regents used to meet with the Trustees. At one of those meetings Arthur said to me, "Joe, did you buy any of those South Mall bonds, yourself?" I said, "No." He said, "Get them. They're great bonds." All of which goes to prove that Arthur Levitt was a very smart man.

FRANK WILLE: Thank you, Chancellor McGovern. I suppose I should call you Counsel McGovern, after all that insight into the South Mall project. Our last discussant is Dick Netzer, and we look forward to his remarks about what he's heard this morning.

DICK NETZER: I'm type-cast as an academic, but I can't resist beginning with a participant observation brought on by Ed Kresky's recollection of the 1966 foot race about the Triboro Bridge and Tunnel Authority money, since I had a small role in this. After John Lindsay was elected Mayor in November 1965, not to be outdone by the 1959 experience of Nelson Rockefeller with his task forces, Lindsay, too, decided to appoint a vast number of task forces. In the jargon of the time they were all "reorganization task forces." For example, the tax increase group was called the Fiscal Reorganization Task Force. Another was the Transportation Reorganization Task Force, which Rod Perkins chaired, and on which I served.

We were beavering away, right away realizing that our job was to find a way of getting access to this Triboro Bridge and Tunnel Authority money. In our number there were a few people who were fairly bold about this, and they devised this scheme which was given to Lindsay. He was to come up here to Albany, on February 6, 1966, present it to the Governor, and make it public.

Well, he made the trip and then came back to New York. There was a meeting of the task force. Lindsay reported that he had delivered it, and Rod Perkins said, "What did the Governor say?" Lindsay said, "Well, Rockefeller said it was a good idea." "No. Wait. What did he really say? What's going to happen now? What did he say?" Perkins kept bearing in on him about this, and Lindsay was getting more and more testy about being grilled this way. What Perkins was saying was, "Is he supporting it or not? What's really happening?" And as this was going on, I suddenly had this blinding revelation. The footrace was over. It was through. Nelson Rockefeller had appropriated the idea!

Ed Kresky posed three questions about innovative financing. Here are my quick answers, followed by the amplifying remarks expected of academics:
1. Was it (the innovative financing) too much, too soon? No.
2. Was it worthwhile in retrospect? Yes.
3. Did it contribute to the 1975 fiscal crisis? Yes, to an extent.

In amplifying, I'm picking up a role I found myself in during the immediate aftermath of the New York City fiscal crisis in 1975. I had rather expected students and academic colleagues to be highly interested in accounts of my own experiences at the center of the crisis in the summer and fall of 1975 as a MAC board

217

member, but what I found was some impatience with war stories. Instead, my auditors wanted to know my views of how on earth the crisis could have come about — my views not as a participant, but as an academic observer. And as an academic observer, I began by rejecting devil and conspiracy theories, because (a) such theories offer complicated rather than simplified explanations, and an element of the scientific method is the principle of parsimony — never look for a complicated explanation when a simpler one will do; and (b) such theories are demonstrably false in almost every case. The academic approach is, instead, to reconstruct the circumstances in which the decision-makers found themselves and thereby to understand how the decisions were made.

We have had at this meeting a good deal of reconstruction of the temper of the times of the Rockefeller years. Let's consider the economic circumstances. To be sure, there was concern at the end of the 1950's that New York's was a mature economy that might not have strong growth prospects, and there had been some sputtering in isolated sectors of the State's economy. But as of 1959 and 1960, the long-term prospects for the downstate metropolitan region (including New York City itself) seemed very bright indeed and were being so put in the volumes of a large-scale study, then being published. Rochester was doing its very successful hi-tech thing; and Syracuse and some other industrial centers were, apparently, thriving — in part because of the completion of the Thruway. I mention the Thruway, because we tend to forget that, as of those years, New York State had the most nearly completed network of limited access highways of any state in the nation; that alone made us poised for growth, not for decline.

In any event, the New York economy grew strongly during the 1960's until the peak in 1969. In fact, relative to other mature states, we did extraordinarily well; New York City itself was one of the few large old central cities with substantial employment growth over that decade. I believe that the performance of government in the decade had something to do with the economic success.

But more to the present point, given the economic growth, it would have been irresponsible for a governor — even a governor far less ambitious than Nelson Rockefeller — to have said: We should be worrying about potential economic weakness sometime in the future and therefore should confine ourselves, in planning and public investment, to conventional and conservative financing mechanisms. That would have been acting as if the State's economy was going to hell in a handbasket when it was doing just the opposite.

218

Now move ahead to 1969-70. There is a national recession. In contrast to the earlier post-World War II recessions, New York's economy was relatively hard hit this time. Even so, given the record of brief and mild recessions over the preceding 20 years, it would have been wrong to assume the worst, immediately retrench, and abandon the hope for the future that underlay the ambitious plans for public investment. Instead, the only reasonable posture was that adopted: assume that the economic adversity would be short-lived. It really was not until 1973, that it was clear that the economic downturn was not a passing thing, and that the State's economy was in serious trouble. I say this as an economist who had been expressing some skepticism about the appropriateness of expansive fiscal policies by New York State and City governments in the late 1960's. But economists of this persuasion were in the minority and could not expect to convince the decision-makers instantly.

That is, given the economic circumstances that actually existed, rather than the forebodings and suspicions, the construction programs and the development policies involving heavy borrowing were, on the whole, appropriate until 1973 or thereabouts. Not everything was appropriate. For example, by 1970, hard demographic data made it very clear indeed that the enrollment projections underlying the plans for further huge construction of public higher education facilities were grotesquely exaggerated. But this was an exception, albeit a large one.

If the development policies were correct, and if the only way to borrow money to execute them required innovative financing methods, then one must allow that the innovative financing methods themselves were justified. Of course, hindsight reveals that there were all sorts of disadvantages in those methods, and that, knowing what we know, any number of tactics, features and details could have been done better, even in the context of the strategy that was employed. Although it seems anomalous to use the word in connection with Nelson Rockefeller, the innovative financing methods amounted to doing good by stealth. By "stealth" I do not mean deviousness, but instead the use of mechanisms that, because they were intricate (like first instance appropriations), tended to allay apprehensions about the large amounts of money involved.

In the end, there were three consequential disadvantages of the innovative financing methods. First, some individual bad investment choices were made; choices that might not have been made under more conventional methods, because the latter involved slower-moving processes. This was real, but applies only to a small fraction of the cases. Second, the innovative mechanisms tended to make it difficult to reverse or correct investment policies and decisions rapidly, that is, as soon as it became clear that things were going wrong. For example, early on, there were indications that Battery Park City was not going to work, and that investment should have been halted, but the financing mode virtually dictated that work continue on hopes and prayers.

The third disadvantage was indirect but, in my view, by far the most serious. Because the State government was doing highly unorthodox financing, it could not hold the City of New York to rigorous, conservative financing practices. When the City government followed the routes pioneered by the State, it went much further, and was far more imprudent. For example, the State invented bond anticipation (BAN) financing, but it was the City (with legislative authorization) that carried the device to the extreme, in perpetual BAN financing of the city Mitchell-Lama Program. Similarly, by far the most irresponsible use of the State-invented moral obligation bond was for the City Education Construction Fund, which was little better than a Ponzi scheme. Logic tells us that there was no need for the Legislature to authorize the City to carry the methods to these extremes, just because the approach had been used previously in more suitable ways. Hindsight tells us that the Legislature should not have been so incautious. But in reality, it would have been difficult, in the expansive climate, for the State to have been conservative in regard to the City when it was being, apparently, so daring in regard to its own practices.

And, of course, the City's practices did lead to, and greatly exacerbated, the 1975 fiscal crisis with its severe impact on the State government. This strikes me as the really unfortunate effect of the innovative financing methods. Nonetheless, my overall conclusion remains, that the innovations were worthwhile, for all the defects. The legacy is a vast increment to the public facilities and services of New York State. A final point: I suspect that had Nelson Rockefeller been Governor in 1974, when things started to fall apart, he would have done what was necessary to stop the rot and turn things around.

FRANK WILLE: I think it fair, in the light of Dick's Netzer's comments, to ask our other three panelists two sets of questions. I'll start them with this first one: "Do you believe, in retrospect, given the political circumstances of the time and the legal and constitutional restrictions that were on the State government, that the projects and the programs that required these vast sums of public monies could have been accomplished in any different way than the innovations that were relied on by Nelson Rockefeller?"

ED KRESKY: Basically, my answer is "No," but I want to qualify that "No" because Dick Netzer made a very good point. It really isn't very healthy for the body politic, for the voters, to really be so unknowing. What I'm saying, is that we could not have gotten the increment that we referred to, of an enlarged and better public service, very rapidly through the alternative of convincing the public in referenda. I don't think that we could have gotten all that we got, if we paid less of a price and waited for referendum approval, for it would have taken another generation to achieve the same goals. So in balance, I really don't think there was much of an alternative.

Ed Logue said something very interesting. You know this all involves you and me. It would have been inconceivable for Nelson Rockefeller to have the patience to do this through referendum methods to get the basic authorizations. I don't think that this particular human being as Governor could have sat around for a generation or two to see these things done. All governors want to do things within their own term of office; that man wanted to do it in that very year.

FRANK WILLE: Joe, do you have anything you want to add to that?

JOSEPH MCGOVERN: I would also answer the question in the negative. Most of these things could not have been done in the context of the times, without the resort to the particular financing devices. Certainly in the case of the South Mall, it's inconceivable to me that the project could come to pass, at least in its present form, without the very unusual and very close cooperation of a Republican Governor and an Albany Democratic Mayor. And I think that this is illustrative of another feature of Nelson Rockefeller's character. He was impulsive, he wanted things done quickly, and he would use every available means, even if that meant working with the Albany Democrats to achieve it. It's to his credit that, when he saw this was the way in which his objective could be accomplished, he went right full steam ahead. And I think in years to come that it will be clearer that this couldn't have been done in any other way. Possibly it could have been done by an authority, but there were other legal problems with an authority located solely within the City of Albany. I think it is good that it was done, and my answer to your question is "No."

FRANK WILLE: Ed Logue?

EDWARD LOGUE: Frank, I'd like to give my response to "Could you have done UDC in another way?" The answer is "Yes." In our development business, five percent of the cost comes from acquiring the kind of property we acquired (we did not relocate anybody) and making detailed plans long enough and strong enough so you can get hard prices. That's five cents out of a dollar. The State of New York could have put up that money over a

Zipper's stuck

Robert Dunn's comment on Governor Rockefeller's desire to maintain a pay-as-you-go policy.

period of time either as a regular appropriation or a so-called "first instance" appropriation. The advances could have been paid back at closing.

The second thing the State of New York could have done was to fund the agency's operating expenses. That is basically how UDC is operating now, because, as you all know, in his second term Governor Carey rediscovered the UDC. If the State put up the operating expenses, it could mean no more fees. The fee business, that all agencies are engaged in, has inflated the cost of housing unmercifully. Those fees are not necessary if appropriations pay for the services of the staff and the outside professionals, architects, engineers, and (to a limited degree) lawyers. You would not have to get that money back. As a consequence, you could do two things: significantly reduce the cost of the final product, and still not take any big money risks.

I loved general purpose bonds. The system was designed for us, and I was determined to see what we could do with it. But that was not enough.

If you had provided the upfront cost of acquiring land and making plans, the upfront cost of the staff and operations and outside requirements and consultant services, you still needed to do something else. One way was to have a friendly relationship, as we did in Boston, with the local Federal Housing Authority (FHA). But if the State of New York had been willing to create an insurance agency to insure the financing it would have been a very easy trick in those days (in my judgment) to have gotten all the institutional financing we required on a project-by-project basis. So there was another way that did not require moral obligations, at least so far as UDC is concerned. If these were projects that could not pass insurance underwriting tests and they were still thought worthwhile, they could be partly subsidized by appropriations.

Joe, I think I agree with you, that, probably, a bit of creative genius would have been required with regard to the South Mall. I don't know of another method. In the case of UDC, there was another method.

AL MARSHALL: I think that we'd be a little remiss, in retrospect, if we just concentrated on the innovative part and suggested that all major capital projects were done in a way that was not open to the public. Just remember that middle-income housing was passed in 1959, that the mass transportation bond issue was taken to the people in a campaign which was equal to any gubernatorial campaign ever taken to the people, and that a billion dollar Clear Water Bond Issue was taken to the people in a campaign that cost millions of dollars of both private and public money.

The point I want to make is that "No," in my judgment these things could not have been done. There was no way to get Urban Renewal bonds passed in this State. There would have been no way to get a bond issue sent through fast for the South Mall. There probably would have been no way, because of the selfishness that did exist in those people who could send their kids away to college — who would refuse to recognize the desperate situation we were in in the State of New York in the way of higher education. So someone, in retrospect, ought to decide whether or not we chose that best vehicle that could get things done in terms of the times.

I don't disagree with Ed; I'm only amplifying what he said. Nelson Rockefeller was not impatient, in the sense that he was willing to spend hours in that damn airplane, and days eating Oreo cookies and drinking Dubonnet, to go out and sell bond issues to the people, when he thought that the bonds had some chance of the people accepting them. The history of New York State has been dismal in connection with low-income housing bond issues and even the urban renewals. (When I first went to Budget the average Urban Renewal project was three years old. It was just nothing but flat land. There was not a damn thing built.) This morning as I listened, I thought, whoever examines our considerations today should put in one more thing. Dick, this I think is the measure. Do you assume the job had to be done and ought to be done? And when we had to campaign, and God knows, Ed and Dick Weibe and the others carry the scars of it — we spent as much enthusiasm in campaigning for bond issues with the people as we ever did in electing Nelson Rockefeller Governor!

FRANK WILLE: Well, I appreciate for all of us that addendum to the record, because it was true that much more was going on at the very same time as we were trying to put in place these various innovative financing projects.

Dick Netzer had something to say.

DICK NETZER: My remarks were not intended to put any of the participants in the Rockefeller administration on the defensive, when I said that with clairvoyance or with the aid of hindsight, some things would have best been done differently. In January, 1959, no one had any right to forecast that Nelson Rockefeller would be Governor for the next 15 years. Had he taken office for a 15-year term on that day, surely many things would have been different, for the administration would have then had the luxury of choosing slow, conventional methods instead of fast but unorthodox ones. The major case in point is the moral obligation bond. One vital reason for moral obligation bonds is that New York's Constitution does not permit the State government or any general-purpose local government to issue honest-to-goodness revenue bonds; only authorities can do so, but authorities are limited in other ways. For example, an authority has no taxing power, so it can't pledge an earmarked tax to a revenue bond. To authorize outright revenue bond financing by the State itself requires amending the Constitution, a slow and uncertain process. But from a five-year time perspective, that might have been worthwhile. In fact, I am in no doubt today, that this would have been the right course of action in 1959. But it's another thing entirely to have made that judgment in 1959; I don't fault the participants for not being clairvoyant.

MILTON MUSICUS: I want to speak as one of Rockefeller's big spenders in terms of uses to which this innovative financing was put. I was called in by a friend of ours, Bill Ronan, and was assigned the Mental Hygiene Facilities Improvement Corporation with $500 million because the Governor felt that changes should take place in mental health treatment. I think what Ed said is terribly important. We should not be talking about Governor Rockefeller as an innovator in finance, or Governor Rockefeller the builder, but about Governor Rockefeller who wanted to have the kinds of programs that would help the people, and that the help be available to all those who needed it.

In mental health, we had overcrowded facilities and we had changes in therapeutic treatment. Different types of facilities were necessary. If we did not have this innovative financing, and we had to depend on the traditional process of appropriations, we might have gotten a couple of million dollars one year and a couple of million another year. As a result, the mentality of our departments was that they thought in small terms.

When we came up with $500 million we approached the Commissioner of Mental Hygiene and asked, "What do you want to have done?" He told me that he needed a paint job in the Harlem River State Hospital, and the roof was leaking in the Hudson River Hospital!

In addition, the innovative financing forced a complete change in the thinking about programming at the State University. I wish Tony Adinolfi was here to tell us what he had to do to get the State University to think in terms of new programs.

We now have completely different programs in higher education and mental health. In achieving this, I think we should not forget that this was not only the result of establishing these public authorities and innovative financing, but there were administrative changes. We did not have to conform with public works procedures. We did not have Civil Service limitations. And although we had some people from Norm Hurd's office still looking over our shoulders, we did have direct access to the second floor. Sometimes budget examiners gave us a bit of trouble, but I think we were able to have them called off.

No, all this could not have been done without innovative financing — certainly not when you got the Governor re-elected on the promise of solving the narcotics problem, and nobody knew what programs were needed. We needed narcotics facilities, and you didn't think of the dollar sign. We had to build.

As far as Arthur Levitt's objections and comments, may I point out that we have an elected Comptroller. There's a powerful body of people who profited from this innovative financing program and they made their voices heard loud and clear. Arthur Levitt's acceptance was not only because he was a great statesman, but also because he was a great pragmatist and politician who argued against all this very properly, but not very loudly.

As for lease-purchase arrangements, we found that our vehicle was awfully good for that, too. When Mayor Lindsay discovered that he couldn't build Bellevue Hospital in less than 15 years, and that he didn't have the money for the hospitals he needed, we amended our innovative financing program to extend to lease arrangements with municipalities, and Lindsay bought it — hook, line and sinker — as *his* innovative financing plan.

FRANK WILLE: That's precisely what the professor was complaining about!

VINCENT J. MOORE: As a planner who worked for the Governor's staff during the early years, I can say we faced considerable frustration in our efforts to coordinate the planning and development activities of the various State agencies with those of the local governments. This was a major objective of the Governor's and could be noted, for example, in the regional development tours he conducted early in his administration. I think, in retrospect, that the planning concept the Governor expressed early in his administration provided considerable incentive for such coordination, but there was a gap between the vision and the political reality.

Consider, for example, the resistance of local governments as well as some of the older State bureaucracies to the changes necessary in such coordination. As a result we spent too much money. For example, Tony Adinolfi, the late former General Manager of the State University Construction Fund, once told me the new State University of Buffalo campus at Amherst probably cost an additional $50 million in "construction penalties," because it was located in the wrong place. It was built in an unserviced, flood-prone area of a suburban community with inadequate public transportation facilities. But I don't think these things could have been avoided, at that time, due to the state of the art of such coordinative planning, and local government suspicion of State government motives.

FRANK WILLE: I'm going to only pose the second of my tougher questions and leave you to think about it. While we focused on how you accomplish certain capital projects, most of which involved construction — was there sufficient consideration given to the long-run operating cost implications of what that construction would mean when fully utilized? While we all can say from our point of view that it was a great thing that Nelson Rockefeller was Governor for 15 years, I have often wondered whether he thought so, as these operating cost implications came home to roost.

Chapter IX

Rockefeller Policies Toward Crime and the Criminal Justice System

VINCENT O'LEARY: This session is devoted to a discussion of Nelson Rockefeller's programs related to crime and the criminal justice system. It is one of the two concluding sessions this morning, and for it we have a most distinguished panel. I have known some of them for so long a time that it would be embarrassing to disclose how long. Others, I met more recently. In addition to the panel, we have a very distinguished audience. I hope some will participate in the discussion. One person in this room, for example, has had a great deal to do with crime from a mental health perspective. He is Dr. Alan Miller, Director of Mental Hygiene at the time of the Rockefeller administration. I hope we may hear from him.

One interesting thing about working in the area of crime and the criminal justice system is to observe recurring themes that surface periodically. I have just finished serving on the Liman Commission, a body appointed by Governor Carey. I must confess, I had the feeling that I was hearing many of the same issues that we faced during the Rockefeller era and before.

The Rockefeller administration in New York occurred at a unique time in this country's history with respect to crime and criminal justice issues. It was a time when these matters were given great national attention — perhaps the greatest ever given them in the history of the country. It is fascinating to observe, how the Rockefeller administration in New York reacted to these national initiatives and, indeed, carried out its own experiments that were to affect the direction of many of the programs on the national scene.

We can trace the national interest in the crime area back to the Kennedy administration in the early 1960's. There weren't too many programs, but those that existed were very important and influential. One of the most important was the Committee on Juvenile Deliquency and Youth Crime, which based much of its national policy on experiments conducted on the lower east side in New York City by a team of investigators from Columbia University. If we wished to take the time, we could trace out the lineage of the "War on Poverty" from that program. Drugs were becoming a preoccupation for the first time on the national scene. Then there were the youth gangs in many cities. And, of course, Bobby Kennedy is identified with the attack on organized crime. We can trace parallels in the State of New York to each of these. Some of the most imaginative programs were carried out in the State of New York.

The Presidency of Lyndon Johnson brought with it the National Commission on Law Enforcement and the Administration of Justice, which made a number of important recommendations and which, in turn, led to the birth of the Law Enforcement Assistance Administration. It was a major national effort which made funds available to the states. It stressed a centralized planning mode at the national and state levels, and state after state established state planning agencies. Coordination was a feature of that effort. At that same time, of course, information systems began to grow very rapidly. They had profound implications for management systems and brought with them the question of identification bureaus and the relationship of the states to the national FBI systems.

Nixon's administration marked the continuing evolution of some of the efforts, with perhaps a greater emphasis on enforcement concerns. One of the chief efforts of the Nixon administration was the recodification of the Federal Code, a task that had been going on for years and is still going on. Standards and goals were another characteristic, as well as an emphasis on corrections.

As these events were occurring on the national scene, New York was being affected by them and influencing them in turn. One only needs to consider the Division for Youth, the NYSIIS system, criminal code revision, centralized planning, the attack on organized crime, and drug programs — all of which were mounted on a large scale in New York. Many were stimulated externally, but often New York was the leader in educating the Nation in the nature of those problems. It is an interesting area in which to study how Rockefeller responded to national concern and played a prominent role in influencing it.

We have a panel today that will provide us a rare opportunity to look at some of the dimensions of the Rockefeller approach. Our purpose here is not to talk about the substance of crime control or criminal justice reform, but about how Nelson Rockefeller in his time responded to these issues.

Those of you who are aware of the Rockefeller admnistration know that the key person in the attack on crime in the Governor's Office was his Counsel, and we have a representative of that office here this morning. In addition, we have a person who was an important leader in the Legislature, who went on to be instrumental in setting up New York's planning agency, and who later became an important court official. Another panelist was concerned about the Division For Youth and drug reform, operated the New York State Information System, and is now involved in legal aid services in New York City. Finally, we have an academic who has studied the Rockefeller crime program and brings a view from that perspective.

So let us begin. Let me introduce our theme setter, Howard Shapiro, who was in the Counsel's Office for a number of years.

HOWARD SHAPIRO: Thank you very much, Vince. I am deeply honored to be selected as the theme setter for this panel on criminal justice and the Governor's policies on crime. I have to tell you, in all sincerity, that there are many others with whom I worked, some of whom are here today, who could very easily fill this same role as well or better than I. That also leads to a little bit of intimidation — an incentive to be very careful that what I say here today is precise and accurate. After all, we have a member of the State's highest court sitting in the audience, Judge Jones, from the Court of Appeals; we have the Dean of the Albany Law School; we have a professor from Union; we have the President of the State University; and we have my good friend, Arch Murray, from The Legal Aid Society in New York City. In fact, their presence reminds us that part of the legacy that the Governor left was the people, a fact that I would like to get back to later.

I did serve in the Governor's Counsel's Office from 1969 until 1973 — from late 1970 until 1973, as First Assistant Counsel. My ticket to the Rockefeller administration, the so-called Hogan Chair, was in itself a Rockefeller legacy. Frank Hogan was a District Attorney for New York County. For many, many years, he was known as Mr. District Attorney in the United States. The Governor, I think, was wise enough to select some of his people, at least in the Governor's Counsel's Office, from Frank Hogan's office. I was one of many in a rather long line of lawyers who served in the criminal justice seat of the Governor's Counsel's Office. Arch Murray was one of my predecessors, and Judge Howard Jones was another. John Sheehey, who is an attorney in

New York City, was still another. A person who succeeded me is Bill Donino, who is still active in the criminal justice system and serves as Elizabeth Holtzman's top aide in Brooklyn. So the Hogan Chair was very much a part of the Rockefeller Administration.

There will be no attempt, on my part, to try to identify, discuss, and analyze each and every program that was part of the criminal justice effort over 15 years of the Rockefeller administration. That would take days, weeks, months of our time — not to mention the additional time that it would take to discuss the merits of all those programs. Instead, I will try to fulfill the role that was identified by Norm Hurd: set certain parameters and give the discussants an opportunity to provide their own experience and insights. And I will try to point out what I think were the distinguishing features of the Rockefeller effort in criminal justice. I'll do that from my perspective not only in the Governor's Counsel's Office, but as an Assistant District Attorney in the Homicide Bureau in New York City and, after working in the Governor's Office, as Chairman of the State Investigation Commission — all told covering about ten years of the 15 year Rockefeller adminstration.

Several of the important features of Governor Rockefeller's crime control and criminal justice efforts were common to all of his administration's efforts, and they bear very importantly on the success of his programs. First, there was the man himself —charismatic, electric. When he walked through a room everyone recognized he was the leader. That rubbed off. He had clout. That was very crucial for the success of any program that was being proposed at any particular moment, especially to people who served as his negotiators on particular programs and issues.

Second, there was not just the man himself, but also his particular personal commitment to the criminal justice area. He felt very, very strongly about crime control, particularly drug abuse and other crime-related matters. I know that he believed that if his economic programs and his social programs were to be successful, the people had to feel safe and protected.

Third, and I mentioned this earlier, the people whom he involved assumed a level of responsibility, after associating with Rockefeller and his administration, that certainly was significantly higher than in previous administrations — just by the fact that they were involved with such a powerful figure.

Vividly, I remember coming to Albany — the end of the world for me. (That was the vantage point of a person who had worked in Manhattan.) A lot of snow was on the ground. I thought that I could do anything in criminal justice; after all, I had tried homicide cases. I was handed an assignment that looked like

Chinese (concerning criminal justice planning and reorganization of a portion of the so-called criminal justice system) and I was asked to attend a meeting of some people who were working with the Governor's staff on this project — people like Dick Denzer, Peter McQuillan, Dick Bartlett, and Arch Murray. I was to "supervise" these people. I remember walking into the room and seeing the looks on their faces that said: Don't worry kid, you just listen to us. Everything will be fine, and you'll learn something about this business.

The people that Rockefeller attracted are truly a legacy. Those in doubt need only look around New York State today and, in fact, the United States, in the criminal justice community (the good guys, I mean), and you will see Rockefeller's very, very strong imprint. These are people of enormous talent, ability, experience, and judgment. Much of that judgment, I think, they got working in the Rockefeller administration. They are the true legacy. If government leaders today have a particular and difficult criminal justice problem, — look at the Liman Commission, for example — you will see people from the Rockfeller days selected and involved, and very often they are the ones doing the heavy lifting.

After the people, Governor Rockefeller's second legacy is the massive, comprehensive series of programs and resources devoted to crime control, rehabilitation of offenders, courts, drug problems, and so forth. If you look back over the 15 years of the Rockefeller administration, I doubt whether you will find an area in any part of what's called the criminal justice system, that was not touched, and touched effectively and forcefully, by the Governor's programs. Perhaps it's a fair measure of the problem of crime control in our society today, that it has resisted an effort as massive and comprehensive as that applied from 1959 to 1973. That effort, I think it fair to say, is truly a blueprint for those who are still involved and still dedicated to improving the crime situation in our society today.

Vince O'Leary mentioned the Liman Commission, the Executive Advisory Commission on the Administration of Justice, which just submitted its report to the Governor. I would not agree with all of what they said, but certainly with much of it. I would particularly agree with the statement that the many local and State bodies concerned with crime share a common general goal, but it does not provide Euclidian rules by which their efforts are interrelated or integrated, nor is there even a neat table of organization for the State's criminal justice system.

I would probably go even further. I don't think that there is a system in the true sense (or even close to the true sense), of the word. I also, as did some of yesterday's speakers, I took to the dictionary. My Webster's says that a system is defined as a "regularly interacting or interdependent group of items forming a unified whole." I doubt whether the criminal justice system today could be characterized as "unified."

Another definition involved the word "harmonious," a "harmonious arrangement". And I doubt whether that's an accurate characterization of our criminal justice system.

During some informal private discussions held yesterday, the opinion was expressed, that perhaps it was impossible to have a true criminal justice system, because there are independent branches of the government involved — particularly the Judiciary. My response to that, is that the Legislature is also an independent branch of government, and yet Governor Rockefeller, as was pointed out over and over again yesterday, found many, many ways to work very effectively with the Legislature toward common goals. He also, especially later in his administration, found many ways to work in a practical, coordinated way with the Judiciary, and solved some serious problems in the process. So I think that there is certainly a good opportunity to have a true criminal justice system.

We already said that we are not going to go through every one of the Governor's particular programs. But there are a few that I would like to touch on, hopefully to set the stage for discussion and some participation from the audience, so as to get a dialogue going as to some of your reactions as you observed Rockefeller's criminal justice programs.

The 1960's are already looked to, as the Executive Advisory Commission's report indicated just a few days ago, as the time that the "fear of predatory crime became a principal domestic concern." And, as I said, there was a great and deep concern by the Governor. Here are some of the areas in which succesful efforts were undertaken. Dick Bartlett was Chairman of the Penal Law Commission, and, for the first time in over 60 some odd years, there was a revision of the Penal Law and Code of Criminal Procedure in this State, with great impetus and support coming from the Governor. We live with some of these modern laws today; how much worse things would have been without them!

There was clearly a major effort at strengthening the court system. We spent a good deal of our time dealing with such things as the Temporary State Commission on the Court System, financing of the courts, the State take-over of much of the local burden, the appointment of judges, and improving the overall quality of the courts, not to mention the tremendous increase in the number of judges and other court personnel that directly resulted from the Governor's programs.

In terms of correctional services, there were many major contributions. Training of correctional officers was basically nonexistent before the Governor's administration came into being. We did something as simple as changing the type of administrator in correctional services to move with the times, going from the traditional Paul McGinnis to a person of a completely different background and approach, Russ Oswald, who came with a parole and probation background.

I have a special fondness and recollection of the area of gun control. Having worked in the Homicide Bureau in New York City and having seen the terrible damage and tragedies caused, very often unintentionally, I had developed a very strong abhorrence for guns of all types. My first assignment, in the dead of winter of February 1969, was to work on a very comprehensive gun control bill. I worked day and night on this particular piece of legislation and drafted and polished, and, finally, after being up all night and having the bill printed and released to the press at 10:00 A.M., I was advised at 11:00 A.M. that the bill was dead. I said, "The bill can't be dead; it hasn't even been introduced." "Well, you have to understand," I was told, "that Senator Brydges already announced that the Senate would not pass the bill." The bill was dead. I learned a lot over the next three years about politics and not placing too much emphasis on pride of authorship. It was an eye-opening experience.

Nevertheless, the Governor continued with gun control legislation attempts; I even used a difficult situation at Cornell on one occasion to write a little gun control legislation. You may remember a takeover at Willard Straight Hall on the Cornell campus, by people with bandoleers across their bodies. The Legislature was in an uproar wanting to impose life in prison on all involved Cornell students. A bill was produced by the Legislature, and we had about an hour and a half to respond with a responsible, yet politically acceptable, proposal of our own. We did so, and you will find in the Penal Law today a fairly effective, modest piece of gun control legislation, at least for college campuses.

Police and prosecutor training is something that a lot of people today think is a very weak point of the criminal justice system. The quality of arrest and the quality of prosecution are all tied to recidivism, and many people feel that if there were better quality perhaps some of our problems would be diminished. We did spend a lot of time on upgrading prosecutor training and prosecutor compensation, to create a better level of district attorneys and assistant district attorneys. A great deal of time and money was spent, too, on training police — for example: creation of the Municipal Police Training Council, the State Police Academy, and the significant improvement of the training of those people who had on-the-firing-line contact.

I have a comment about funding, generally. Funding permeated the Rockefeller administration. Those were very different days than today. If you had a legitimate proposal, the Governor was more than likely to adopt it, and you knew that the money to do it would be there. It's one thing to have this great idea about reforming something and, yet, know, at the same time, that the resources will not be there. The effort will fall flat. That was not the case.

Organized crime was something that the Governor felt very strongly about. I had a personal interest and involvement, especially when I was appointed to head the State Investigation Commission which was charged, among other things, with the investigation of organized crime. The Governor had very, very strong personal feelings about organized crime, particularly, his sense that it was responsible for drug selling and distribution and the ravages of drugs.

Crime victims benefits: There was a Crime Victims Compensation Board established by the Governor. It started to sink into certain peoples' minds during the 1960's, that victims should be given some attention after they had been the subject of the crime, that they should get more than just protection.

Official corruption: There was always, during the modern history of the State, attention paid to corruption, especially when there was scandal. You may remember something called the Knapp Commission, which investigated corruption, particularly in the New York City criminal justice system. I think another governor would have looked at that situation, tipped his cap to what had already been developed and done, introduced a few pieces of legislation, and what had been going on forever would continue to go on. But this was a different person, and he had a somewhat different approach.

For the first time in the history of the State, five district attorneys, all in New York City, were superseded at one time and replaced by a special prosecutor to investigate corruption in the criminal justice system. I remember, vividly, the reaction from some D.A.'s on the day that the superseding took place, and they were not pleasant conversations. I asked specifically not to be assigned to call Frank Hogan, my former boss, who took this very personally. But that was a very dramatic thing, and most people believe it was a good thing.

The State Investigation Commission was directed to conduct

a study of the whole criminal justice system in New York City and identify some of the weak spots and recommend improvement. If you look at the document produced by the Commission, which unfortunately became another one of those commission studies which are placed on the shelf with reports by other commissions, you will find again some of the blueprints for improving the system.

There was also a great deal of attention paid to the information system, coming into the 20th Century and developing computerization. We saw the development of NYSIIS, and subsequently the Division of Criminal Justice Services, and the School of Criminal Justice here at SUNY.

So there was an enormous, massive, comprehensive effort covering all aspects of the criminal justice system, with a very special emphasis on drugs, which I guess I didn't appreciate until I went back and looked at the annual State of the State Messages in preparation for this panel. There is a constant theme from the beginning to the end of the Rockefeller administration about his concern for drug abuse. It starts off with deep concern about the addicted: extensive effort, many programs and lots and lots of money (over a billion dollars — and those were big, big dollars in those days) spent for the treatment, rehabilitation, and education of the drug users. There was strengthened enforcement. There were the Special Narcotics Courts. There was the beefing-up of the State Police. There was an effort to try and establish an effective coordination between Federal and State and New York City drug enforcement officials, not always successful or harmonious, but it was a major effort. Then, finally, to cap this theme, in late 1972, out of the blue, the Governor announced to his staff that he would seek very harsh penalities for drug crimes.

I would suggest to you that despite what you hear from various people as to the reasons for his decision to seek to impose these penalities, no one alive today really knows the reasons why Governor Rockefeller suggested this program. I think he took *that* legacy with him. This is my own conclusion based on talking with a lot of people. It may have been a combination of all the theories that I've heard. I think that he may have developed a deep personal frustration. Here was a problem that he felt very strongly about, to which he had devoted a great deal of his own time and attention and a lot of the State's money. Yet the efforts had been unsuccessful. It was very frustrating. The most sophisticated thinking had gone into Narcotic Addiction Control Commission (NACC), then later Drug Addiction Control Commission (DACC), to deal with this problem and we were losing the war against drugs.

I had some personal discussions with him, as did most of his staff, on various aspects of this Drug Penalty Bill, because, although he delegated much of the responsibility for most of the details in his administration, he wanted to understand virtually every provision of this life-without-parole program that he announced to a very enthusiastic Legislature. He wanted to know all the details. When, for example, someone went into his office and said: Governor, you know that there is a provision in your bill that would allow a person who gave a diet pill to a neighbor to escape the impact of the bill? I immediately got a telephone call and was questioned up-and-down as to what this was all about. I had to give him a long explanation of the history of drug penalty legislation, the difference in weights and amounts, and why the possessor of a certain small quantity was assumed not to be a user as opposed to a seller, and so forth.

This was a very complicated piece of legislation we had produced; it made most tax bills look simple. He listened, not very patiently, for a few seconds and said, "I understand your logic. It makes perfectly good sense. Please come down to my office right away. I want to talk to you further about this." And he was not at all happy. He wanted that piece of legislation to go to the Legislature just as he had described it.

There has been a lot of hindsight and reflection on this Drug Penalty Bill. It subsequently was changed and repealed in part. I think the historians probably will be spending a lot of time looking at the reasons for these proposals and what their true impact has been, and there are going to be more. You only need to pick up last week's copy of *New York* Magazine. Right on the cover is a graphic illustration as to why the drug business is florishing today, and how one timely trip to Colombia, if not detected, makes you and your family multimillionaires for the rest of your lives. The drug problem is getting worse rather than better, and, I suspect, you will see other proposals being made to deal very harshly with people in the drug business.

A couple of closing comments and then I will be anxious to hear the critique or comments or filling-in or whatever from my co-panelists.

Today I am much more an observer than a regular participant in the criminal justice system, and somewhat of a pessimist in terms of society's ability and effectiveness in dealing with the current crime problems. I think that when we talk about the crime problem, we have to talk really about large cities and other heavily populated places. I don't think that the crime problem, for example, in Albany, is really very serious; at least, it's not perceived to be. And perception is all-important. The average citizen's feelings about walking out on the street, and worrying about whether the person coming up quickly behind him is to be feared or not, is very important.

But the crime problem in the big cities, I think, is certainly not getting any better, and the statistics, I think, would probably bear that out. My rationalization or my conclusion with respect to the massive effort that I was involved in (and criminal problems over those 15 years) is that things might have been much worse had some of these efforts not been made. If some of these major changes in the criminal justice system, in the court sytem, in correctional services, and in police training had not been undertaken, how much worse off — less prepared — we would be!

I watch with great interest the appointment by Governorelect Cuomo of a Criminal Justice Coordinator, and I understand that the gentleman selected for that position is extremely well thought of and qualified and able. Much of that assignment in the Rockefeller administration was the responsibility of the Assistant Counsel for criminal justice. I wish the new coordinator a lot of luck. He's going to need it.

I'll close by sharing a little secret with you. I think some day the State of New York will come to the conclusion that there needs to be a State Justice Department, just as there is on the Federal level. Not only a coordinating, but an implementing and planning body. Now I'm not suggesting that there was any calculated grand design, but if you look around the statute books of New York, then you will find more than just the seeds of a State Department of Justice. You will find many of the necessary components already in place.

You will see State Police. You will see a state-wide prosecutor. (Although it's called the Organized Crime Task Force, it has state-wide jurisdiction, and, with some minor tinkering and major political discussion, it could have a broader role.) You will see planning and funding in the Division of Criminal Justice Services. There are a few other pieces as well. If it was a decision of the State today to go for an overall state-wide entity to at least coordinate effectively the criminal justice system, the blueprint and many of the pieces are available to be used.

VINCENT O'LEARY: Richard Bartlett was a very prominent member of the Assembly associated with the revision of the New York Penal Code - a very important reform. He then became head of the Crime Control Planning Board for the State of New York, our match in the LEAA World, and, after that, left there to become, as a judge, the quartermaster for the whole task of court administration. It was a distinguished career. Then he became

Dean of the Albany Law School, where he is serving today with great distinction. Dick Bartlett.

RICHARD BARTLETT: Thank you very much, Vince. I suppose that introduction prompted you to think: He's had trouble holding onto a job. Maybe there's some truth in that.

I'm going to start with the Counsel's Office, because it became a very different kind of unit in the Rockefeller years than it had ever been before. Perhaps it can be said that during the Dewey years the seeds were planted for an organized, structured Counsel's Office, but, I have a feeling, that kind of lapsed during the Harriman years and then was pretty much a one-man show. Then, beginning in 1959 (when I was a very green new legislator) I saw the development of a structured, highly competently staffed Counsel's Office for the first time in this State.

I think it's important for us to have that in mind, not just as we look at the criminal justice system, (where the role of Counsel's Office was so very dominant), but in terms of how the government operated in the State of New York during the Rockefeller years. We had as Counsel, over the fifteen-year period, Rod Perkins, Bob MacCrate, Sol Corbin, Bob Douglass, and Mike Whiteman. They were aided by an enormously talented staff, many of whom went on to do other important things in government (including two of our panelists today, Howard and Arch, as well as Frank Wille in the next room). If we were to take the guest list here and just check off people who had been in Counsel's Office, it would amount to a fairly significant portion of the attendees. I think it is well for us to have that in our minds, not only as we discuss this topic, but as we think about how Nelson Rockefeller ran his show for fifteen years, because the Counsel's Office was really an extremely important part of his success.

I want to say a little more about the Hogan legacy — the Hogan Chair — because that was very important. Bill Rand was the first, then Howard Jones, then Arch Murray, then John Sheehey, then Howard Shapiro and Bill Donino and Paul Gioia —all top-flight people, all graduates of the Hogan office. Was it because Frank Hogan had special influence on Nelson Rockefeller? I think not. In fact, there were a number of showdowns over the years that Frank consistently lost. I think that someone told Nelson: You ought to have somebody who knows something about criminal justice, and the place to go is Frank Hogan's office because they have very talented people there. It's to be noted that they had very talented men and hardly any women in those days, but that's been changed. If any of you are interested, I can still visualize the desk that was occupied successfully by those people.

239

It never changed over the years. You might have thought it was located on the right of Counsel's Office, but it was to the left — only slightly to the left. I worked with all of them, and I can tell you that their influence in the second floor structure was much larger than one would expect from a lowly Assistant Counsel.

That influence was due to the attention that criminal justice matters got, not just in the Counsel's Office but on the rest of the second floor. Programatically, criminal justice (at least throughout the years we are reviewing) was peculiarly and precisely the responsibility of Counsel's Office.

Now let me talk a little bit about the Penal Law Commission, because that's the part about which I know most. To tell the truth, I don't know how it actually started. For the first two years I was in the Legislature, 1959-60, I was largely concerned with getting the ski development going in Warren County (at the expense of the taxpayers of the State), and I was concerned about the daily limit on the catch of lake trout in Lake George among other equally important issues. I did not trouble myself very much with crime. It was not a big deal in Glens Falls. I don't know, to this day, just how I came to be selected as chairman of the commission. I suspect, more than anything else, that it had something to do with the fact that MacCrate and I were classmates in law school. Anyhow, in the Governor's Message of 1961, he called for the creation of a Temporary Commission to thoroughly revise the Penal Law and the Criminal Code. It hadn't been looked at in a long time. The Penal Code was first proposed by a fellow named Field in the 1860's. The proposal languished until the 1880's, before it was passed by the Legislature in 1884. There was a subsequent structural revision of the procedural aspects of that code in 1909. That was the state of those two bodies of law in 1961. They were just incredibly confusing and layered — a hodgepodge, it's fair to say, of statutes. And so, the Governor asked for the commission, and the Legislature approved it, without, I am sure, giving the matter a great deal of thought. I have no recollection of voting on the bill at all. That summer, I got a call from Bob MacCrate, who suggested that I might interest myself in being on the Commission. I promptly consulted the speaker, Joe Carlino. I was named to the Commission by the Speaker and appointed Chairman by the Governor. Timothy Pfeiffer, a Milbank and Tweed partner, was the Vice-Chairman. The other members were: William Kapelman, then an Assemblyman; Nicholas Atlas, New York City practitioner; John Conway, the D.A. of Monroe County; Phillip Halpern, one of the brightest judges in our court system; Howard Jones, Assistant Counsel to the Governor; William Mahoney, Walter Mahoney's brother and also the most prominent criminal lawyer in western New York, at that time; and Herbert Wechsler, the great professor at Columbia who had been the recorder for the American Law Institute's Division of Penal Law. That was the team.

If your quick thought is that Bartlett alone among them appears to have no experience or background, you're right! Herbert Wechsler deserves particular mention, because he contributed so enormously to the work of the Commission. As the draftsman of the Model Code, he was incredibly knowledgeable in the field and remarkably skilled, for a professor, in the give and take of compromise and getting things accomplished. Some people later associated with the project were John Hughes, a State Senator; Julius Volker, Assemblyman; and Whitman Knapp, a lawyer in New York City and Chairman of the Knapp Commission. Frank Hogan joined us, after a while, as did Arch Murray and Charlie Rangel. Earl Brydges, Jr. was a member. (There were a few legacies around like Earl Brydges, Jr., but he was a very good member.) Senators John Dunne and Bernard Smith also served on the Commission.

We had virtually a free hand in selection of our staff. That deserves emphasis, because it didn't often occur with legislative committees. It was understood that we would hire the best professionals we could find.

Where did I go to look for staff? Frank Hogan's office, of course! We chose Dick Denzer as our director, and a great choice it was. He had been chief of the Appeals Bureau, a very scholarly fellow. We also selected Peter McQuillan, who had been an assistant district attorney, as had Peter Preiser. These three were the mainstays of our staff. You may be thinking: All D.A.'s — no defense people. One of the remarkable characteristics of the Frank Hogan office was that it turned out people who were amazingly balanced about the criminal justice system. I think this demonstrated itself in our product. In fact, all of the people associated with us reflected that kind of balance.

Now, what was the relationship of the Commission and its work with the Rockefeller administration? In the beginning, not much. We were given a mandate to go clean up these two bodies of law — the Penal Law and the Code of Criminal Procedure — cast out the superfluous and unnecessary, examine the substantive law that's left, and make recommendations for revision.

We went about our work and in February 1962 we filed a modest report on our plan of work. We did propose a couple of bills in 1962. *Mapp v. Ohio* had been decided, and so we drafted a bill providing for the procedure for suppression of illegally siezed evidence. Also in 1962, Governor Rockefeller issued a Special

Message relating to the administration of criminal justice. It proposed doing something about municipal police training and suggested the establishment of a school of criminology at SUNY. It was several years later (I believe it was in 1965) that the School of Criminal Justice was established. The School of Criminal Justice is a very special school; it's the only place I know where problems associated with the administration of criminal justice are looked at in a scholarly, if sometimes abstract, way. It represents a very important development in both the criminal justice and education fields, in my view.

The first bill involving the death penalty that I had anything to do with was in 1963. When Nelson Rockefeller became Governor, New York was the only remaining state in the nation with a mandatory death penalty for persons convicted of premeditated, first-degree murder. Felony murder was not mandatory, it was optional. It was suggested that we look at that and develop a proposal for the so-called "two-stage trial." In the first stage, the jury determines innocence or guilt. In the second stage, the jury hears matters relevant to punishment and recommends life imprisonment or the death penalty. That bill passed and was signed by the Governor with an approving memorandum, which noted that we were the last of the states to abandon mandatory capital punishment.

That same year, the Commission considered the report of the Foster Committee, which made recommendations concerning the insanity defense. We first proposed a bill loosening up the strict rules regarding psychiatric testimony to let psychiatrists testify in terms familiar to their discipline, instead of the straight-jacket imposed by legal definitions. The definition of the defense of insanity remained unchanged until our revision package was adopted. We also continued with an examination of the principal work: revision of the Penal Law and Criminal Code.

During that time, the relationship between the Commission and its efforts with the Governor's Office was not a close one. I made it my business to keep the Counsel's Office informed of what we were doing, and, of course, some of our work was in response to requests from that office. Beginning in 1964, a closer relationship began to evolve. We participated in drafting and sponsored two little bills called "No Knock" and "Stop and Frisk" — great titles. "No Knock" was in response to the claim of the police that — in executing a search warrant in a drug raid — between the time they demanded entrance (as the law required), waited to see that there was no response, and the time they broke the door down, the drugs were all flushed down the toilet. "Stop and Frisk" established the right of a police officer to stop someone

242

behaving suspiciously, to demand to know what the person's up to, and to search for weapons.

Now I want to discuss capital punishment. It was understood from the beginning that one of the things we would look at was capital punishment. We dealt with the mandatory character of the penalty as it existed in New York in 1963. By 1965, we had finally come to a conclusion regarding the main issue: retention or abolishion of capital punishment. The Commission voted eight to four to recommend its abolition. There was no consultation with the Governor's office, except to alert them that we were about to come out with a report on the subject. Members voting for abolition were Bartlett, Pfeiffer, Kapelman, Mahoney, Atlas, Wechsler, and Knapp. Ray Barratta, who was then the D.A. of Dutchess County; John Conway, the D.A. of Monroe County; Howard Jones; and Julius Volker were for retaining the death penalty. Howard Jones wrote the minority report, and Herbert Wechsler wrote for the majority.

We sponsored a bill to abolish the death penalty, which was amended by the Legislature to carve out exceptions to the abolition for the killing of a police officer in the course of duty and for murder committed by someone already serving life in prison. Before the bill came to a vote, I was trying to get some kind of a signal from the second floor. To be frank about it, what would happen to this bill if it passed? And no signal emerged. So we went ahead. After great debate, the abolition bill passed and was sent to the Governor. I got very nervous. The clock was running, and it was a ten-day bill. I was getting all kinds of conflicting reports. I finally called Sol Corbin and said, "I really want to see the Governor about the death penalty bill." He said, "I don't know if he wants to see you on that subject or not." Another day went by. I called again and he said he would get back to me in a few minutes. He got back to me and said, "You don't need to meet with Nelson, he just signed the bill." He signed the bill without memorandum or comment of any kind. The Governor was very troubled by the bill. Two of his very closest advisors, both of whom are at this conference, urged against signing. Others urged for it, and he finally decided to sign it — a very major piece of legislation that he just quietly put his name to.

Later that year, the bill providing for a new Penal Law for the State was passed. After amendments reinstating criminal penalties for adultery and consensual sodomy were added, the bill passed with ease. The Governor signed the bill without particular comment. He called me at home to tell me the Commission had done a great job. You know, those calls from the Governor never ceased to impress. One of the kids would answer the phone and excitedly announce, "The Governor is calling," and it is fair to say that not just the children were impressed! The Commission then went on to develop a Code of Criminal Procedure which was passed finally in 1970. Thus, the principal responsibilities of the Penal Law Commission were discharged.

Over the years, in addition to our major work of statutory revision, the Commission staff became an adjunct staff to the Counsel's Office. We were delighted to be asked to participate, and we did regularly, in drafting many of the other measures related to criminal justice not specifically within our mandate. Denzer, McQuillan, Preiser, and I were regularly in and out of the office, and we developed a very close association. So I admit to some bias with regard to Counsel's Office, but do not think I have been overly effusive in describing the quality of their work.

A couple of other things are worth mentioning, post-Penal Law Commission. Crime control planning: If anything can be said to have characterized the Rockefeller years, it was the emphasis on planning, and that has impacted on everything that has happened since in State government. Planning went on in every conceivable area, in a more organized way than had ever been the case before.

A good example would be the crime control planning effort that pre-dated the Safe Streets Act passed by Congress in 1968. In 1967, during the Constitutional Convention, Al Marshall called and asked me to come down to chat with him. The administration wanted to form a Crime Control Council — one of the recommendations of the President's Commission on Crime — in anticipation of the Federal government requiring the states to involve themselves in planning. So we geared up a year ahead of time and we had a planning component, a planning staff, in place and at work by the time the Safe Streets Act passed. I continued to be associated with that effort, as Chairman, for many years. I can tell you that we regularly heard from Counsel's Office and Al Marshall when he was secretary, reminding us that the Governor wanted to be sure that we were looking at every area of the criminal justice process in planning for the future.

There is one last thing I think ought to be mentioned in looking at the Rockefeller policies toward crime. That is how the Governor responded to the tragedy of Attica. Immediately after the Attica riot, the McKay Commission was appointed to conduct an inquiry into what had happened and how and why. Within a few days of that action, another committee was appointed, not to look at Attica, but to look at our prison system as a whole. The chairman is in this room today, Judge Hugh Jones, and I was pleased to be a member of that committee. Peter Preiser was staff director. We spent the next one and a half to two years looking at the prison system and produced a whole series of recommendations, nearly all of them implemented. They included: better training for guards, manuals of operation; better food, better clothing, and better housing conditions for inmates. And, of course, that's a classic Rockefeller response to a problem. No cover up — everything out in front: the McKay Commission to look at what happened and why, and the Jones Committee to look at the penal institutions as they functioned and make recommendations for their improvement. Thank you.

VINCENT O'LEARY: Arch Murray was one of the holders of the Hogan Chair. He was involved in the Counsel's Office and spent some of his career in drug control activities. Arch spent a good deal of his time in the legacy that Dick Bartlett spoke of in the State of New York: the planning agency that received millions of Federal dollars and spent them here. In addition, he was responsible for NYSIIS, an information system that is a prototype across the United States. New York started it very early and it has responsibiity for the fingerprints system and the statistical system.

After a distinguished career there, Arch is now the head of the Legal Aid Society in New York City. Arch and I were on the Liman Commission together, and there was a sense of deja vu.

ARCHIBALD MURRAY: Four characteristics stood out as I stopped and began thinking about the Rockefeller administration in recent days. First, one has a sense of responsiveness on the Governor's part in his approach to crime — a responsiveness to perceived problems. Another characteristic was persistence. Governor Rockefeller was the most persistent person I have ever met. He got hold of something, and he did not let go until he finally got what he wanted out of it in the way of a solution. I think that, more than anything, explains the ultimate drug proposals that he made. It is part of a larger pattern of persistence.

Third, there was the scope of his vision. Most of us then tended to come to a problem and wanted to take a little piece of it and see how that worked and then maybe deal with another piece of it. Rockefeller had to grab it, and he had to deal with it, and he had to solve it. If that meant that he had to marshall massive resources, then he marshalled massive resources and got the job done. Another unusual characteristic was his capacity to anticipate national plans — trends elsewhere in the country and in the world. Usually he became quite a pacesetter because he did that sort of thing.

One of the small by-products of all of this was that he tended to be a very appreciative boss to work for. The Governor encouraged intiative, and if you seemed to be getting a job done, he was very, very supportive. Now, that's not to say that if you were not getting the job done, he would not let you know how unhappy he was.

Something about the responsiveness: it seems to me that every year, if we were to go back and look at the Annual Messages of the Governor, there would be something in them, of a major sort, reflecting current concerns about crime as perceived by the population or as reported by the media. One of those concerns related to drugs. I went back and looked at the Annual Messages for 15 years and there were at least 11 major initiatives over those 15 years having to do with attacking the drug problem. He tried. He tried, and tried on a bigger scale. He then tried on a massive scale.

On the question of his ability to anticipate: Dick already has alluded to the fact that Rockefeller anticipated the creation of LEAA and the planning capacity that was later installed in the Justice Department, and the funding of programs. I came back to the State government in December 1967, because they were creating this agency called the Crime Control Council. We were to get geared up and be ready to beat the Federal government before they got LEAA in place about a year later. That was important, because New York was about the first state to arrive in Washington and pick up the money. We even arrived and picked it up before the law permitted us to do it!

Interestingly enough, the Safe Streets Act was passed, but the President did not name the LEAA immediately. At the Justice Department, the Attorney General had no authority under that statute to spend that money. But, there was a provision in there that said unless certain portions were spent by some date in September of 1968, that the money would lapse. The Attorney General of the United States, therefore, took it upon himself to send notices to governors saying that they might apply for this money. We looked at the statute in New York and said that he had no authority to do it, but we would not look a gift horse in the mouth. So we dashed off to Washington to pick up the money, and I think that we were probably the first ones to do so. Because of that head start, New York State was probably able to get more than its fair share of those discretionary funds and, of course, all of the money we were entitled to on the basis of the formula.

Also, looking back at the "anticipation," one of the things that struck me was that several years before OEO Legal Services came into being or were even thought of by the Federal government, New York (since 1961, I think) had authorized the larger counties in this State to provide funding for civil legal assistance for the poor. This was something that was not really thought of, in a serious way, elsewhere for another three years.

I was an assistant counsel to the Governor after the Supreme Court of the United States decided *Gideon v. Wainwright*, saying that indigent people who were charged with crimes had a right to be provided with a lawyer at government expense. One day an Assemblyman from Glens Falls dropped by my office and said, "Gee, this year we are about to increase per capita aid to localities, and I am sure that, unless we give them something worthwhile to do with that money, they are going to put it down the rat hole. What about doing something about providing representation for people who are charged with crime and cannot afford to pay for legal service?" So, out of that came what is now called Article 18B of the County Law. Then, it was referred to (it depended on whether you were in Binghamton or Glens Falls) as the Bartlett-Anderson law or the Anderson-Bartlett law. The Governor was very willing to support this kind of enterprise.

I think that as Governor Rockefeller saw the system, there were probably two major things that had to be accomplished. One was improving the quality of personnel dealing with the problem, and the other was bringing together the kinds of resources that they needed to deal with it. If you were to go through and look at all the program proposals made over his 15 years of service, you would find a constant theme of professionalizing the personnel dealing with the problem of crime. Early legislation provided for the training of police officers; the creation of the Municipal Police Training Council; the creation of the Bureau of Municipal Police; requirements that police officers, before they were promoted to first-line supervisory positions, undergo certain kinds of qualifying training; and that standards be set centrally before people could qualify for appointment to police positions. Governor Rockefeller tried to bring professionalization to the office of the District Attorney, with requirements that the district attorneys in counties of a certain size be full-time, and at the same time made provision for easing the financial burden that that brought. Later, other laws required training for correctional officers.

When we took these training resources, and the structures to implement the new standards, we ultimately had in place the variety of pieces which could have become the base for a Department of Justice. In those days we were more modest, so we came up with a Division of Criminal Justice Services. New York had evolved a criminal justice planning capability over the period from 1967: we had, since 1965, the beginnings of an information system, and we had the training and standard-setting capacity since about 1963 or 1964. And one day in 1972 all of these pieces were brought together in one place. The State, with the assistance of Federal dollars, now found itself in a position to begin to influence what happened in the larger criminal justice system.

By using grants-in-aid, we attempted to influence what localities did. It was not very easily done. People sometimes tend to forget that much of what happens in criminal justice is really done at the local level of government and is very much under the control of local government. Police are, for the most part, local officers. The Division of State Police is just one tiny drop in the ocean of all the police forces and police officers serving in the State. Detention and the correctional function for misdemeanors are done at the local level. Prosecutors are county officials. They run in counties and they respond to the electorate in the localities. The biggest piece that the State controls is the adult correctional system. Except for that, what you're dealing with in terms of numbers of personnel is overwhelmingly local. So the Governor did not really have direct control, but by a system of grants — giving or withholding assistance — an effort was made to influence these localities in the direction of improving their capacity to perform. I think some headway was made.

In addition to that, we had within this enterprise the beginnings of the information one needed to go about making change happen. It was not designed to be a management information system, but simply a system for keeping track of people who had been arrested and sent to prison. We started off with the fingerprinting system from the Department of Correction which, with the introduction of computers, became a system that kept track of people who were arrested and then passed through the system. The system was not designed initially to do many of the things that we later attempted to do with it. That is part of the problem with what is called NYSIIS. Out of the information in that system, we began to identify trends; we began to do some planning, dealing with larger problems beyond what the State would normally have been able to do.

In all of this, the Governor was especially supportive. When, in 1972, he started creating some additional court parts around the State — particularly in the City of New York — he was especially supportive. What we had to do, in those days, was to persuade five district attorneys to begin functioning together. As separately elected officials, they were not at all inclined in that direction, but he was willing to make the phone calls when necessary to push people into cooperation. As a result, we finally got them to participate in a number of cooperative ventures in the

City of New York. The Governor's ultimate massive effort, superseding the district attorneys, was possible because he had determination and he was willing to push for those things that he thought would bring about the kinds of solutions he sought.

The creation of the Office of Special Prosecutor in the City of New York and the creation of the massive program for dealing with narcotics, both in the treatment phase and the prosecution and enforcement phase, reflect the Governor's determination on these matters and his willingness to bring to the task whatever effort he thought it would take. There were those who thought, when he proposed the massive enforcement side of the drug program, that he was particularly insistent, astute, forceful and probably likely to be successful.

Those who looked at the creation of the additional judgeships were particularly impressed with the political astuteness that went into that. It guaranteed a rather significant number of votes in the Legislature, because there were an awful lot of people who were willing to vote for the creation of those judgeships — with the hope that they themselves might one day hold those positions. There were others who felt the same sense of frustration that the Governor did and, out of that, voted to support those enterprises. I guess that, in my view, the proposals went much further than necessary, and since then, they've been modified. But they were a reflection of his willingness to push for a solution, to go the distance and to hang in there as he attempted to develop all the resources required to carry out this program in a very short time.

One small story about that: the Governor was willing to give support when I undertook the job of trying to get the facilities in place — creating courtrooms in places that courtrooms had not existed before. He called almost every couple of days to find out how things were going. Because of his interest, we were able to get resources that we would not otherwise have had. We got a number of judges together one day to identify where we might find space. (In New York City, courthouse space is not something you find very easily.) It turned out that there was an entire floor available in the City's Civil Court building, which no one really knew was there. After meeting together, and with a little bit of telephoning by the Governor to the right people, the space was made available. In very short order we got these courtrooms built and furnished.

The people who designed them, however, had not had great experience in designing courtrooms and so there were some awkward moments. The judges who were going to be handling these cases were particularly anxious. They said that they were going to be imposing penalties of life imprisonment. People would therefore be desperate and the judges were very concerned about security. So I promised them that we would have a system of security which provided a foot alarm under the bench. Immediately on hitting the foot alarm, substantial numbers of court officers and others would respond.

The first day the courts opened, I got a rather urgent call from one judge. I went dashing over to the courthouse and he said, "Look at this, look at this." He was a rather short man, and when his chair was at full height, so he could see and be seen, he couldn't reach the button on the floor. When he spun his chair down to reach the button, he disappeared. So the question was, "What to do? Should I cut the bench down?" It was much too much trouble; so, that became a courtroom for tall judges!

These were some of the difficulties one got into when asked to implement a massive program on very short notice. This was not a characteristic of the administration. Normally there was lead time — time for planning — time to test before putting programs in place. This drug problem, I think, was the ultimate response to a continuing frustration: it led to massive action without quite enough lead time.

Overall, you have an administration that brought into position a number of pieces of legislation and programs, which will provide future administrations the capacity to influence the entire criminal justice system, both at the State level and, particularly, at the local level. These were built incrementally over the fifteen years of the Rockefeller administration. They reveal continuing interest in the system of criminal justice, and indeed "criminal justice" as a term actually only became prominent during those years of the Rockefeller administration. Before that you used to hear about "law enforcement." The system began to be viewed comprehensively during those years, and people began to realize that by changing one portion of the system, one would, of necessity, affect the others. If you increased the number of police, you ultimately created more work, and needed to address the question of how many more judges were required. And if you created more judgeships devoted to dealing with criminal cases, you could inevitably expect to increase the work load of the correction departments, the probation departments, and the parole boards. We installed the notion, too, that if you increase the capacity to prosecute, you would also have to recognize the need to increase the capacity to defend. Otherwise you merely introduce imbalance and cause the system to choke on itself.

VINCENT O'LEARY: One of the purposes of the retrospective is to understand the history of the Rockefeller administration. After all, this is an Institute concerned with understanding government. So on each of the panels we invited a scholar to sit, listen, and reflect on the information, views and attitudes of those who were actually in the Rockefeller administration. To play that role here, we have a professor from Union College — a political scientist, Bill Daniels, who was for a while an Alfred E. Smith Fellow and a Fulbright Fellow and has written about the Rockefeller administration. At the end of Bill's presentation, I will ask five people in this room, who had commanding posts in the Rockfeller Administration, what one piece of advice, from their days with that Administration, they would give Governor Cuomo, if he were to call them today.

WILLIAM J. DANIELS: My assignment, when asked to participate, was to assist in the effort to place the Rockefeller administration in perspective. As a political scientist — a student of government — I am gratified at the attention now given to Governor Rockefeller's development of programs, how he related to his advisors, his use of task forces, committees, commissions, and the like.

My colleague, James E. Underwood, and I have recently completed a comprehensive treatment of the Rockefeller years, entitled *Governor Rockefeller in New York: The Apex of Pragmatic Liberalism in the United States.* As the title suggests, this book represents an effort to view the Rockefeller administration from a broader perspective, and, interestingly enough, many of the participants over the past day and a half have attempted to do just that. May I call your attention to some of the comments that have been made? For example, Rockefeller was called a "contradiction of terms," "pragmatic in the most effective sense of the word." Also, it was said that "the environment in which we lived was conducive to action," namely, "his programs were expensive when we could afford to be expensive." These thoughts by some of the panelists, most of whom were "insiders," should serve in our efforts to fix the boundaries of the Rockefeller administration and to make comparisons across time.

Governor Rockefeller did not like labels. For example, he said in 1958:

> We must be conservative, for we know the
> measureless value that is our heritage to save, to
> cherish and enrich. We shall be liberal — for
> we're vastly more interested in the opportunities
> of tomorrow than the problems of today, and we
> shall be progressive — for the opportunities and

the challenges are of such size and scope that we
can never halt and say: our labor is done.

His reluctance to be labeled notwithstanding, my colleague and I suggest that Nelson Rockefeller is part of an ideological legacy that we call "pragmatic liberalism".

Let me explain briefly. The political mood of the times from the conclusion of World War II into the decade of the 1960's was liberal and was initially firm or ideological. But with the passage of time into the 1960's, liberalism became less ideological, it can be argued, and more pragmatic. Thus we call the ideological mood of the times, that which prevailed during the Rockefeller administration, "pragmatic liberalism." But what is particularly important here is that Nelson Rockefeller became a prominent figure in national politics during the time liberalism was becoming less ideological, and he later moved into executive power in New York State shortly before the components of pragmatic liberalism gained full currency — in part due to his efforts, we argue.

What are the major components of pragmatic liberalism? Briefly, that all problems can be solved with sufficient effort on the part of the government; that a primary test of a good policy is its pragmatic nature, as opposed to considerations of abstract principle; that government and the private sector should cooperate to solve social problems; that the government should place a higher priority on meeting human needs; that all segments of society should receive an equitable share of the benefits allocated by government; and that science and technology provide the key in solving many of society's problems. These key components provided the foundation for much of the political thinking at the national level, especially following the presidential election of 1960. They are important in assessing the Rockefeller years in New York State. They are being mentioned by participants at this conference, and they relate well to the subject of this panel. In fact, a case can be made that Nelson Rockefeller represented an epitome of pragmatic liberalism in action. When he no longer had the means to function as a pragmatic liberal, that's when he left New York State politics. It can also be said that his leaving New York signaled and symbolized the decline in the currency of pragmatic liberalism, nationally.

It has been said repeatedly at this conference that Nelson Rockefeller was constantly identifying problems and offering solutions. I think that sums up his approach nicely. He was program-oriented, rather than management-oriented, and his programs reflected his beliefs and his style. He was a person with strong convictions, persistent, even stubborn. He expected loyalty and was not keen on people who were trying to save him from himself. He expected loyalty within the framework of the policy as it was established.

Nelson Rockefeller used experts; he used task forces; he delegated details and, frequently, enormous responsibility to others. He loved information. He loved to work in groups and used them extensively. His programs usually contained something for everyone; if one is familiar with the particular issue area the use of experts could readily be seen. A systematic review of the program areas over the years shows that he believed in covering all important areas — there were no gaps.

An examination of the Governor's policies toward crime and related topics demonstrates his tendencies, beliefs, style, and approaches. A point should be made about responsiveness. Rockefeller was always polling: he wanted to know how the public felt. In this regard, if we look at the capacity to anticipate trends and programs in government, New York State was considered to be a bellweather State with regard to the innovative quality and management of its programs. If we look at the issue of drugs, Rockefeller had this to say in 1971:

> How can we defeat drug abuse before it destroys America? I believe the answer lies in summoning the total commitment America has always summoned in times of national crisis.... Drug addiction represents a threat akin to war in its capacity to kill, enslave and imperil the nation's future; akin to cancer in spreading deadly disease among us, and equal to any other challenge we face and deserving all the brain-power, manpower, and resources necessary to over come it.... Are the sons and daughters of a generation that survived the great depression and rebuilt a prosperous nation, that defeated Nazism and Fascism and preserved the free world, to be vanquished by a powder, needles, and pills?

That's how strongly he felt about this issue. He viewed this persistent problem as a crisis; a challenge akin to war. The Governor tackled the problem incrementally — a range of alternatives were brought to bear including treatment, rehabilitation, education; then harsh punishment and strengthened enforcement. For the Governor, fighting narcotic addiction, and the crime addiction it surrounded, had become a crusade. His 1973 drug program represented an effort to defeat drug abuse before it destroyed America.

Even Attica, viewed as an aspect of Rockefeller's policy on

corrections, reflects his beliefs, style, and pattern of acting. Without getting into why he did not go to Attica (because that would take more time than we now have) some broad generalizations are apparent. For example: innovation and government reorganization are evident in the 1971 creation of the Department of Correctional Services. This involved the merger of the Department of Corrections and the Division of Parole. Attracting the best minds is exemplified in the appointment of Russell Oswald, a respected and reform-minded professional, to head up the new Department; authority was delegated, for Oswald had freedom to make key decisions during the negotiating process. Rockefeller was fair, because he negotiated. He was tough, because he ordered the reopening of the institution.

Beyond these two issue areas, an analysis of the Annual Messages to the Legislature shows that, in large measure, the tone of his administration's policies toward crime can be captured on a continuum. To wit: in the early years the Governor emphasized prevention — in the later years, control. He seemed to become more pragmatic as time progressed. The carrot was offered earlier, later the stick. The area of crime prevention and control is not exactly politically attractive, nor was it a high priority area for the Governor. But even here — even here in this unattractive policy area — there was something for nearly everyone.

One final observation. As a political scientist, I ask why things happen. I am interested in the subject of political leadership, as we all are, and I believe this conference can contribute in a significant way to defining, exploring, and explaining the legacy of Nelson A. Rockefeller. I am convinced of one thing, that a part of the Rockefeller legacy was the ability to convince some of the most knowledgeable persons in the country to come to work for New York State government. I would only urge those of you — who have and are serving in the government of our State — who have not participated in this oral history project to do so before this conference is adjourned. I look forward to the results.

ALAN CHARTOCK: One question to those of you who have seen Rockefeller reaching for major solutions. I once wrote a piece on Rockefeller and drug addiction, and in it I wondered, at the end, if the next thing was going to be legalization of heroin. It may seem way out, but with his experimental nature, the disposition that Rockefeller had to get a solution, and his impatience with things that weren't working, it seemed possible. It seems to me that first he tried the soft approach — the motels, essentially creating a nice place for people to be when they would be detoxified. He then tried the hard approach, and that didn't work. I was wondering what else he might have tried, had he stayed on as Governor and not gone on to Vice-President.

HOWARD SHAPIRO: I will never be convinced that he would have gone in that direction.

VINCENT O'LEARY: What about marijuana?

HOWARD SHAPIRO: These subjects were discussed among the staff. Heroin — never. Hard drugs — never. I think you would have seen, had he continued on as Governor, his making the program that he had passed in 1973 more effective. Regarding marijuana, I honestly don't know — though I tend to doubt it, because I think he believed it was part of the whole drug culture. But I could never believe that he would have gone for legalization of hard drugs.

There was a lot of discussion, you may recall, about methadone. We once had an in-house suggestion, early on, that methadone would be available on every street corner in certain places in the City of New York; it being the alternative to heroin. That got quickly shot down.

It's an interesting question, and it's one of the few questions on which I, personally, can give you a definitive answer. In 1973 he was at the opposite end of the spectrum, having been through the whole range.

COMMENT

I think that Howard is right. It's very unlikely. But he had this streak of pragmatism in him that, if someone could demonstrate to him that legalization would in fact solve the problem, he would be willing to try it. But I don't think anybody was likely to meet the burden of proof that he would place on them.

The whole idea of moving more and more toward the enforcement side of it, at least internally, was discernable in 1963 and 1964 and 1965 and the program in 1966. There was an awful lot of discussion internally about doing more enforcement. Some on staff tended to try to change the direction, discourage that, and encourage the notion of treatment. But the theme had been there for a number of years when it came forth in 1972 and '73. It wasn't a new thing.

ALAN MILLER: I would agree with Howard and add a general proposition. I think there is a suggestion when you speak about "pragmatic realist," that almost implies an amorality, with solutions being a primary objective. Certainly, in my brief comments yesterday, I cited many examples in which he was really excited by new propositions — new ways of attacking problems. But there was a certain scruple — a certain strong, highly personal belief that sometimes (unreasonably you might say, depending on how you thought about these things) overrode what you'd consider logic and pragmatism.

His views about treatment did fluctuate. Just after I was appointed in 1966, a new Narcotics Control Commission was established. He sensed that I and many other people in the health professions didn't agree with what he was doing, even though we had nothing better to suggest. He did me the great service of not asking me to support him publicly, even though it was closely related to the Department of Mental Hygiene. He knew that he was on his own in some respects, and he didn't oblige the professionals to give him some kind of professional respectablility. I appreciated that enormously. Four, five, or six years later he came back, and we had a long talk about how the treatment part of it was going. He was not happy with it and asked us if we might make some suggestions, or perhaps, assume some responsibility for it. I think Howard was suggesting that never happened, because he was becoming more and more interested in the enforcement part.

But I think the flavor — the passion — in that comment you just read about drugs is important. He was talking about something that was wicked. He told me that one of the reasons he was driven to develop proposals in the field of drug addiction, was because he had friends — friends living in Harlem — whose children were jeopardized. He was concerned about people, and I don't see him finding the solutions in legalization.

HOWARD SHAPIRO: It would have taken a very special individual (given the time in late 1972 and early 1973, given the staff interaction on development of that program) who, shortly thereafter, within the next few years, would come to the Governor and say: I have a solution and it's the opposite of what you've just done.

HOWARD JONES: But you would concede that he might listen to someone else?

HOWARD SHAPIRO: He listened to a lot of people outside of the administration. That was one of his unique contributions to the State. He didn't isolate himself in Albany or New York City or anywhere else. He had an enormous number of contacts in the outside world who would all of a sudden show up in a meeting. We had never seen or heard this person, and there they were speaking with the Governor, and he was listening.

VINCENT O'LEARY: That gives a staff person fits.

HOWARD SHAPIRO: As a lawyer, you could very easily develop schizophrenia, because your training is to approach things very logically, sort things out, and look at each detail. Then, as in the drug program, a situation develops in which you're required to use enormous imagination. His program was, in a short period of time, in apparent deep trouble in 1973. The press had pointed out that he could not devote the resources (namely, a large number of new judges) to the problem, because the Constitution said that the number of Supreme Court judges was limited by population. Because of his insistence that his staff be imaginative, the concept of developing new Court of Claims judges, without constitutional amendment, and moving those newly appointed judges to the Supreme Court, making political gain as well (this was a nice side benefit, although it certainly was not the main intention), gave him the ability one day to stand up at a press conference and tell reporters, "No. I can create a hundred judgeships if I need to." They were stunned.

COMMENT
Talking about outside influences, I met one the other day. In 1962, I saw countless memos saying, "Oscar said this; Oscar said that." Just about three years ago, the guy got elected President of the City Bar Association, and I met him for the first time: Oscar Ruebhausen. I hadn't seen Oscar before in my life.

HOWARD SHAPIRO: He really exists?

COMMENT
He does exist, he's the great god!

VINCENT O'LEARY: Governor Cuomo. What piece of advice would you give him?

HOWARD JONES: My observation is that the correction system is unlike any other phase of political activity. In other areas you have a balancing of political interests with forces on one side weighing against the other: there is a political mix — an opportunity to resolve things fairly. In this one, unlike any other, there is no political jazz in representing the point of view of correction officers. There is no political jazz, just some emotional detachment to defendants and prisoners. You don't get votes by providing money to build prisons. There is no input from the private sector. Unlike most areas of government, you don't have the private sector on which you can draw for management.

I would suggest that any Governor should be very aware that corrections is going to be an enormous responsibility for his leadership to provide any solutions in, because you don't have the interplay of societal and political forces which characterize almost every other focus of government activity. Governor Rockefeller was great because he did have this enormous capacity to enlist interest.

When I was appointed as Chairman of the Committee on Correctional Institutions and Purposes, the press came to me and said, "How do you feel about what the Governor did at Attica?" I said, "I have a point of view, but I'm not inclined to disclose it, because I think it's only going to be diversionary." "Well, doesn't he know about how you felt?" I said, "As far as I know, he never knew. He never asked me how I felt." "He didn't ask you before he appointed you?" I said, "Never. I never talked with him about what I thought of what he did at Attica." And they couldn't believe it.

This type of leadership — that let you go, that drew you out —gave you a much greater degree of responsibility. This is what his great contribution was.

RICHARD BARTLETT: The greatest danger Governor Cuomo faces is overpromising — overestimating what can be done with criminal justice. The statements already made, in connection with Larry Kurlander, make his job burdensome and difficult. *The New York Times* editorial suited me very much. It said the notion of a czar presiding over a system is nonsense. If we can do something about the information systems that need to be integrated, that is a big step.

We have to go back to an initiative at the start of the Rockefeller years which petered out. That is the focusing on police, on good police services. We've seen the police force in New York City drop from 30 thousand to about 23 thousand now, during a period of enormously rising crime. We have the problem of gap and overlap with these fragmented forces all over the State. I think he has to go back to that.

HOWARD SHAPIRO: You have to look at big cities and at other areas differently. I think there are very, very different problems. We used to say that despite all the legislation we draft, if you get the right people working in a coordinated way, you can solve a lot of problems. If you have bad laws, you can make them work. If you have great laws and bad people, they're just not going to work. One of the biggest problems — making the people in the criminal justice system work together and give up some of their prerogatives — is going to be very difficult. If there was more coordination and cooperation, I think you'd see much better results.

Chapter X

The Manager

RICHARD DUNHAM: Our panel discussion concerns "Rockefeller as Manager." I have no general comments to make, except to say that I had the privilege of working with Nelson for quite a few years. Subsequent to that, I had an opportunity to work directly for President Ford, and then, subsequent to that, for President Carter. Without going into details, Governor Rockefeller lost nothing by comparison with those two distinguished former Presidents.

We have on our panel many people who don't need an awful lot of introduction. On my far left is Senator Warren Anderson. I think his comments will be particularly appropriate. Most of us here at this conference were working on the Executive side, and one comment might be that Senator Anderson was on the reactive or receiving side. He and Stanley Steingut used to get and read —with great trepidation, I'm sure — the Annual Messages and Budget Messages that the Governor conveyed to the Legislature.

Next to Senator Anderson is Professor Connery, who has watched, from the academic side, Governor Rockefeller and his administration, and who cooperated with Gerald Benjamin on a book entitled *Rockefeller of New York.*

Next to Professor Connery is Joe Swidler. I have just one quick anecdote to tell about Joe. The Governor was, as we all know, an excellent administrator. He was also an excellent salesman. And when he inveigled people to join his cabinet, the tradition was to take them and tell them they could have everything that they wanted — anything they needed, to manage their department, and he would back them all the way. He would go on and on. And, as Al Marshall used to say after some cabinet members had gone through this, "Oh, now we've got to go and break them into the traces."

Joe had some considerable previous government experience

and when he went to the Governor's office, the Governor did his usual putting the arm around him and said, "Anything you want and I'll back you 100 percent." I remember Joe saying to the Governor, "I believe you, Governor, and I'm certain you mean it, but I'd like to hear you say it in front of your Budget Director." I was called into his office, and I knew after this had been repeated that I had lost opportunities to change the Public Service Commission budgets.

Our theme setter this morning is Dr. William Ronan who, at least on the Executive side, preceded all of us. The Governor, I know, considered Bill in a way as his professor — his teacher. Some of us viewed Bill in a different light. He used to be accused of being the Cardinal Richelieu or the "grey eminence" of the administration. I think we'll proceed now to our discussion and first, our theme setter, Dr. Ronan.

WILLIAM RONAN: I never really thought of Nelson Rockefeller as a manager, and I doubt many people did. At least I didn't, that is, until I was invited to share in this discussion. For Nelson was so pre-eminently charismatic — a political leader, a personality with a charisma rarely found in public office and very rarely in the state houses of the Nation. His consuming concern was really policy, problem-solving, and program-setting. He pounced on problems. He hammered away at solutions. He forced decisions. Except for some matters of personal interest to him, when he would pursue details with a vengeance, day-to-day administration bored him.

Administration — management, if you prefer — in its broadest aspects interested him. But the details of processes and procedures found little space in his attention span. Such matters he freely left to others.

However, for this occasion I looked up Webster's definition of "manage." I quote key elements of it: "To have charge of, to direct, to conduct; to get persons to do what one wishes, especially by skill, tact, persuasion, flattery, and so forth; to bring about, to continue, to manipulate, to succeed in accomplishing, to succeed in handling matters." In these terms, surely Nelson Rockefeller was a unique manager — and as a governor of New York, the most impressive such in the State's history. He certainly persuaded; got persons to do as he wished by skill, tact, persuasion, mayhap —even by flattery!

To direct or conduct, one must have goals. Certainly no candidate for governor, before Nelson or since, ever offered so comprehensive a program for State government. His 1958 campaign presented a broadly conceived agenda for New York State; a spectrum of programs designed to promote its economic growth and enhance opportunities for its people. His concept challenged a then widely prevalent view that New York was "a mature State with a mature economy" and could not expect substantial growth.

His agenda recognized the inter-relationship among the various forces that support growth — education and higher education and scientific endeavor — and provided incentives for industrial and commercial development. It included improved transportation, increased electric power resources, and modernization of the State's labor laws, banking structure, and business relationships. It also called for making New York a better place in which to live and work through housing assistance, more parks and recreation facilities, and safeguarding and enhancing the State's natural resources through conservation and environmental protection. Health and mental health programs and health insurance improvements were also major items on his list.

The uniqueness of his "platform" was the overall concept and the inter-relationship of the items — all geared toward growth and development. The means to pay for the additional services was to come from the economic growth produced by a better business environment — a better business climate — and the stimulus provided by the State programs. It was consonant with Rockefeller's thesis that government was to provide a framework within which the enterprise economy could flourish.

Where did this amazing agenda come from that he offered in his 1958 campaign and in 1959, his first year as Governor?

Nelson Rockefeller's method of dealing with a problem was to bring together people knowledgeable about it and how it might be resolved or at least pragmatically approached. He drew on their expertise and, to the extent feasible, sought a consensus on possible solutions or remedies. The Rockefeller Brothers Fund studies and reports had used this methodology. A series of expert panels produced reports dealing with major items on a national agenda. Ironically, these studies provided much of the grist for John F. Kennedy's presidential mill.

Knowing very little about New York State or its government back in the 1950's, Nelson learned quickly from his chairmanship of the Temporary Commission on the Constitutional Convention, a post to which he was appointed by agreement of Governor Harriman; Ozzie Heck, Speaker of the Assembly; and Walter Mahoney, President Pro-tem of the Senate. It was at this time that George Hinman, Nelson, and I became associated — George as Counsel to the Commission and I as its Executive Director.

We did a wide spectrum of background studies for the Commission that gave Nelson a grandstand seat from which to view State government and the State itself. That experience also brought Nelson into contact for the first time with many local and State officials and business and labor leaders.

A special point was made of getting to know key legislators. I well remember Eugene Bannigan, then Minority Leader of the Assembly, saying after meeting Nelson, "He has commission, he will travel!" Travel he did, winning the Republican nomination over Ozzie Heck and Walter Mahoney, who had appointed him, and winning the election over Averell Harriman. Harriman, at a luncheon meeting when he entertained the Commission on the Constitution, said to Nelson, "Nelson, you ought to look around this place, some day you might want to be in it!"

Prior to his nomination and the 1958 campaign, Nelson also started his own personal research activity, developing specific background papers for a possible candidacy — with Rod Perkins, Stacy May, and I giving it major direction. As the campaign itself got underway, we added Dick Wiebe, June Martin, Ken DeKay, and others to the staff. The campaign offered a plentitude of programs. There were program items for every day of the campaign; press releases or promises for both AM and PM newspapers. I remember one night — in fact at 3 AM one morning, as June Martin will recall — we were stuck for an appropriate pitch for Nelson at a Columbia County affair being held by a Republican County Chairwoman (you could say it in those days) with the wonderful name of Myrtie Tinklepaugh! At about 3:15 AM we came up with the idea of State urban parks and Ken DeKay drove the speech to Nelson and Myrtie.

In an upset of tradition, Rockefeller unseated a sitting governor, Averell Harriman, after one term. Now the challenge was the program — how to enact it, how to implement it. Well, we had a meeting. George Hinman was assigned major responsibility for getting candidates for appointed offices — cabinet and sub-cabinet — to find the right persons for the jobs. I was assigned responsibility for program — implementation of campaign promises and program development. "Bill, you make the spitballs and I'll throw them," said Nelson. Rod Perkins became Counsel to the Governor and Norm Hurd, experienced in the ways of State finance, became Budget Director. I was also given the privilege of firing the holdover Democrats. I recall going to see George Bragalini, who was Carmine DeSapio's Deputy Secretary of State. When I walked into his office George said, "Well, there go twenty barbershop inspectors."

To assist them in their office, up to this time, Governors had had four principal aides: the Budget Director, the Governor's Counsel, the Press Officer, and the Secretary to the Governor.

The latter statutory post was whatever the Governor made of it. It was a peculiar position, and I was surprised that I was given an honorary membership in the National Association of Secretaries!

The Secretary was usually a political aide; an appointments officer and an overseer of communications to the Governor, and so forth. However, for this administration a very different approach was taken. It was decided that the implementation should have central direction. It was accordingly determined that the Secretary to the Governor would take on program responsibility — both program development and major responsibility for seeing programs implemented. Hence there came into being the first program staff in the Executive Office.

Not surprisingly, the first "program associates" were Dick Wiebe, June Martin and Ken DeKay. Although the Secretary to the Governor in earlier administrations had provided a communication route for cabinet members to the Governor, the Secretary had never had the sweeping responsibility and authority for program and departmental supervision that Rockefeller established beginning January 1, 1959. Under Rockefeller, the Secretary to the Governor became his "chef de cabinet" — his principal deputy in the operation of State government. His stunning defeat of Harriman projected Rockefeller into the national scene, and the budding presidential sweepstakes necessitated considerable travel and absence from New York State. He looked principally to the Secretary to the Governor "to keep the store" in his absence. I recall one absence being so long that he came back to the legislative correspondents' Albany dinner and took the audience by storm, saying: "I have returned!"

As an executive, Nelson delegated enormous authority to individuals he trusted, not only for their ability, but also their loyalty. He also held them strictly accountable and required that he be fully informed. I remember one morning, when he and I were breakfasting at the Mansion — each with our newspaper as we polished off the perennial eggs, bacon, and coffee — when Nelson put down the *Times* and said, "William." (We had two ways I was addressed: "Bill," if things were good; "William," if I was to be reprimanded or given a new assignment.) Nelson said, "I just read a fine statement I made, but I didn't know I made it till now!" Somehow the press release had not gotten to him before release! Such occurrences were rare indeed, as speech and press release drafts were all pre-cleared — a standard operating procedure. He could be meticulous to the point of exasperation, changing words, changing records of programs with a red or black pen, even on the finished copy right up to the last minute.

To the Secretary, Counsel, Budget Director, and Press

Officer, was added a new post — Appointments Officer — in recognition of the Secretary's shift in function. These five plus his personal secretary constituted his own inner office cadre. But here Nelson also departed from precedent. To this inner group he added the Lieutenant Governor, Malcolm Wilson, and the Attorney General, Louis Lefkowitz. To my knowledge, no independently elected officials, such as Lieutenant Governor or Attorney General, ever had such intimate association with a Governor before or since. Their addition to Nelson's "kitchen cabinet" — or "Mansion Mafia" — was invaluable for their knowledge, experience, and political insights.

I do not want to give the impression that the 1958 campaign promises were the sole agenda of the Governor in 1959. Taking office meant problems not only of implementing promises already made, but new policy problems as well. To assist in both, we employed a modification of the panel techniques of the Rockefeller Brothers Fund and studies that we used successfully in the Constitutional Convention Commission. Only this time we didn't create panels — we created task forces. We had task forces on housing, highway safety, health insurance, education, railroads —you could almost name it, and we had one. If memory sustains me, I believe we had some 42 of them at one time, and the Secretary to the Governor was charged with their coordination. Task forces came forth so thick and fast that "task force" became a dirty word in the legislative halls.

Yet these task forces — later called committees or, constituted more formally with legislative participation, commissions — brought forth many of the programs that made history from 1959 to 1974 in areas ranging from medical education to housing, from automobile seat belts to the Long Island Railroad, and from the South Mall to the Adirondack State Park. Some were never formalized or even appointed. One of the most important in developing the revenue bond program of financing was a most informal series of meetings we had with Bill Morton, Obie Brewer, Del Pfeffer of First National City Bank, and John Mitchell (one of the ablest bond attorneys I've ever known).

Now, I don't want to indicate either that all of these things developed just out of task forces and out of an in-group in the Governor's circle. In fact, Nelson reached out very far and wide: he brought in people from all kinds of activities in which he had been involved and consulted other sources of information and expertise. Many of these key elements were brought together at his Sunday night meetings at the Mansion. They were, if you never experienced them, incredible and very productive. The inner group was always there: Malcolm and Louie, Bob MacCrate or whoever was Counsel, Carl Spad or whoever was Appointments Officer, the State Party Chairman, and a lot of other people, too; I never quite knew why some of them were there, except that they did fill the table for dinner. Occasionally the Governor, very graciously, would ask one of these people, whose expertise was unknown or at least ill defined, what their opinion was. It was usually freely given, and sometimes it was even appropriate. But, as was said as we left those meetings, "They also served who merely sat and ate."

A public manager — a public executive — has to live with his Legislature. Rockefeller courted the legislative leadership of both houses and both parties. During the legislative session, his Sunday night meetings with his staff and "inner group" (always including Malcolm and Louie) were followed by Monday morning meetings with the leaders. And indeed, legislative leaders often had dinner at the Mansion, or a noonday lunch. In the first years of his Governorship, party unity and discipline were so strong that an agreement by the Governor and the Republican leaders on bills meant passage of the legislation. It was almost as though New York had parliamentary government. When Heck and Mahoney (or later Carlino) would meet with Rockefeller and agree on a course of action, it was virtually done.

Indeed, when Democrats controlled both houses it also worked. Tony Travia as Speaker and Joe Zaretzki as President Pro-tem met at the Mansion with the Governor, admired the modern art, came to agreement, and passed the bills. What a different world it is today! I shall always cherish Joe Zaretski's looking at a Miro in the mansion dining room and saying, "Governor, I know that one — it's that Assembly district we gerrymandered in Brooklyn."

A key to his approach was that Nelson Rockefeller respected the dignity of the governorship, but he never sat on it. He went to the "third floor" of the State Capitol to the leader's offices to meet with them on occasion — not always having them come to his second floor office. He frequently met with and addressed groups of legislators. He was outgoing and informal — clearly not an "imperial" Governor. He made friendships with legislative leaders and legislators. He invited them to the Mansion and danced with their wives to the tune of "Sweet Georgia Brown". His success at managing relations with the Legislature is recorded in the broad sweep of legislation enacted in his time — much of it innovative, much of it challenging and controversial. Remember, he passed the largest fall-out shelter program ever enacted!

Rockefeller considered the coordination of State policy and State activities as the responsibility of the governor. His relationship to the independent offices of State government reflected this concept. He looked to direct communication with such offices and expected response from them. I have already referred to the close relationship he established with the Attorney General and the Lieutenant Governor. Malcolm Wilson played a major role in legislation. Louis Lefkowitz did also and offered important legal advice as well.

The independently elected Comptroller presented a different problem, partly because of the nature of the office and partly because its incumbent was of the opposite political party. Although the incumbent was invited to cabinet meetings and many functions, a distance was maintained. Nevertheless, personal relations were cordial.

By passing legislation often with bi-partisan support, and by mounting outside support for such projects as the South Mall, the State University Construction Fund, purchase of the Long Island Railroad, and the like, Rockefeller succeeded in getting Comptroller Levitt's acquiescence in such major projects and programs, although the Comptroller frequently expressed disagreement or doubt about them. No major project was "vetoed" by the Comptroller, although his office on a number of occasions filed negative or apprehensive reports — but after the fact.

Another constitutionally independent body is the State Board of Regents which appointed the Commissioner of Education. To establish the State University as the kind of statewide higher educational force that would help build a greater New York State, the Board of Regents had to be tackled. Nelson cultivated them as a group, and sought out individual members. He cultivated the Commissioner of Education assiduously. The Commissioner, Jim Allen, found it a sometimes harrowing experience.

Fortified by his task forces, special committees, and commissions on education, the Governor actually shaped much of the major education policy. If he did not necessarily persuade the Regents, he moved them. He respected the Board's dignity. He entertained it. He outflanked it — a key factor in establishing the strong, vital, well-financed State University of New York and the Scholar Incentive Program to aid the private colleges. Not unexpectedly, these became great Education Department accomplishments as well — especially the latter. But the legislative correspondents' dinner show recognized the reality when it sang, "At Fordham and St. John's they put Rocky up in bronze."

Coming into office with the avowed purposes of improving rail transportation and adding to the State's electric power resources, Rockefeller understood he could expect little positive action by the Public Service Commission. The heavy, deadly hand of Milo Maltbie and the Commission under his leadership had held back progress and helped speed the commuter railroads into insolvency. So he looked elsewhere to encourage electric power development, as had Governor Dewey before him, to the State Power Authority, which was then completing its monumental hydro works at the Saint Lawrence and Niagara. He also sponsored the State Office for Atomic Development to pursue nuclear research and nuclear industry.

To improve transportation, he sponsored the legislation that created the Metropolitan Transportation Authority in New York and transportation authorities in the Niagara Frontier, the Rochester area, Syracuse, and then Albany-Troy-Schenectady and other areas. All were exempted from Public Service Commission regulation.

For a change in approach by the Public Service Commission, Rockefeller looked to improving the quality of the Commissioners. By his appointment of strong, balanced and informed leadership, the Commission re-established confidence in its regulatory activity.

The independent State Board of Social Welfare presented a difficult situation. It was not a board whose role was fixed by the Constitution of the State, but the Board appointed the Commissioner who was responsible to it. In a major reorganization, growing out of the Reorganization Plan for State Government prepared by the Office of Secretary to the Governor and a Moreland Act Commission (and after a prolonged struggle), the Commissioner became an appointee of the Governor, and the Board became a quasi-legislative, quasi-judicial body.

The Governor's cabinet meetings under Rockefeller were few and far between. They were largely pro forma, but did give some agency heads one of the rare opportunities they had to see the Governor personally. The cabinet never made a decision. It never had a show of hands. When summoned, it listened.

Clearly, Rockefeller was a management centralist. Through his control of budget, and administrative oversight of the State agencies and legislation, he enhanced the executive power in New York State government. Under Rockefeller, a governorship already powerful became even more so. His institutionalization of the staffing of the Executive Office, plus his own personal influence with the Legislature and the independent agencies of State government, assured that State operations were under tight administrative control by the Governor's Office.

A program associate from the Secretary to the Governor's office was assigned to a set of departments for policy and program. An Assistant Counsel covered a set of agencies for legislation and law enforcement. The Appointments Officer was involved in the initiation of political appointees within departments with a further check by the Governor's counsel and the Secretary. The Budget Office maintained a rein on all financial matters. But the Governor, himself, worked longer hours at his job of Chief Executive than I believe any others ever did. Over time, he came to have more knowledge of the workings of the State government than any of his predecessors.

For policy responsibility and program implementation, however, the governor relied principally on the "chef de cabinet" — the Secretary to the Governor. The responsibility devolved not out of theory but from practical necessity. Someone ultimately has to answer for the governor if he is not available. I was interested that when Hugh Carey became governor, he took an early strong stand that he was not going to have any such "chef de cabinet" — "no Bill Ronan." So Hugh left the impression that he would be dealing directly with his commissioners. Well, he didn't have a Bill Ronan. He had a Bob Morgado.

From time to time Rockefeller added or subtracted other staff officers to his Executive Office coterie: a special assistant for Federal-State relations, a special assistant, an administrative officer, or a director of operations. The titles, functions, and influence of these varied with the time, the incumbents in the other staff offices, and his own needs. Early in 1966, when the problem of his re-election was raised, and when he was told by a consultant that he "couldn't be elected dog catcher" the coming November, the Secretary to the Governor was freed from "detailed administration" to concentrate on "substance." This created the basis of what is now the Director of State Operations. I suppose I should say this was done on the basis of management philosophy. It wasn't. It was the pragmatic thing to do and obviously made management sense.

Nelson was always concerned about the input of information to him. He was restless, and from time to time he would establish a chart room, or he'd get someone else to get information from his principal deputies. Usually, these things didn't work out. But he was never a prisoner of his staff. He had friends and associates and advisors outside State government. Some of these people came from the Rockefeller family and associates. People like the John Lockwoods, Oscar Reubhausens, Frank Jamesons, Stacey Mays, Victor Borellas — all had very significant roles in advising the Governor at one time or another, as did others who came in from time to time, some of them from out-of-state — Sam Lubell, Emmett Hughes, Ted Braun. Nelson reached out for all sorts of information and talent, sometimes to the great surprise — if not dismay — of his principal deputies. Hence, he appointed at various times "administrative assistants" whose functions were not clearly defined and who usually wound up as fifth wheels.

Nelson was fond of graphic presentations and talked often of the "chart room" he had had in the U.S. Department of Health, Education & Welfare. Some of these "assistants" or "operations assistants" were given "chart room" responsibility — to keep up-to-date graphics on both basic data and State operations. From my observation, it never really worked. The pace of development outran the ability to chart it. The Budget Division had the statistical data or could get it.

Physical planning was a major interest. He himself said, more than once, that he was a frustrated architect. The pace of New York State construction appalled him. When we pointed out bizarre examples, like the mental hospital laundry building which was designed for tubercular mental patients' laundry, took eight years to be built, and, by then was not needed, he got a "task force" of leading architects and builders to improve matters. He was equally aghast at the ugliness of State buildings in the post-war period. By the time the Public Works Department, the State architect, the budget bureaucracy, and the parsimony of the finance committees of the Legislature did their respective bits, the resulting structures were "public works renaissance" and "budget bureau baroque."

His determination to improve State physical planning and plant led to the Office for Planning Coordination, the creation of various construction public authorities, an increase in archi-tectural fees, and the engagement of some of the world's leading architects on State projects. He took an active part in the development of the South Mall, and he sat down with Burch McMorran and some of us to lay out some State highway routes.

One of his great accomplishments, here in Albany, was the elimination of the pigeons and their daily contributions to the State Capitol. After the Public Works Department had failed, after the General Services Administration had failed, Nelson delegated the task to Eddie Galvin, his State Trooper aide. Ed succeeded where others failed. As to how he did it, there are no reports. But he never got the Audubon Society Award for the year.

In the reconstruction of the grounds around the Capitol, the Governor told Cortland Schuyler how to select and place the trees, the walks and benches. Of the South Mall — now appropriately the "Governor Nelson A. Rockefeller Empire State Plaza" — Wallace Harrison is the principal architect of record, the *de jure* architect, if you will. Actually, the *de facto* architect was the firm of Harrison and Rockefeller. Many a weekend at Tarrytown,

Nelson and Wally poured over the drawings.

As a manager, Rockefeller had an appreciation of the importance of the work force. As a Governor, he had an unusually close relationship with organized labor. Others had had labor political support and had taken "pro-labor" stands. Nelson, however, involved labor leadership in his task forces, in his advisory activities, in his consultations. He sponsored the State's first minimum wage law out of conviction, as he did the liberalizing of other labor law restrictive measures. He raised the salaries of State workers, which had been languishing behind those of the Federal government and comparable private employers. It was no mean task to get the Legislature to raise commissioners' salaries so that the State could raise others as well. He stopped, thereby, a developing talent — and brain-drain from State government.

Financial management, as such, held little interest for Rockefeller. His principal concern was finding the money to do things on his agenda. You may remember, however, that period of his incumbency when he preached and tried to follow the path of "pay-as-you-go" financing. There was his 1962 pledge of no tax increase, but he found, as Al Smith had put it, "You don't pay and you don't go". Not to go forward was anathema to Nelson; he and Norm Hurd proposed raising "fees," not a tax increase. The uproar that followed still echoes over the Helderbergs.

However, let's remember that Rockefeller came into office in those years when Americans were told that theirs was a "consumption economy," an "affluent society," and our horizons were unbounded. It was the era of JFK and LBJ's "Great Society." The more we spent, the more we consumed — the greater the production, the greater the society.

Nelson was not an executive or manager in the sense of a supervisor or an umpire to decide among contending forces. Nor was he a custodian. He was an activist. He believed New York State, and for that matter, the Nation, could not stand still. And he certainly couldn't! Either you went forward or you went back. You had to go ahead to meet the problems, before they became crises and overwhelmed you. And you didn't have to wait for prolonged "in-depth" research. You summoned the available expertise and acted upon the best information available. He liked "conceptual thinkers" and had scant patience with small minds. He usually dealt in broad strokes.

He was persistent — and even stubborn. An obstacle was to be overcome, a challenge accepted. When a liquor executive told him, in the privacy of his office, that the industry had already killed the reform bill in the Legislature, and he might as well drop it, its passage became an absolute must, with a special session, if necessary, to achieve it. In its first year, the Council on the Arts bill floundered because some Democrats tried to trade additional city judges for ballet dancers. The next year, Nelson said its passage was mandatory or none of the Legislature's own bills would be approved. His determination to see the South Mall completed was a factor in his seeking his fourth term.

Returning to Webster's definition of "manage," how does Nelson fare? Certainly he took charge of. Surely he directed. Clearly he conducted. Indeed he not only conducted, but usually managed the stage as well. No one there will ever forget when we took the Emancipation Proclamation — which New York State owns — to Washington for its Centennial Celebration. As owners we insisted, much to the chagrin of John F. and Robert Kennedy, that Nelson present it over national television at the Lincoln Memorial ceremony. When the Marine Band began to play "The Battle Hymn of the Republic," guess who got up and led the band and the impromptu singing? Nelson A.!

Clearly he got persons to do what he wished. He succeeded in accomplishing. After all, what better measure of a manager than his results? This great University; this reborn State Capitol; the vast network of highways and other transport facilities; the health, hospital, and social welfare programs and institutions; the State's educational system; the new and improved parks and recreation facilities; the Pure Waters Program — are but part of the panoply of his accomplishments.

It has been rightly said, he undertook so much, it could not be truly comprehended by the public. And mayhap, as some have said, he tried too much, but, before that phrase gained its now banal popularity, he reached out — reached out to touch not one, but everyone, particularly after his 1966 re-election. For in that contest, our campaign lead was not the candidate, but his record —not promise, but performance. Our success impressed him. So he featured more of his pioneering "town meetings," which may well be an established institution for all future governors. He liked to speak, he liked to meet individuals, and he liked to appear before audiences. He liked repartee. Few present will ever forget his Long Island town meeting, when a very fat, probably three-hundred-pound-plus woman berated him on a welfare matter and accused him of "neglecting the hungry." His reply began, "I think it's remarkable that you are their spokesman."

But he was an effective salesman. I often chided him that he was the "second coming" of his great-grandfather, who had sold snake oil remedies.

Above all he was a planner and a deviser of action. The felt-tipped black pen and the ubiquitous yellow pad were his

Governor Rockefeller meets with his staff, July 16, 1973. Far side of table, left to right: Lt. Governor Malcolm Wilson, Governor Rockefeller, Robert R. Douglass, Dr. T. Norman Hurd, Richard Dunham, Joseph Boyd, Charles Lanigan, Ann Whitman. Standing: Harry W. Albright, Jr. Near side of table, left to right: Abraham Lavine, Mary Kresky, Richard Wiebe, Hugh Morrow, Michael Whiteman, Ronald Maiorana, James Cannon, Louis Lefkowitz.

principal tools. His speech thoughts went on the yellow pad. His points to take up with Dick Nixon for the famous "810 Fifth Avenue Summit" were on the yellow pad. Everything was on the yellow pad. The first time I saw him — and the last time, the day before his untimely death — he dashed some thoughts for the next day on that yellow pad. I shall always remember and cherish the memories of that yellow pad. What a fabulous distance we all traveled on the "yellow pad" road!

RICHARD DUNHAM: Thanks, Bill. We'll now proceed with the second part which, I must admit, is kind of a new word for me. It must be a new academic term: "discussants." The first discussant is Warren Anderson, whom I first knew when he was Chairman of the Senate Finance Committee. So we'll be interested in his comments on Malcolm's definition of Nelson as a "fiscal conservative."

While I reflect on that — Bill referred to the famous bomb shelter program. Well, I remember the appropriation very well. It was a $100 million appropriation, and some in the Legislature didn't view it with the top priority status that Nelson did. When Senator Anderson and I were working, one time, on the final appropriation, with me trying to find out what the Legislature would approve, this subject came up. And the compromise which was suggested was a little footnote in the appropriation bill, which, as Malcolm would say, was "back with the depilatory advertisements." It had a little footnote: $100 million appropriation was there, but no more than $112,362 could be spent.

This enabled me to assure the Governor that his appropriation was, in fact, in the bill and at the $100 million level. About a year or two later, he asked me how the program was doing, and I said, "Well, Governor, so far only $112,362 was spent." He said, "Why is that?" I said, "Well, there haven't been any applications." I was glad that he didn't go on with the questions. I probably would have thrown in Senator Anderson's name.

WARREN ANDERSON: Thank you, Dick, Bill. I guess I have rather a unique role here today, because I'm one of the few remaining people still on the active State payroll. How long that will continue, I don't know. I think there might be some people in the Executive Branch who might have a contract out on me.

But it has been kind of a unique experience to live through the days that Bill and Malcolm certainly know more about and told you in better detail, because they were closer to the picture than I. But I was always a good friend of the Governor's, and I was a great admirer of his. And I have had some experience since, so as to be able to compare his handling of the office with some others with whom I've had more recent contact.

I looked up too, Bill, how the word "manager" is defined because, though I thought he was a hell of a leader, I didn't really think of him as a manager. But after looking it up, I agree with you. I have a Random House Dictionary. It says a manager is one who "manipulates resources and expenditures." If that doesn't make Nelson a manager, nobody will ever be one. But maybe I shouldn't repeat those kinds of things.

I'd like to give you just a little bit of a perspective from the Legislature's viewpoint, the other side of the coin, as it were. You must know that I had only one year as Majority Leader while Nelson was Governor. But, as Dick has said, I had served as the Chairman of Finance for seven years, and I was a very close personal friend of Majority Leader Earl Brydges, so that I saw and heard secondhand a lot of things that others have described to you. And I will attest to the accuracy of about 99 percent of what everyone else has said.

I certainly will attest to the fact that he courted the Legislature, and I wouldn't want that to appear to mean that he did it in any kind of an artificial fashion, or that he did it for the sole purpose of accomplishing his end, though I'm sure that was a big factor. But, as Malcolm said, here was an individual who truly liked other people. He liked people from different kinds of backgrounds. I guess Louis Lefkowitz talked about that more than anybody else here. I know he liked Joe Zaretski very, very much. I know he liked Stanley, and I know he liked Tony Travia, and the things that he would do — little personal things for them, unrelated to any particular objective that he might want — are so numerous that I can't recount them all.

For example, he would visit Earl. Earl's health towards the end wasn't the greatest. He would come to see him in the hotel room and talk about things there — not by telephone. He did it personally. And he would, as Bill said, come to the offices on the third floor, alone many times, not with a trailing staff of people. Because, generally speaking, when he was up there, he was involved in a specific objective, and, at that point, he knew as much about the problem as the people who had worked with him in analyzing it. He was a good delegator, I'm sure, but in the process of delegating, he learned a lot about the problem at hand.

He was a fast study — I think anyone would say that that's so — and an enormously effective presenter of the problem. He would get right into it, and then he would, as it has been said, do virtually anything to bring the solution about. As an aside at this point — it is a sad note that Joe Zaretski was defeated in a primary contest, because certainly no one, with due respect to other legislative leaders in New York City, ever got more for the City of New York in the process of working out programs with Nelson than did Joe Zaretski. Joe was not a holdup artist in this process, but he would just indicate that something was needed here or there to help out his city, which he loved dearly, and it was brought about.

And another thing that should be said (and I don't know that I heard anybody say this directly, but it's been inferred) is that if Nelson said he was going to do something for somebody else, it was as good as done. You didn't have to write notes on your own yellow pad about what was said, because whatever he agreed to do, whether it was to sign a bill or to make a visit to your district, or to put some additional numbers in some program for next year, it was done.

It's true, as Bill said, that he would sometimes send delegates to us, but he would always back them up. We would know that when an Al Marshall or Bill Ronan or whoever came to see us about a particular program — Dick Dunham or whoever — we would know that what that person said was going to be backed up. Nelson wouldn't undercut anybody whom he had sent up as the go-between.

Now, that didn't necessarily mean that all of these delegates or proxies were always successful. There was a time in 1966 when

Medicaid was first developed, and the person who was advancing that to the Legislature, who was giving us judgments as to how much it was going to cost, was Al Marshall. Helping him, I think, was Ed Van Ness. And it wasn't very many years later that we learned that those first evaluations, as to the cost of that program, had been grossly underestimated — which is still haunting us, as a matter of fact, though it's still a fine program.

Be that as it may, there was another program which the Governor always had on his list for legislative action, which, as far as I remember, never got any place in either house. It had something to do with universal health insurance and was drafted in various guises through the years. It was traditionally always on the "must list" of things that, before the Legislature adjourned, should be addressed. (Addressed in this context doesn't necessarily mean passed.) This is one item where, I think, for the good of the State, it's just as well we didn't get behind it as we did get behind some other things.

But in any event, the Governor did ask Earl, one time, if somebody from downstairs couldn't come up and at least talk about universal health insurance. How could Earl turn him down? He said, "Sure, we'll set up a conference." So there was such a conference, and I'd guess it was 1968, or 1969 — somewhere in that area.

I well remember that John Hughes was still alive, and, knowing that this was going to be the subject and that someone was coming up from the second floor to discuss it, the people sitting around the table at our conference meeting were scribbling on their yellow pads and almost pawing their feet in vengeance for whatever individual had the temerity to come to a conference on that subject after the way Medicaid had mushroomed. That was the setting when the door to our conference room opened and in comes Marshall, again trailed by Ed Van Ness — the same two that we remembered so well. When Earl introduced Al, everybody was just waiting to see how this thing was going to be presented. And Al, in his customary style of being able to define a problem said, "You know, gentlemen," (I don't think we had any women Senators at the time) "we thought downstairs that the same two people who had screwed up Medicaid ought to come up and explain this program." That broke everybody up and he went on from there.

Well, I think that's all I need to say. If there are any questions I'll try to answer them — but there was a definition of "manage" that I didn't find in Random House. I guess Bill didn't see it in whatever dictionary he was looking at either. But, in the true sense, Governor Rockefeller managed to get done what he wanted to do, and, if that doesn't make him a good manager, I don't know what does.

RICHARD DUNHAM: We'll proceed now with the next discussant, who is Joe Swidler. Joe was Chairman of the New York State Public Service Commission and, before then, was Chairman of the Federal Power Commission in Washington under President Kennedy. That was one of the reasons Nelson asked him to come here. So I think, again, he has a different perspective on Rockefeller as manager than perhaps some of the others do.

JOSEPH SWIDLER: I wish I had the qualifications to speak to you about Nelson Rockefeller from close association over many years, like some people on the program and in the audience, who were a part of the Rockefeller political family. My own experience was more limited. I guess my coming to Albany was a sort of political accident, and I was different in a way from the other members of his team. For one thing, I served in the last term. Although I was nominally head of the Department of Public Service, my role was basically a quasi-judicial one which was insulated from executive management. I was and still am, much to the dismay of this audience, a Democrat. Having served in a bi-partisan agency as a Democrat, I was not privy to the political aspects of Rockefeller's work.

The manner and reasons for my appointment would say something about Nelson Rockefeller as a manager. I think in 1969 Nelson was told — as Bill Ronan says, he was told before the previous election — that he couldn't win. Arthur Goldberg was supposed to be the candidate against him, and this proved to be right. And Nelson had the need to shore up what was regarded as a weak and vulnerable part of his administration, the Public Service Commission, which had run down through the years.

I didn't know him at the time. I was happily practicing law then in Washington. I was not a political figure. He sought me out in 1969, because he had heard, perhaps erroneously, that I had had a good record as the Chairman of the Federal Power Commission in Washington, and he thought that I was a person who not only could divert some of the political lightning, but also reform the Commission and assure the health of the energy industries, do something about telephone service in New York City (which was then collapsing), and try to meet the problems of inflation as they affected regulated companies.

I told him I was a very illogical person for the job. I then represented some utilities (including one or two in New York) and said that it would be very inappropriate for me, having taken on the representation of utilities, to be placed on the Public Service Commission. He said, "Don't worry about that. The public will look at your career as a whole. The press will regard your appointment as a balanced one. And I'm sure that it will be well met." The risk of criticism didn't scare him off. I told him also that I thought that some major legislative changes were necessary, and some additional funding. He agreed to both, and, as a matter of fact as I recall, I put it in writing and he agreed. (It turned out to be wise.)

I think that this says a lot about the Governor. As a number of other people have pointed out, he was resourceful. He did not want to be limited in his use of people to those who were already about him or, even, the people who lived in the State. He was determined to get the help of whomever he thought he needed to help him do his job.

One of the words that I have not yet heard about Nelson is integrity. He was a politician, of course, but he practiced politics with great fundamental integrity. He would not descend to subterfuge. He told the same story to everyone, and he was not deterred from acting according to conscience by criticism or political risks. At the same time he prided himself on being a quick learner. I don't mean that he emphasized the same points to every audience. He did not!

The fascinating thing to me, as I watched Rockefeller, was to see how he combined the qualities needed to manage one of the great enterprises of the country with his political responsibilities. This is, of course, the test of a public manager. He was not only managing the expenditure of billions of dollars a year and the employment of many thousands of people, supervising and creating programs in the process; but, in order to be able to do all this, he had to win elections. He had to respond to political necessities. This requires a lot of tightrope walking. And it's how you walk the tightrope that tells a lot about a man's character.

I mean that if he told you he would support you up to the hilt, that didn't necessarily mean your program would always have his highest priority. It wouldn't, and shouldn't. And frequently you were left pretty much to your own resources, but he never withdrew his support. He simply had to spread his time in the way he thought was most effective for the dispatch of the business of the State.

When we talked about the qualities of the job, before I came to Albany, he never asked for any substantive commitment, but we did talk in terms of approaches to government. What he liked — and I think it fits my own description of myself — was "tough but fair." This was, in a way, his own self-characterization. He thought of himself as tough-minded, skeptical, politically sophisticated, testing the claims of people — not prone to be pushed around, but never acting unfairly. I don't think that it could ever be said of him, as with some other people in political life, that his programs lacked basic fairness, as between groups of the population or in the treatment of, for example, the disadvantaged and the poor.

He was greatly interested in the internal capability and efficiency within the agency, and in the program of combining consumer protection with assurances that utility industries would be able to carry the load of providing a sound infrastructure for industrial growth and employment in the State. You have to remember, in connection with my job, that in a way it was a small one. It was the cabinet position that had the fewest appointments —a total of six hundred or seven hundred people — with an expenditure for the agency (fully reimbursed by the regulated industries after 1970) that you couldn't find in the budget. But it had a lot of importance in the way of stress, especially in a period of economic turmoil in the budget, and its influence on major industries.

A public utility commission has no supporting constituency. It can't do the right thing. Any rate reward is going to be too small for the utility companies and too large from the consumer point of view. Inherently, a utility commission is a political liability. There are more consumers than utilities and the consumers vote. A lot of governors have reacted to that problem by, in a way, undermining the authority and integrity of the commission by insisting on unrealistic expectations of how utilities can survive in a critical situation. Nelson Rockefeller recognized what the economic imperatives were, and he was prepared to take the heat.

I've said that there was never any effort to influence my substantive views, but of course there was a little test on the periphery. To see the man whole, these matters need mention. For example, not personally from him, but through one of his aides, I was asked to advise his office in advance of the results of important decisions of the Commission, by at least a few hours, before the decisions were released to the public. I declined politely. I said that, unless he was going to change it or do something about it, a few hours of notice wouldn't make any difference, and I couldn't contemplate the possibility that a decision of the Commission would be influenced by him. It was not a head-to-toes confrontation, but it was an example of his need to protect his political fences to the extent that he could, within the framework of independent agencies with quasi-judicial responsibilities.

The party hierarchy was another problem. The party people came around and said that the Governor thought I didn't have

279

enough good Republicans on the staff. Well I explained that this was an agency where all of the people except the support staff were professionals, engineers, economists, rate experts, and lawyers, and that there wasn't room for political appointments. We wrestled with that for quite a while. And we worked out a compromise, that I would interview anyone that the party people recommended, that I would show them no preference, but I wouldn't discriminate against them. Well, actually they sent around a number of very good people, some of the time.

One of the things that always amazed me was the extent to which Nelson kept on top of the work of the State. During the period of blackouts and brownouts in the State and the period of collapsing telephone service, I developed the practice of reporting to him weekly on the New York utility developments. These were rather dull reports after the first few months. I would report how much excess capacity each company had; the extent to which its units were on line that week; what problems they were confronting; where brownouts had occurred; where they might occur; how many complaints we had had on telephone service — that sort of thing. He released them. They were designed for his own information, but he thought the public was entitled to it all, and it was made available as soon as he reviewed it. But, what really surprised me was how often I would get back these reports with his comments scribbled in the margins. With all the other things he had to do, he found time, somehow, to stay on top of the job that I was doing. I always felt that I was being watched, and I performed better as a consequence.

RICHARD DUNHAM: Professor Connery, you're cleanup man. We have just about ten minutes so I hope we don't shortchange your remarks too much.

ROBERT CONNERY: We have heard a little bit this morning about the facts of the Rockefeller administration. That is the first stage of doing what the Institute is supposed to do. If we accept everything that has been said this morning, the big question is: So what? Should we point to the Rockefeller administration with pride ... or view it with alarm? Isn't there some objective means of putting it in a framework so we can get some measurement — some yardstick of the Rockefeller administration's efforts? How did this administration differ from others? In many ways, Rockefeller as Governor served as other governors did. Dr. Ronan spoke this morning about the preparation of the State of the State address to the Legislature. But every Governor presents such a Message to the Legislature each year. In some states the message is the governor's and he has few real powers thereafter.

It seems to me that there are two or three ways of considering the Rockefeller administration. One is to compare Rockefeller's administration with the administrations of his predecessors. Certainly New York State was unique in that it had a very distinguished group of men who had served as governors since 1900. A number of them went on to other things, including the Presidency of the United States. Most of Rockefeller's predecessors were famous for one thing they accomplished as governor. Al Smith, for example, was noted as a reformer of the administrative structure of the State's government. Rockefeller, however, presented a whole series of proposals rather than one at a time. His achievements, in improving State mental hospitals, highways, and parks, were outstanding.

Another means of evaluation would be to compare Rockefeller with governors of other states. Unfortunately, most people assume that all governors have the same power in their states. The governor, because he's the governor, does certain things and has certain power. But, this is not true. To give one example, take California, the state with which New York is most frequently compared. In New York it's said, "The Governor proposes and the Legislature disposes." That is, the Governor submits a program and the Legislature accepts or rejects it. But in California, even under Mr. Reagan, the legislature proposed to build a larger state university and the governor accepted it. In California, the governor's staff was relatively small, because it was only concerned with preparing the speeches and controlling his agendas. The legislature has the large professional staff. In New York State, the Governor's staff is the professional staff.

One contender for the nomination of President of the United States in the last election claimed his chief advantage was that he served as governor of Texas. The governor of Texas has very little real power: most state officials are elected. A former governor of Texas undertook to improve state highways, only to discover that he had no authority over highways. The highway commissioner was elected, and the gasoline tax was appropriated to his agency and spent under his direction. The governor was only an innocent bystander to both highway building and administration and financing.

The great challenge to the Institute, over time, will be to provide means of evaluating the Rockefeller era, either by comparing that era with the previous administrations in New York State or by comparison with the performance of governors in other states. However, care must be taken to understand that no governor in any other state has the power and authority that the Governor of New York has. I think that when this is done, Nelson Rockefeller will emerge as a giant among pygmies.

Chapter XI

Nelson Rockefeller and the New York Governorship

Gerald Benjamin

A decade after he stepped down from the governorship, controversies still raged over Nelson Rockefeller's legacy in New York. With surprising regularity, given the scant attention generally paid to the records of even the most visible and long serving governors, books continued to appear on "The Imperial Rockefeller" well after his death in 1979. There was seemingly endless fascination with Rockefeller's personal drive and magnetism, his uncertain ideology, his penchant for large-scale solutions, his monument building, his financial policies, his political prowess, and, of course, his great, unsatisfied ambition for the presidency.[1]

In New York, during the post "wine and roses" years, criticism from the right focused upon the Governor's "tax, tax, tax; spend, spend, spend" behavior that, it was argued, brought the State to the brink of fiscal collapse. And from the left, it was charged that Rockefeller never had a "real" commitment to the liberal social policies of his first two terms, but that these were simply instruments for gaining power in New York, and abandoned when his pursuit of the Republican presidential nomination dictated that the Governor assume a (more personally comfortable) conservative stance.

Some of the continued interest in Nelson Rockefeller is due, no doubt, to the fact that the Governor was not only a man of great wealth but, as the preeminent Rockefeller of his generation, the bearer of a name and tradition symbolic of the power of wealth in American society. His entry into the public arena necessarily exposed Rockefeller and his family to a degree of public scrutiny that they had theretofore avoided. The Governor himself became a lightning rod. His visibility fed the re-emergence, after decades, of Rockefeller-based conspiracy theories from both ends of the political spectrum.[2] And, in such forums as the 1974 vice-presidential confirmation hearings, more thoughtful critiques emerged on the desirability of merging, in the hands of one person, both great private and great public power.[3]

Nelson Rockefeller attracts continued interest not only as a symbol, but also for his record as New York's longest serving governor in modern times — a governor who placed an indelible stamp upon the State during his 15 year tenure. The visible evidence is everywhere: in the billion-dollar mall named after Rockefeller in the State Capital; in the sprawling State University campuses in every corner of the State; in the hospitals, highways, and public schools built during his administration; in the public benefit corporations he caused to be designed to attain his goals; indeed, in the very size and scope of State government itself.

Three major focal points emerge from this retrospective discussion of Nelson Rockefeller in New York by his aides, political allies and adversaries, journalists, and academic observers: his personal and leadership qualities; his political successes and failures; and the wisdom and impact of his policies. In the course of addressing these central concerns, a variety of answers, some conflicting, are offered to such questions as: Why did Rockefeller achieve such enormous success in New York politics and yet repeatedly fail on the national scene? Were the benefits of the programs Rockefeller brought to New York offset by the negative long-term fiscal consequences for the State? What was the actual role of this Governor, seemingly so interested in concentrating power in his own hands, in the management and direction of the State government? and, How was the structure and functioning of State government permanently altered as a result of Rockefeller's long service?

The Man and the Leader

In 1942, Nelson Rockefeller was the 33 year old Coordinator for Inter-American Relations, the leader in Washington of the anti-Nazi effort in Latin America, and a rising young Republican in a Democratic administration with regular, back-channel access to the war-time Roosevelt White House. It was most fitting, then, that *The New Yorker* profiled this quintessential New Yorker as "the protegé of a New York Governor turned President." The magazine found the "most ambitious of all living Rockefellers" to be a "buoyant type," "optimistic about everything," with the "resilience of youth, of the believer, of the very rich." "A wavy-

haired, handsome, boyish, aggressive, idealistic young man,"
Nelson Rockefeller appeared "impetuous" with "no patience for
subtlety" and "used to acting with the directness which is
instinctive in a man accustomed to power."[4]

"I perfectly frankly love competition," the young Rockefeller
declared to *The New Yorker* writer, Geoffrey T. Hellman, who also
noticed that there seemed no feeling of "guilt," no "interior
tension," in this third-generation Rockefeller about his great
inherited wealth. John D. Rockefeller Jr.'s second son brought
great energy — "an almost fanatical application" — to his job as
Coordinator and inspired "considerable hero worship" in his
staff, but, perhaps surprisingly, was "philosophical" about errors.
"When he gets slapped down he shows a willingness to eat crow
and start all over again."

But Hellman's inquiries also unearthed some "shrewdness"
to balance Rockefeller's "easy going charm." The techniques he
used when President of Rockefeller Center during the Depression,
to lure new tenants, led one competitor, August Heckscher, to
characterize young Nelson as a "modern Frankenstein." And
another former associate anonymously commented: "The Rockefellers lean against their good will hard. They fool you with this
gentlemanly thing."

More than a third of a century later, *The New Yorker* returned
for the last time to the subject of Nelson Rockefeller. The former
Vice-President and four-time Governor of New York State, now a
"hoarse-voiced, winking, high spirited, and on occasion low-
dealing figure," had withdrawn entirely from New York politics.[5]
(Of the State's politicians Rockefeller said: "I don't talk to them.
Don't talk to anybody. Don't see 'em.") Uninvolved in the 1978
race for Governor, Rockefeller was nevertheless remembered for
his "Borghian" behavior in helping to scuttle an earlier bid for the
State's top office by the Republican candidate in that year, Perry
Duryea. Duryea (the Assembly Speaker who sought, in 1974, to
challenge Rockefeller's Lieutenant Governor, Malcolm Wilson,
for the gubernatorial nomination) found himself indicted at the
initiative of another Rockefeller ally, Republican Attorney General
Louis Lefkowitz, for campaign "dirty tricks" and was effectively
immobilized, if only for the short term.

Another essay written less than a year before his death found
Rockefeller not at all retrospective. "I don't believe in guilt," he
said, echoing the sentiment of his earlier life, "and I don't believe
in worry."[6] With the privacy that accompanied the withdrawal
from politics of this once "wily, driving, demanding, ruthless
politician," some of the mannerisms, the famous wink and grin,
seemed gone. Rockefeller did express regret at never having

reached the White House, but he expected to live to be 100 and to face and solve new problems. "If I don't have enough," he concluded, "I create them."

From these observations, bracketing as they do a career at the upper reaches of public life that spanned almost two generations, we can begin to perceive the complexities and ambivalences in Nelson Rockefeller's personal style. The strengths, identified over and over again by his close colleagues in State government during this retrospective, included enormous energy; courage; self-confidence; great tenacity; an ease with power; an ability to inspire extraordinary loyalty in others; an unwillingness to accept limits; and an assumption that all problems were solvable if enough effort, talent and resources were brought to bear upon them. Permeating all was a certain "toughness," a quality somewhat unexpected in a person born to great wealth. As Joseph Persico, Rockefeller's long-time speechwriter, commented, "He could bite clear through the silver spoon in his mouth."[7]

One characteristic frequently commented upon by Rockefeller's close political associates was his persistence. In his remarks in this volume, Malcolm Wilson mentions his predecessor's "determination," "energy," and "staying power," and William Ronan calls the Governor "persistent, even stubborn." Jacob Javits, New York's Republican U.S. Senator during all of Rockefeller's tenure, recalled him as "stubborn" and "hard to change in his views."[8] Henry Kissinger remembered his patron and friend as "incredibly persistent."[9] And George Hinman, a long-time political associate and Republican National Committeeman, compared Rockefeller to a polar bear: "You shoot him and he just keeps coming on."[10]

It is a commonplace among politicians that persistence is a virtue; if you "hang in there" long enough, ultimately you will be rewarded. But now, in addition, scholarly work by a leading political scientist, William Riker, suggests that persistence not only may produce victory but is also a major source of political creativity. In a presidential address to the American Political Science Association, Riker demonstrated that the innovative constitutional design of the American presidency "...emanated from the will to win of such men as James Wilson in the face of prospective loss...," at the Constitutional Convention. Like Wilson, Rockefeller's will to win led him to continually seek alternative means to his ends, to structure situations so as to create the context for present or future victory.[11]

Yet clearly, each of Rockefeller's positive characteristics might be manifest in a less attractive way. It was not only the Governor's political enemies who translated "persistent," "hard driving," and "ambitious" into "stubborn," "ruthless," and "obsessive." "In the service of his beliefs," Henry Kissinger wrote, "he could be cold-blooded and ruthless."[12]

A problem-solver's unwillingness to accept limits might also be regarded as an unhealthy disregard for legitimate constitutional restraints and economic realities. Rockefeller attracted extraordinary people and inspired great loyalty, but he also tended to "use people up." And staff was not always positively motivated. As Al Marshall, Rockefeller's former Secretary, once commented: "As soon as you stumbled, he already had his eye on somebody else..."[13]

These ambivalences about Rockefeller were, to a degree, reflected in the physical descriptions made of him. One indicator of the man's personal force was that people expected him to be taller than he actually was. Many came away from a first meeting surprised that Rockefeller's height was no greater than 5'10". His physical image was one of solidity and squareness: a square thick torso, square shoulders, a square head, a square jaw, even square hands.[14] Writing during the 1968 presidential campaign, Norman Mailer remarked that "Rocky had an all but perfect face for a President: virile, friendly, rough hewn, of the common man yet uncommon..." Yet for Mailer there were also physical flaws: his complexion (Rockefeller himself said that his "Aldrich skin" made him look as though he'd just "crawled out from under a stone") and an unnaturally wide, thin-lipped "catfish mouth."[15]

Mailer liked the Governor's famous voice, "...an honest voice, sincere, masculine, slightly hoarse, full of honest range-rider muscle, with injections from the honest throatiness of New York," but he was not sure whether it was natural or part of a contrived image, one that had been presented so long so as to appear natural. Joseph Persico's physical descriptions reflect similar dichotomies, with Rockefeller's public persona - hand shaking, back slapping, kissing and winking - belied by his slate blue eyes, "veiled and remote."[16]

Finally, the varied interpretations of controversial events or practices during Rockefeller's governorship illustrate these ambivalences about Rockefeller's personal characteristics. Gifts and loans to associates in government, for example, were seen by some as acts of friendship and support, and by others as attempts by a super-rich man to cement loyalty with money. Another example was the pardon of L. Judson Morhouse, an early political supporter and Republican State Chairman, who was later caught in scandal. Recalled in this retrospective as an act of compassion and loyalty, the pardon was also interpreted at the time as a cynical suspension of ordinary justice for a political friend.

What was the genesis of this complex man's ability to create a "magnetic field," to "suck up all the authority" in a room when he entered it, to consistently convince others that he was enlisting them in causes "bigger than him or you?"[17] Some have suggested that it was simply the marriage of great private wealth with public authority, a marriage that provided either enormous potential for public good or "conflicts of interest...so pervasive ...that they exemplified the conflicts inherent in the system itself."[18] Others saw it as the fortuitous arrival on the public scene of the right "active-positive" style and pragmatic-liberal philosophy at an appropriate place and at the correct moment in history.[19] But the drive was very personal: it came from somewhere else.

Rockefeller's grandfather had amassed an enormous fortune, and his father had made a profession of giving money away. He revered both, defending the first John D. Rockefeller in his Senior Honors thesis at Dartmouth and quoting the second when asked by the *Saturday Evening Post* for the saying he most admired.[20] But though Nelson Rockefeller repeatedly denied feeling any guilt over his wealth or heritage, he also commented that his name made it hard for him to "know who his friends were" and that his inheritance "didn't provide any inner sense of having made good."[21]

Public life, an arena presumed for two generations to be impossible for a Rockefeller to successfully enter, was a challenge. It provided a setting in which Nelson might make an independent success. F.D.R provided both the opportunity and the model, but appointive office, it became clear, was too dependent upon the whim and approval of others. Success there was not independent, not meritorious. It did not flow from personal effort alone. There was always someone in the hierarchy, someone with a different agenda to whom one had to answer.

The solution was to run for high office, to become an "autentico represente del pueblo" and, in doing so, to submit to a different measure of success than that used by other Rockefellers —votes rather than dollars. This course allowed both independent achievement and prominence and held the ultimate promise of an opportunity to follow in F.D.R.'s footsteps. The great irony was, of course (as Henry Kissinger has noted), that Rockefeller could never separate himself from his wealth, and therefore could never really know if he could have "made it on merit alone." And this lack of certainty simply served to drive him harder.

Political Successes, Political Failures

The battle for the 1964 presidential nomination was the

Armageddon of modern Republican national politics. In that year, Nelson Rockefeller, "...the tribal chieftain of what used to be called the Northeastern Liberal Republican Establishment...," lost the nomination to Barry Goldwater, and the party turned permanently rightward.[22] Looking back, Rockefeller's political associates, represented here by Malcolm Wilson, attribute this, and other failures on the national scene, to the unique political circumstances of each moment — disadvantages that were impossible to overcome. Thus, in 1964, it was the Governor's divorce and remarriage (with the birth of a son by his new wife on the eve of the critical California primary). Previously, in 1960, it was Vice-President Nixon's early start and consequent iron grip on the convention delegates. And finally, by 1968, New York Republicanism was permanently out of sync with the national party, and in addition there was the residual effect of the divorce and Rockefeller's apparent buckling under to the sanitation union during its strike in New York City.

In contrast, the view from outside the inner circle, represented here by journalist Jack Germond, stresses poor advice and missed opportunities as the reasons for failure on the national scene. Rockefeller, Germond insists, too often took political advice from those who knew little about national politics. Emphasizing the Governor's freshness and personal magnetism when he came on the scene in 1958, a generally bad year for Republicans, Germond believes that Rockefeller might have prevailed in a series of state primary challenges to Nixon. (Recall, however, that the ability to produce national convention majorities solely through the primary route is a phenomenon of the 1970's.) Then the Governor could have gone on to defeat another millionaire, John Kennedy, for the presidency, with the wealth issue neutralized, as it had been in his gubernatorial race against Averell Harriman.

Unstated in Germond's analysis is the view that, in national politics, Rockefeller "...lacked the particular hunger, the edge, the requisite totality of desire for the office."[23] In 1968, as in 1960, journalist Henry Fairlie wrote: Rockefeller, "the All-Star Born Loser," "...was indecisive; his vacillation undermined the liberal hopes..."[24]

Though Malcolm Wilson here defends Rockefeller's commitment to his party, citing his declination of Hubert Humphrey's offer of the Democratic vice-presidential nomination and his refusal to consider switching parties to gain the presidential nomination, others have raised the question of "his real commitment to progressive Republicanism as a movement." Citing Rockefeller's efforts to seek the presidency through personal organization rather than party building, two young Republican leaders wrote in 1966 that "...the organizational follies of the Rockefeller staff betrayed the organizational ailment attributed to New York Republican politicians since Dewey — parochial inattention to the rest of the country."[25]

Johnny Crews, the legendary Brooklyn Republican leader, once said of Tom Dewey: "It's a funny thing with this guy. Every time he runs for President, he gets re-elected Governor."[26] The same may be said, of course, of Nelson Rockefeller. And as Burdell Bixby reminded us in his closing remarks on the Governor's "Party and Political Relations," Rockefeller's difficulties on the national scene should not be allowed to obscure the magnitude of his political successes in New York State.

In a *Life Magazine* story entitled "A Voter's Choice of Millionaires," Theodore H. White called the 1958 campaign for the governorship of New York "...the greatest pitting of fortune against fortune in the history of the Republic."[27] Even Soviet Premier Nikita Khrushchev was moved to comment upon the choice offered New Yorkers, between "a naked monopolist" (Harriman) and "a man whose millions for charity only cloaks the predatory nature of capitalism" (Rockefeller). In his remarks here, Malcolm Wilson, who was present at the creation, recalls for us how Nelson Rockefeller traveled the State by car to capture the 1958 Republican gubernatorial nomination; emerged as a "political natural"; and, wrapping Harriman in the cloak of the Tammany machine, went on to beat an incumbent Governor (and potential Democratic presidential nominee) by more than half a million votes.

Rockefeller's most difficult campaign was in 1966. The Governor prepared himself psychologically for defeat as his approval ratings in the polls sank to all-time lows, the voters reacting to a series of tax and fee increases that he had said, in 1962, he would not have to seek. Jack Germond comments here that the Liberal Party candidacy of Franklin Delano Roosevelt Jr., which attracted over half a million votes, contributed decisively to Rockefeller's victory (though there is no way to tell where those votes might have gone if there had been no Liberal in the race, or if that party had endorsed Rockefeller's opponent, New York City Council President, Frank O'Connor). That campaign is most memorable, however, for its early use of the techniques of the "New Politics," high-powered consultants, regular and repeated polling, and extensive media advertising.[28]

As a candidate and as Governor, Rockefeller was at the forefront in the development of these innovative methods, all of which cost money. Estimates of the amount spent for his four gubernatorial campaigns (excluding the national efforts, or contributions to the campaigns of others) range between $14 and $18 million, much of it from his family, and far more than was available to his Democratic opponents. Interestingly, one commentator on the use of money in politics has noted that the Governor had difficulty raising funds from the general public, primarily because he couldn't convince people that he needed it! Nevertheless, "there [was] a feeling in any Rockefeller campaign that money [was] there not only in great depth, through at least three generations of Rockefellers, but also in breadth, from the many financial resources of their empire."[29]

In his remarks during this retrospective, Charles Holcomb likens Governor Rockefeller and his principal associates to a "cork" in New York State's political bottle, with new Republican leadership blocked from top positions for almost a generation by their dominance. Indeed, the Governor's continued success at the polls masked vast changes in the New York electorate. While Rockefeller continued to win time after time, statewide Republican enrollments began a long decline. Upstate and suburban areas once dominated by the GOP became more competitive, and increasing numbers of New Yorkers registered "Independent." Rockefeller's withdrawal from the State political scene in 1973 occurred simultaneously with the Watergate crisis in Washington. Totals for statewide Republican candidates in 1974 appeared to have "dropped off a cliff," and regular control of the governorship and the State Assembly was lost to the Democrats.

Despite former Republican State Chairman Richard Rosenbaum's description of Nelson Rockefeller as his political "co-conspirator," the Governor did not leave a healthy State party behind him in Albany. During the Rockefeller era, the State party was an adjunct to the personal political organization of the Governor. It responded to him, not he to it. At first hostile to the use of patronage as a political tool, Rockefeller came to accept, then master, what remained of New York's patronage system. "Once in the game," Robert Caro has written, "he played it like a master — as if he had been raised in the Fourth Ward instead of Pocantico Hills."[30] The result, however, was not a strong State party organization but a machine that depended over much upon Rockefeller's personal patronage. When he left State office, the party, bereft of resources and with a declining base of Republican voters, entered a period of decline.

Post election studies in New York showed that Nelson Rockefeller was able to attract to his electoral coalition voters from ethnic and racial groups — Blacks, Jews, Hispanics — whose support was not transferable to other Republicans.

One normally Democratic group that offered Rockefeller

extraordinary backing was organized labor, even when he ran against Arthur Goldberg, labor's long-time legal champion. It has often been suggested that labor's support for Rockefeller was given in exchange for the enormous range and number of construction projects that the State entered into during his governorship, and this was surely a factor. There were, however, at least two others. The first was Rockefeller's assiduous efforts (cited here by William Ronan, Louis Levine, and Milton Musicus) to treat union representatives as equals, grant them access, and incorporate them fully into his administration's decision making processes. A second was the Governor's close personal relationship with George Meany, a tie that dated back to the days when Rockefeller was Chairman of Rockefeller Center and Meany was business agent for the plumbers and the voice of the Building Trade Unions at the Center. Of Rockefeller, Meany said: "Nelson is satisfied with his own share, and he doesn't try to keep the other feller from getting his. He doesn't have the mean streak you find in some of these Republican businessmen."[31]

Rockefeller's mastery of the Legislature in New York was legendary, and a feel for the way he personally worked both sides of the aisle, and reached legislators indirectly through such local party leaders as Democrat Meade Esposito of Brooklyn, is evident in the remarks here of William Ronan, Richard Rosenbaum, and Stanley Steingut. It is also true, however, as Ronan recalls, that Rockefeller had to learn from his first session, in 1959, not to try to overwhelm the Legislature with too great an agenda each year. And as Warren Anderson reminds us, the Governor did not always get what he asked for even when he wanted it badly and kept coming back for it. The example Anderson used was Universal Health Insurance; others, such as the Rye-Oyster Bay Bridge, might be cited as well.

One quality Anderson valued in Rockefeller in his dealings with him was that the Governor kept his word and backed his people. Legislative leaders could thus strike deals with the Governor and his top aides and sell the results to their colleagues knowing that the agreements would be kept. This quality was also valued by the Governor's commissioners. It was not always easy to get Rockefeller's agreement or commitment, but once it was obtained, as Joseph Swidler remarks here, subordinates knew that they could rely upon it.

Perhaps the longest-lasting effect of Rockefeller's dominance of the State Legislature in New York, as Alan Chartock notes in his remarks, was the development, in both houses of that body, of large professional staffs so as to balance the Governor's control of information and expertise in policy-making. The Legislature, which had a total budget of $8.5 million in 1958, had, by 1983, become a $108 million institution. Growing legislative capacity and independence reflected the influence of reapportionment and social change: it was not solely a reaction to a dominant executive. But this reaction was a major factor. And the irony was, of course, that Nelson Rockefeller, whose initiatives in part induced the Legislature to strengthen itself, if just in self-defense, only briefly had to deal with this strengthened institution. It was his successor, Hugh Carey, who felt the full impact of these changes.

Manager and Policy Maker

If Nelson Rockefeller, who was enamored of experts and expertise, thought of himself as "expert" in anything it was in politics. Certainly he did not regard himself as a "manager," a view reflected in the skeptical reaction of the many former aides, associates, and adversaries at this retrospective to the notion that the Governor had "managed" State government during his tenure. Rockefeller was a charismatic leader, a politician, a policy innovator, they said, but certainly not a manager.

Indeed, Rockefeller's forte was large-scale policy design. When he became interested in some area, he met intensively over relatively short periods of time, with Executive Chamber advisors, commissioners, and outside experts (the famous task forces), ultimately reaching decisions that set broad policy directions. After legislation was passed or direction otherwise set, the details of day-to-day management were left to others, with the Governor called in only if his special involvement was needed to overcome political or administrative roadblocks. For some programs (Rockefeller's early and ambitious effort to build fallout shelters throughout the State, for example), this detachment from detail actually allowed aides to satisfy the Governor, in the face of legislative opposition, without any real action or achievement. Generally, however, he could count on his subordinates to get the job done. In fact, they were so used to being given broad latitude in implementation that when Rockefeller insisted on detailed involvement, as in the case of his draconian drug abuse program of 1972, staffers thought it both exceptional and remarkable.

But if effective management meant the ability to achieve goals through others, to recruit very able people and effectively mobilize and direct their energies, then Rockefeller was indeed a manager. The Governor had an extraordinary ability to focus upon others one at a time, and capture them for his purposes. "He collected people," Joe Persico noted.[32] Again and again in these proceedings, Nelson Rockefeller's associates report their inability to say "no" to him, from the moment they were first recruited to his administration, to the times he made clear his great expectations of the departments or programs they headed. He enlisted them by convincing them of their indispensability, drove them with visions of goals larger than any one person or career, and rewarded them with shared credit, a late night phone call, or a supportive remark to a spouse. He had, one observer noted, "an ability...to grasp and judge the inspirations of other men."[33]

Though little remarked upon here, Governor Rockefeller exhibited another characteristic of the public manager throughout his career: a preoccupation with the formal structures and channels of government. During the Eisenhower administration, Rockefeller was an active member of the President's Permanent Advisory Committee on Government Reorganization, and helped structure and direct the Department of Health, Education and Welfare. Later, after he became Governor, he made sweeping suggestions before a Congressional committee for structural reform of the American national security apparatus.[34]

Governor Rockefeller leads a press conference in the Red Room, New York State Capital.

One might speculate that Rockefeller, a frustrated architect and a dyslexic, was naturally drawn to thinking about government in visual, structural terms. (Additional evidence for this, mentioned here, was his preference for graphic presentation of information and his fascination with the educational possibilities of television.) In any event, one of the Governor's very first initiatives was a massive reorganization effort, the Ronan Plan, which sought to drastically reduce the number of State departments and agencies. The plan even went so far as to suggest, in accord with orthodox public administration theory, that two statewide elective offices, Comptroller and Attorney General, might better be filled by gubernatorial appointment!

This proposal produced opposition from so many different quarters (as might easily have been predicted) that it was bound to fail. Later, as Malcolm Wilson, William Ronan, and Ed Kresky note in their remarks, Rockefeller was able to either co-opt or deal with other statewide elected leaders, even the Democratic Comptroller, Arthur Levitt. Over time, reorganization came to be a tool the Governor used to respond to practical necessities rather than to implement comprehensive plans. Creation of new structures, as with innovations in finance, was a means to an end and not an end in itself.

Though perhaps not interested in centralized, day-to-day gubernatorial management, Rockefeller was very much interested in centralized gubernatorial power. If the consolidation of this power required reorganization, or even constitutional change (as it did to bring social welfare policy firmly within the orbit of the Governor's control) then this was the route that was taken. If it required the aggressive pursuit of Federal funds (largely controlled by the Governor in New York State until 1982) and their use to gain leverage over local governments, as in the criminal justice area, then this was done.

In the panel on elementary and secondary education, participants credit Rockefeller for the immense expansion of State aid during his tenure, and for a significant re-definition of aid formulas. But despite this, Alton Marshall recalls Rockefeller's great frustration at his inability to control educational policy in New York, an area for which the State had constitutional responsibility and in which it spent billions, but one that deliberately was removed from direct gubernatorial or legislative dominance. Rockefeller's attempts to influence this area — both formally through the State budget process and commissioned studies and informally through contacts with the Regents, the Commissioner of Education, and school groups — were continuous. Nevertheless, the frustration at the lack of complete authority was always there.

The fact that the Governor chose not to immerse himself in detail does not mean that the Rockefeller Administration was lacking in centralized direction. Commissioners were given great discretion but were overseen in the traditional way through the Budget Division, and reported regularly, too, through an augmented gubernatorial staff. One major and enduring structural change accomplished by the Governor was a re-definition of the role in State government of the Secretary to the Governor. Rockefeller almost immediately built up the staff of his Secretary, William Ronan, who came to serve as first among equals in his inner circle. As is noted here by Alton Marshall, Ronan's program associates, working in specific program areas, emerged as strong advocates of innovation and change, balancing the cost conscious approach of the Budget Division with the Counsel's legal emphasis. Later, a Director of State Operations was added to free the Secretary even further for his policy role. All of these structural changes survived into succeeding administrations, though a context of fiscal stringency later helped return the Budget Division to predominance.

Rockefeller's belief in delegation to subordinates and later support for them, cited by Melvin Osterman and a number of others in this retrospective, was seen by most of the Governor's associates as a great virtue. It did, however, have another side. Rockefeller used the distinction between "gubernatorial power" and "gubernatorial management" to help explain his actions in response to one of the most traumatic events of his governorship, the Attica prison uprising. During the House of Representatives Judiciary Committee hearings on his appointment as Vice-President, Rockefeller identified as "the most serious mistake" he made during this crisis his failure to override his Commissioner of Corrections, Russell Oswald, and quickly retake the prison during the first few hours, while the situation was still fluid. As Rockefeller recalled it, his Commissioner said, "I can do this. I can handle it. I know these men. I know how to handle this, and I will do it," and the Governor "supported him." "I supported him as I do people I appoint."[35] Elsewhere he commented more formally: "After the policies were determined, I have always tried to pick the ablest people to carry out those policies...Having done so, I've given them my full support and backing, following the operations through a top flight staff."[36] The question here, of course, is the credibility of a Governor, so interested and skilled in centralizing power, explaining his reluctance to use it in crisis (and to take responsibility) on the basis of a theory of delegation of authority.

If one major theme of this retrospective concerns whether

Nelson Rockefeller was a "manager," another concerns whether he was an "experimenter." Certainly, as Alan Miller points out, for the mental health area, Rockefeller was willing to try new approaches, even if the fiscal and political costs might be major. Across policy domains innovation abounded, and much of it provided models for other states and for national action. This was the case, for example, regarding State aid for handicapped children, initiatives in the arts, and, as Robert Helsby comments, the establishment of collective bargaining for public sector labor relations.

But innovation differs from experimentation. As Barbara Blum notes, Rockefeller's approach was not to test new solutions in a limited way and under controlled conditions, as a social scientist might, before applying them statewide. He was not, Alton Marshall argues, a social experimenter, but a pragmatist interested in solutions — big solutions that would work quickly and throughout New York.

Rockefeller's rapid build-up of the State University system, to meet the demand for higher education created by the post-World War II baby boom, is the archtypical example of his penchant for large-scale answers to problems. But the gamut of State programs that, over 15 years, physically transformed the State and attacked its social problems are all illustrative of the Governor's unwillingness to accept limits, his conviction that all problems were solvable. And this was combined with an insistence on speed, an impatience typical of a politician serving a limited term, uncertain of re-election and desirous of seeing the results of his efforts. "I like to see some tangible result of what I do," Rockefeller once said to Jacob Javits. "I go out and see a housing development or an office building or a ski run, as a result of something I have done. I can see it and touch it."[37]

But an emphasis on large solutions sometimes led to large mistakes. In his comments on Rockefeller's social policy initiatives, Alton Marshall notes that incipient problems were sometimes addressed prematurely by the Administration, for political reasons, and in ways that occasionally had one set of solutions running headlong into another. Both Marshall and Senator William Smith are highly critical, for example, of the scale of New York's initial commitment to Medicaid under Rockefeller, an effort largely structured to maximize the State's access to Federal funds. Here, an overcommitment — the result, in part, of a bidding war during an election year between the Governor and Assembly Democrats — created a range of benefits to a defined constituency that later had to be painfully cut back, turning a short-term political asset into a long-term liability.

And an emphasis on speed often led to waste. In Albany, the simultaneous construction of numerous public works projects drove up the cost to the State of all of them. A specific, oft-cited example of speed leading to waste concerns the construction of the South Mall. In trying to meet State schedules, contractors for different portions of the project interfered with each other on the job, creating conditions under which some were able to successfully sue the State.

In addition, one era's large-scale solutions may be the next's large-scale problems. The State University was built to meet a burgeoning demand for higher education. At the same time, means were found to subsidize the State's private colleges, which had long resisted the emergence of an integrated State University system. The facilities were built and the demand met, and with great skill and verve, as the remarks in this retrospective attest. But the problems of the 1970's and 1980's then became excess higher education capacity and the need to maintain a now middle-aged physical plant. With fewer resources available and new priorities emerging, the rapid growth of the Rockefeller era contributed to the need for painful decisions by the Governor's successors, the parameters of which are evident from the discussion of higher education in this volume.

Such developments bring into question the utility of the operating assumption that the problems faced by the State, especially in the social problem areas, were "solvable." Neither a "medical" nor a "criminal" approach held out real promise of "solving" drug addiction. Neither large scale institutions nor community-based care were "solutions" to the problem of mental retardation or mental illness in New York. Problems like these may be constrained, answers may be found to some aspects of them, progress may be made, but to hope for ultimate solutions, especially through State government with its limited resources and reach, is to create unrealistic expectations and to preordain failure. The goal, then, as William Ronan reminds us here, is to make progress, to go forward.

For major areas of State policy, then, a crucial question becomes striking a balance between costs and benefits. In his remarks, Edward Kresky emphasizes that Rockefeller's financial innovations — moral obligation authority bonds, lease-purchase agreements, and massive first instance appropriations, to cite three examples — should not be viewed apart from the policy goals they were designed to facilitate. The ends, all of which might not have been achieved, included improved public transportation, low-income housing, college and university facilities, and hospitals and nursing homes. Generally, the participants in this retrospective agreed with Kresky; they saw the benefits as worth the costs incurred. The Governor himself succinctly summarized this view when he commented at the hearings on the Urban Development Corporation (UDC) financial collapse: "Let's not talk as if we are running a bank. We are running a social institution to meet the people's needs."[38]

Nevertheless, as Senator William Smith points out here, Rockefeller's spending in a variety of program areas left New York with a tax structure and debt burden that ultimately came to threaten the very viability of its private sector economy. To cite just one example: half the public authorities in the State were created during Rockefeller's tenure. Their long-term debt in 1974, $12 billion, was by then four times the size of the State's general obligation debt. As a consequence of State and public authority commitments and practices, fiscal constraints and service cutbacks (already evident before the end of the Rockefeller era) came to be the dominant theme of Albany decision-making through the 1970's and into the 1980's.[39]

Participants in this retrospective disagreed about the contribution of Rockefeller administration decisions to New York's fiscal crisis of the mid-1970's. Clearly, as its former chief Paul Belica points out, the Housing Finance Agency's (HFA) massive difficulties were not based upon unsoundness in its practices, but upon a panicky market reaction to all New York related securities. But Edward Logue's attribution of the UDC default not to agency shortcomings but to unanticipated events outside of its control, is more questionable. Logue cites the suspension of Federal housing programs early in Richard Nixon's ill-fated second term, and the alteration of Port Authority bond covenants in 1973 — an action that led the major New York City banks to force a "test" of the State's moral obligation commitment to its authorities' bonds — as critical blows to his agency. Both were important, but Logue's go-go, results-oriented style, so compatible with Rockefeller's, led to a series of borrowing practices and optimistic assumptions about the availability of aid and the size of the market for higher risk agency bonds that significantly contributed to the UDC's difficulties.

For Logue and most others at this conference, New York City, not New York State, was the progenitor of the fiscal crisis. Edward Kresky even suggested that Rockefeller's fiscal practices were "out front," when compared to those of the City. Dick Netzer disagreed. He thought the State administration's techniques "stealthy" and ultimately contributory to the crisis, if indirectly, by making it impossible for the State to discipline the City for what it was doing.

Whatever their views on the causes of the crisis, participants in this retrospective agreed with Nelson Rockefeller's view that if he had remained Governor, especially *after* 1974, it might have been avoided entirely, at least in Albany. "Nelson we know," Logue recalls the bankers saying in 1974, "Malcolm Wilson we don't know." But, in the end, one man's credibility was a thin reed upon which to prop the fiscal viability of the entire Empire State.

By Nelson Rockefeller's final year as Governor, he had become such a dominant figure that one journalist, seeking to name the ten most powerful people in New York, awarded him the top three places on the list![40]

Rockefeller's were a unique combination of personal characteristics, family resources, and high public office, brought to bear in pursuit of a vision of the future of the State and its people in an era in which it was believed that State government could indeed make a difference. If his reach exceeded his grasp it was because of the ambition of his goals, both for himself and for New York. The Governor's failures flowed from the excesses of his virtues. Ultimately, not all problems were solvable, even by the best minds working with unlimited resources. And ultimately, too, resources were not unlimited.

Even before he stepped down, experts had begun to number Nelson Rockefeller among America's greatest governors — one who had built the "most socially advanced state government in United States history" and had changed the physical face of New York more than any Governor since DeWitt Clinton built the Erie Canal."[41]

And the accolades continued as time passed.[42] Certainly, those who worked with Rockefeller, observed him in action, or even opposed him during his governorship were convinced that, largely because of his leadership, they were engaged in events at a unique and transforming moment in New York history.

The value of this retrospective is the added insight it offers, from these participants, into the controversies of that time and the qualities of that governorship.

Notes

[1]Recent books include: Joseph Persico. *The Imperial Rockefeller* (New York: Pocket Books, 1982); Peter D. McClelland and Alan L. Magdovitz. *Crisis in the Making* (New York: Cambridge U. Press, 1981); William Daniels and James Underwood. *Governor Rockefeller in New York* (Westport, Ct.: Greenwood Press, 1982); and Michael Turner. *The Vice-President as Policy Maker* (Westport, Ct.; Greenwood Press, 1982).

[2]For an example of a view from the left, see Joel Andreas. *The Incredible Rocky* (Berkeley: The North American Congress on Latin America, 1974), and from the right, see Hamilton A. Long. Rockefeller, *A Menace to the Republic* (New York, 1968).

[3]See generally, United States House of Representatives. Committee on The Judiciary. *Hearings Concerning the Nomination of Nelson A. Rockefeller To Be Vice President of the United States.* 93rd Congress, 2nd session; November 21-27, December 2-5; 1974.

[4]Geoffrey T. Hellman. "Best Neighbor," *The New Yorker*, April 18, 1942, pp. 26-27.

[5]Andy Logan. "Around City Hall," *The New Yorker*, August 10, 1978, p. 64.

[6]H. Dudar. "Nelson Now," *New York*, September 25, 1978, p. 65.

[7]Persico, *op.cit.*, p. 53.

[8]Jacob Javits and Rafael Steinberg. *Javits* (Boston: Houghton-Mifflin, 1981), p. 362.

[9]Peter Collier and David Horowitz. *The Rockefellers* (New York: Holt, Reinhart and Winston, 1976), p. 356.

[10]Henry Kissinger. *The White House Years* (Boston: Little-Brown, 1979), p. 5.

[11]"The Heresthetics of Constitution Making," (Chicago: Annual Meeting of the American Political Science Association: processed, 1983), p. 30.

[12]Collier and Horowitz, *op.cit.*, p. 496; Theodore H. White. *The Making of the President, 1964* (New York: Atheneum, 1965), p. 73; and Kissinger, *op.cit.*, p. 4.

[13]Persico, *op.cit.*, p. 205.

[14]*Ibid.*, pp. 51-52; and Kissinger, *op.cit.*, p. 5.

[15]Norman Mailer. *Miami and the Seige of Chicago* (London: Weidenfield and Nicholson, 1968), pp. 12-13; Persico, *op.cit.*, pp. 51-52.

[16]Persico, *op.cit.*, p. 53.

[17]*Ibid.*, pp. 54 and 199.

[18]Collier and Horowitz, *op.cit.*, p. 488.

[19]For a description of the active-positive type see James David Barber. *Presidential Character* (Englewood Cliffs: Prentice Hall, 1972). The term "pragmatic liberal" is from Daniels and Underwood, *op.cit.*

[20]Nelson Rockefeller. "My Favorite Quote," *Saturday Evening Post*, December 1, 1962.

[21]Persico, *op.cit.*, pp. 169 and 172.

[22]Theodore H. White. *America in Search of Itself* (New York: Harper and Row, 1982), p. 234.

[23]David Halberstam. *The Best and the Brightest* (New York: Random House, 1972), p. 66.

[24]Henry Fairlie. *The Parties* (New York: St. Martins Press, 1978), pp. 61-62.

[25]George Gilder and Bruce K. Chapman. *The Party That Lost Its Head* (New York: Knopf, 1966), p. 113.

[26]Richard N. Smith. *Thomas Dewey and His Times* (New York: Simon and Shuster, 1982), p. 543.

[27]Theodore H. White. "A Voters' Choice of Millionaires," *Life*, September 22, 1958, p. 104.

[28]Robert Connery and Gerald Benjamin. *Rockefeller of New York* (Ithaca: Cornell, 1979), Chapter 2; James Perry. *The New Politics* (New York: Potter, 1968).

[29]George Thayer. *Who Shakes the Money Tree?* (New York: Simon and Shuster, 1973), p. 161.

[30]Robert Caro. *The Power Broker* (New York: Knopf, 1974), p. 1068.

[31]Joseph Goulden. *Meany* (New York: Atneneum, 1972), p. 404.

[32]Persico, *op.cit.*, p. 198.

[33]Caro, *op.cit.*, p. 1068.

[34]Cited in Daniels and Underwood, *op.cit.*, p. 110.

[35]House Hearings, *op.cit.*, p. 164.

[36]Cited in Connery and Benjamin, *op.cit.*, p. 156.

[37]Javits and Steinberg, *op.cit.*, p. 377.

[38]Cited in Annamarie Hauck Walsh. *The Public's Business* (Cambridge: MIT Press, 1978), p. 264.

[39]See McClelland and Magdovitz (1981), which is cited by Senator Smith in his prepared remarks, for a detailed critique of Rockefeller Administration fiscal practices.

[40]Robert Daley. "The Struggle for Control of the City," *New York Magazine,* January 14, 1974, p. 34.

[41]Neal R. Peirce. *The Megastates of America* (New York: Norton, 1972), pp. 25 and 27.

[42]See, for example, George Weeks. "A Statehouse Hall of Fame," *State Government* (Volume 55, #2, 1982), pp. 67-73.

Rockefeller In Retrospect
Conference Participants

(With positions held during the Rockefeller Administration:

1959 to 1973)

Senator Warren M. Anderson
1953 to date, Member, State Senate; 1966-1972, Chairman, Senate Finance Committee; 1973 to date, President Pro Tem and Majority Leader, State Senate

Richard J. Bartlett, Esq.
1959-1966, Member, State Assembly; 1959-1973, Private Practice of Law; 1961-1970, Chairman, State Commission on Revision of Penal Law; 1973-1974, Justice, State Supreme Court

Paul Belica, Esq.
1959-1962, Private Practice of Law; 1962-1974, Executive Director, State Housing Finance Agency; Chief Executive Officer, Municipal Bond Bank, State Project Finance Agency, State Medical Care Facilities Finance Agency, and State Mortgage Agency

R. Burdell Bixby, Esq.
1959-1974, Chairman, State Thruway Authority; 1959-1974, Private practice of Law

Samuel Bleecker
Author of scientific and technological works, including "The Politics of Architecture: A Perspective of Nelson A. Rockefeller"

Dr. Barbara Blum
1967-1971, Deputy Commissioner for Mental Hygiene and Mental Retardation, New York City; 1971-1973, Assistant Administrator/ Commissioner New York City Department of Social Services; 1974-1976, Director of the Metropolitan Office, State Board of Social Welfare

Kenneth Buhrmaster
1959-1974, Chairman of the Board, First National Bank of Scotia; 1956-1961, Area Director, State School Boards Association; 1961-1974, President, State School Boards Association; 1968-1974, President, State Teachers Retirement Board

Professor Alan Chartock
1959-1964, Student; 1965-1974, Eagleton Institute of Politics, Rutgers University; John Jay College of Criminal Justice, City University of New York; Professor of Political Science at State University of New York College at New Paltz and Professor of Communications at State University of New York at Albany

Professor Robert Connery
1959-1966, Professor of Government, Duke University; 1966-1976, Professor of Government, Columbia University; Co-author with Professor Gerald Benjamin of "Rockefeller of New York"

Professor William Daniels
1959-1966, Student; 1966-1974, Professor of Political Science, Union College; 1970-1971, Alfred E. Smith Fellow, State Division of the Budget; 1973-1974, Fulbright Scholar, Foreign Service Institute and Waseda University, Tokyo

George A. Dudley
1960-1962, Director, State Office of Regional Development; 1962-1965, Trustee, State University Construction Fund; 1967-1972, President, State Environmental Facilities Corporation; 1967-1975, Chief Executive Officer, State Council on Architecture

James W. Gaynor
1959-1969, State Commissioner of Housing and Community Renewal; 1970-1974, Private Consultant

Jack Germond
1959-1962, Gannett News Service, Albany; 1963-1973, Gannett

Mrs. Lee Goodwin
1959-1962, Assistant to Chairman Joint Legislative Committee on Housing; 1962-1973, Executive Assistant to State Commissioner of Housing; 1963-1973, Assistant Director, Housing Finance Agency; 1973-1974, Commissioner of Housing and Community Renewal

Dr. Robert Helsby
1956-1966, Executive Deputy State Industrial Commissioner; 1966-1967, Dean of Continuing Education, State University of New York; 1967-1974, Chairman, State Public Employees Relations Board

Charles Holcomb
1959-1966, *Rochester Times-Union*; 1966-1973, Gannett News Service, Albany

Hollis S. Ingraham, M.D.
1959-1963, First Deputy Commissioner of Health; 1963-1974, Commissioner of Health

Dr. John Kirkpatrick
Prior to 1971, Vice President, College Entrance Examination Board; Vice President and Treasurer of Pace College; Comptroller of the University of Chicago; 1971-1974, President, Commission on Independent Colleges and Universities, State of New York

Dr. Edward Kresky
1959-1961, Associate Director, State Constitutional Revision Commission; 1961-1965, Program Associate, Office of the Governor; 1965-1971, Secretary, Metropolitan Transportation Authority; 1971, General Partner, Wertheim & Co.

Dr. Oscar E. Lanford
1959-1961, Dean of the College, State University of New York at Albany; 1961-1971, President, State University of New York College at Fredonia; 1971-1974, Vice Chancellor for Campus Development, State University of New York and General Manager of the State University Construction Fund

Dr. Abe Lavine
1959-1961, Assistant Chief Budget Examiner, State Division of the

Budget; 1961-1969, Deputy Director, Division of Employment, State Department of Labor; 1969-1972, Director, Office of Employee Relations; 1972-1974, Commissioner of Social Services

James Lawrence
1959-1961, Student; 1961-1962, Intern, State Labor Department; 1963-1974, Progressed from Junior Budget Examiner to Assistant Chief Budget Examiner, State Division of the Budget

Louis L. Levine
1959-1965, Director of Rehabilitation, New York City Central Labor Council, AFL-CIO; 1966-1969, Deputy State Industrial Commissioner; 1969-1971, Commissioner of Labor Affairs, State Department of Labor; 1979-1974, State Industrial Commissioner

Dr. Edward J. Logue
1959-1960, Development Administrator, City of New Haven; 1961-1967, Development Administrator, City of Boston; 1968-1974, President and Chief Executive Officer, State Urban Development Corporation

Robert MacCrate, Esq.
1959-1962, Counsel to the Governor; 1962-1974, Partner, Sullivan & Cromwell; 1971, Counsel, State Court on Judiciary

Alton G. Marshall
1959-1961, Secretary, Public Service Commission; 1961-1965, Deputy Director, State Division of the Budget; 1965-1966, Executive Officer to Governor, Executive Chamber; 1966-1970, Secretary to the Governor; 1971-1974, President, Rockefeller Center, Inc.

Joseph McGovern, Esq.
1959-1974, Private Practice of Law; 1959-1966, Part-time Professor of Law, Fordham University Law School; 1961-1968, Member, State Board of Regents; 1968-1974, Chancellor, State Board of Regents

Alan Miller, M.D.
1958-1961, U.S. Public Health Service; 1961-1963, National Institute of Mental Health; 1964-1966, Associate State Commissioner of Mental Hygiene; 1966-1974, State Commissioner of Mental Hygiene

Dr. John J. Morris
1959-1960, Student; 1960-1970, Assistant Professor, Associate

Professor, Professor, Philosophy and Religion, Colgate University; 1970-1972, Director, Division of Humanities, Colgate University; 1972-1973, Provost and Dean of Faculty, Colgate University; 1974, Acting President, Colgate University

Archibald R. Murray, Esq.
1960-1962, Assistant District Attorney, New York County; 1962-1965, Assistant Counsel to Governor; 1965-1970, State Penal Law Commission; 1965-1967, State Drug Addiction Council; 1967, Counsel to State Crime Control Commission; 1971-1972, Administrator, State Division of Criminal Justice, Office of Planning Services; 1972-1974, Commissioner, State Division of Criminal Justice Services

Dean Dick Netzer
1959-1960, Assistant Vice President, Federal Reserve Bank of Chicago; 1961-1974, Professor of Economics, New York University; 1969-1974, Dean, Graduate School of Public Administration, New York University

Dr. Vincent O'Leary
1959-1962, State Director of Parole, Texas; 1962-1964, Director, National Parole Institute, Texas; 1964-1965, Executive Assistant to Director, National Council on Crime and Delinquency, New York City; 1965-1968, Director, Division of Research Information and Training, National Council on Crime and Delinquency; 1968-1974, Professor of Criminal Justice, State University of New York at Albany

Melvin H. Osterman, Esq.
1959-1961, Private Practice of Law; 1961-1964, Assistant Counsel to the Governor; 1964-1966, Private Practice of Law; 1967, Special Counsel, Public Employee Relations Board; 1968, Special Counsel to the Governor; 1969-1974, Director, State Office of Employee Relations

Dr. Stanley L. Raub
1959-1968, School Principal; 1968-1970, Assistant Commissioner of Education; 1970-1974, Associate Commissioner of Education

Dr. William J. Ronan
1959-1966, Secretary to the Governor; 1965-1968, Chairman, Metropolitan Transportation Authority; 1967-1977, Commissioner of the Port Authority of New York and New Jersey; 1974-1977,

Trustee, Power Authority of the State of New York

Richard M. Rosenbaum, Esq.
1959-1970, Private Practice of Law, 1970-1973, Justice, State Supreme Court; 1973-1974, Chairman, New York State Republican Committee

Max J. Rubin, Esq.
1959-1974, Private Practice of Law; 1961-1963, President, New York City Board of Education; 1965-1973, Member, State Board of Regents

Dr. Donna E. Shalala
1959-1962, Student; 1962-1964, Peace Corps; 1965-1970, Assistant and Instructor, Maxwell School, Syracuse University; 1970-1972, Assistant Professor, Baruch College; 1972-1974, As ociate Professor, Columbia University

Howard Shapiro, Esq.
1959-1964, Student; 1965-1968, Assistant District Attorney, New York County; 1969-1971, Assistant Counsel to the Governor; 1971-1973, First Assistant Counsel of the Governor; 1973-1974, Chairman, State Commission of Investigation

Senator William T. Smith
1962 to date, Senator from 51st District; Chairman, Social Services Committee; Chairman, Temporary State Commission to Revise the Social Services Law; Deputy Majority Leader

Hon. Stanley Steingut
1959-1965, Member, State Assembly; 1969-1974, Minority Leader, State Assembly

Jospeh C. Swidler, Esq.
1961-1965, Chairman, Federal Power Commission; 1966-1970, Chairman, State Public Service Commission; 1970-1974, Director, Institute for Public Policy Alternatives, State University of New York at Albany

Professor James Underwood
1959-1963, Student; 1963-1974, Professor of Political Science, Union College; 1966-1967, Congressional Fellow, Washington, D.C.

Paul T. Veillette
1959-1962, Director of Operator Control, Connecticut Department of Motor Vehicles; 1962-1964, Director of Management Analysis, Chicago Police Department; 1964-1967, Deputy Director, State Identification and Intelligence System; 1967-1970, Chief of Management Analysis, State Division of the Budget; 1970-1974, Chief of Education Budgeting, State Division of the Budget

Lois J. Wilson
1959-1960, Graduate Study; 1960-1965, State Assembly Office of Legislative Research; 1965-1973, Director of Studies, State Teachers Association-State United Teachers; 1974, Deputy Secretary to the Governor

Governor Malcolm Wilson
1959-1973, Lieutenant Governor; 1973-1974, Governor

R. Frank Wille, Esq.
1959-1960, Private Practice of Law; 1960-1964, Assistant Counsel to the Governor; 1964-1970, State Superintendent of Banks; 1970-1974, Chairman, Board of Directors, Federal Deposit Insurance Corporation

Dr. Joseph F. Zimmerman
1959-1965, Professor of Government, Worcester Polytechnic Institute; 1965-1974, Professor of Political Science, State University of New York at Albany; 1968-1973, Research Director, Joint Legislative Committee on Mass Transportation.

Advisory Committee

Dr. T. Norman Hurd, Chairperson

Professor Gerald Benjamin, Secretary

Robert R. Douglass, Esq.

Manly Fleischmann, Esq.

Robert MacCrate, Esq.

Alton G. Marshall

Hugh Morrow

Dr. William J. Ronan

Dr. Donna E. Shalala

Honorable Stanley Steingut

Professor James Underwood

Honorable Malcolm Wilson

Dr. Joseph F. Zimmerman